Understanding Fairy Mythology

By Ty Hulse

TyHulse.com

Table of Contents

Just on the Tip of Your Tongue

Remnants of a magical past

Like a word stuck on the tip of your tongue that you can't quite remember, fairy tales aggravate us with deeper meanings we're almost certain we know, but can't quite recall. For just enough of the old fairy faiths survive within them to tantalize us with their forgotten mysteries; teasing us with a hidden past filled with dark guardians to the underworld, bright and beautiful fairies[1], and long winters nights people feared would never end. There is still a mysterious heart to fairy tales, giving us a peek into a primal world, beckoning us to recall old traditions. This book will seek to explore these old traditions, to answer questions about the hidden origins of fairy tales.

Unfortunately, many of the most intriguing questions that would give us the answers we seek are heavily debated, such as; "what impact the Huns had on Germanic religious beliefs?" or "What is Stonehenge?" No one alive today can definitively know the answer too many of these questions, no matter how tantalizingly close they seem. Yet even if they can never be found, searching for the answers is still of value because, by searching we can come to a greater understanding of ancient society, religion, history, and perhaps, in a way, even a better understanding of ourselves.

When trying to understand the origins of and meanings behind fairy tales, it's important to understand that almost no fairy tale is a single story. Rather, they are typically made up of the pieces of many stories and ideas which all came together over time to create the stories we know today. Fairy tales, after all, don't belong to a single era or a single culture, but instead are an odd soupy mixture of different times and places, as they were handed down from one generation to the next, and from one land to another.

The multi-cultural origins of fairy tales leads us to an interesting question; to whom do

---

[1] Fairy – This is perhaps the most confusing of all terms utilized in this book. A fairy, as referred to here, was, in essence, one who controlled human fate. Thus, a fairy could be anything from the spirit that made grain ripen in the fields to the ones who caused people to stub their toes or controlled the fate of even the gods themselves. This definition is very broad and would include everything from pixies to Odin. Instead, then, I will define fairies as magical beings who spent much of their time on the earth and controlled human fate. It is important to note that this is not necessarily a statement of power but, rather, one of proximity. Fairies were beings believed to live alongside humans, unlike the earlier example of Odin, who was believed to live in Valhalla but would come and act as a fairy on occasion. Other figures are more confusing, such as Zeus, who was at the same time believed to live in each person's house in the form of a snake, on every mountain top, and in the heavens. In this sense, Zeus could be considered both fairy and deity, depending on the situation.

3

fairy tales belong? Were they a product of the generation which last told them, even if that generation didn't create them? For example, does the story of "Hansel and Gretel" belong to 1812, when the Grimm Brothers published it? Or does it belong to the era of the Great Famine of 1315-1317 when parents began to abandon their children in the woods and from whence the story may have originated? Does the story belong to Germany where it was collected, or does it belong to the peoples of North Eastern Europe where the idea of a protagonist using a chicken bone to trick a witch into thinking they were too skinny to eat may have originated?

Because they have so many origins, and have been altered so many times, it's nearly impossible to discuss a single meaning for any one fairy tale. Instead, fairy tales have multiple meanings and multiple purposes, to the point that the people telling them to the Brothers Grimm or other folklorists may not have fully understood them. Olive Tolley states that "It is therefore clear that any poem may have served one purpose at the time of its composition and another at its recording." Indeed, "Stories do not belong to storytellers and story listeners because all stories are "reassembles of fragments on loan" and "depend on shared narrative sources" (Zipes, Jack.)

Folk Religion in Fairy Tales

Perhaps the most interesting origins of fairy tales, and the ones this book will focus on, are the many fairy tales built on the remnants of older folk religions. These fairy faiths in many places effectively remained the beliefs of the peasants' right up into the modern era, such that even until the beginning of the 20th century:

> The cunning[2] folk of the English countryside were the leaders and practitioners of the people's religion as well as their folk medicine. The medical, divinatory, and other religious services provided by these wise women and men possessed of special supernatural powers and religious techniques were far more important in the lives of the people than the official religion (Horsley)

In fairy tales these cunning folk appeared as advice givers, as a hen wife who told people how to rescue the moon when she was captured by monsters in one fairy tale from Lincolnshire, or as wise women who told a knight how to slay dragons in a tale from Essex.

---

[2] Cunning – Cunning folk could be defined simply as "good witches" or at least as witches that are not specifically evil. This term must be fluid, however, as many "good" people do bad things. People went to them for magical advice, cures, love potions, etc. However, they lived in a society with a codified religious leadership (i.e., the Catholic Church, Puritan Church, Orthodox Church, Buddhists, etc.) of which they were not members. Though many cunning were shamans who would talk to fairies to learn their cures or enter trances in order to be possessed by fairies, not all of them were. Many cunning learned their magic from books or utilized herbs for most of their powers.

This is similar to their role outside of fairy tales as well, in which they advised people by telling them about the fairies that humans believed shared their world. Thus for thousands of years they influenced the way people thought about the spirit world, and the stories they told.

These cunning folk and their kin in countries across the world didn't have official political power. Instead, like the shamans[3] of the past, they gained power through influence. People trusted them and were afraid to go against what they said. In many ways this is far more important than any official title, in so far as fairy tales are concerned, because it means people believed the stories they told, and were likely to share those stories with others. Because of this, folk religions were able to exist side by side with the official state religion for thousands of years, and sometimes prove themselves more important to the lives of the lower classes, and at times even the nobility, who would secretly seek the cunning folk's advice. To understand fairy tales, then, one must understand the folk religion of the people who told them:

> Unlike codified religions, folk belief is extremely diverse in character and difficult to define precisely." It is made up of vague magico-relegous beliefs, many of which are survivals or successors of archaic and primitive elements; these beliefs or primitive elements themselves remain systematized theoretically and ecclesiastically, but in many ways have penetrated and become interrelated with institutionalized religions." (Ichiro Hori)

In other words, like fairy tales, folk religions are made up of pieces of many religions from many places and times. This makes them difficult to understand because they don't generally have a single coherent cosmology, but rather they are made up of the remnants of many different religions and systems of thinking (Horsley). The cunning folk of England, for example, used ideas from multiple sources of previous English Paganism, from Roman Paganism, from books that were based on Middle Eastern Ideas, from Catholicism, and the Church of England in order to explain and cure illness.

Because folk religions are made up of so many ideas they tend to be a series of ideas about how to deal with the spirit world, such as leaving clean water out for fairies to bath in, or throwing salt over ones shoulder to keep away evil spirits, wishing upon a star with a rhyme, or knocking on wood for luck. In other words, it could be argued that folk religions are a series of superstitions rather than a cannon of laws; superstitions which people believed were extremely important to their survival, which is why they were passed on from parent to child for thousands of years.

Unlike state religions which focus on creating a single coherent cosmology to explain the metaphysical/philosophical world and the larger social structure of a nation or group of nations, folk religions typically focus on surviving from one day to the next. More than this, however, folk religions are about building and maintaining relationships between

---

[3] Shaman – While I discuss shamanism in greater detail in the chapter entitled "Shamanism," I use the word with some frequency throughout this book, so it is worth defining now. The definition of shamanism is often debated; however, for the purposes of this book, shamans are those who enter into states of ecstasy in order to communicate with and gain help from the spirit world. They do this either by sending their souls to travel the spirit world, working with helping spirits, meeting with fairy beings, or being possessed.

people, and with the spirit world (Bock). This is why social morality is an important part of many folk religions and therefore fairy tales. It is also largely why folk religions persist over time, because they are centered on specific social norms, often of a subgroup within the larger culture, although such social moralities don't always resemble the morals we might think of today. Indeed, the morals of the past are often shocking to modern ideas. To certain groups such acts as kidnapping women, stealing from neighboring villages and more were all perfectly acceptable, given the right set of circumstances. Today parents often view stories, such as "Jack and the Beanstalk" as being immoral, because this story is about a thief:

> *Then Jack crept out on tiptoe from his oven, and as he was passing the*
> *ogre he took one of the bags of gold under his arm, and off he pelters*
> *till he came to the beanstalk, and then he threw down the bag of gold*
> *which of course fell in to his mother's garden, and then he climbed*
> *down and climbed down till at last he got home and told his mother*
> *and showed her the gold and said: "Well, mother, wasn't I right about*
> *the beans. They are really magical, you see."*

In lore theft was oftentimes not only acceptable, it could at times be considered a heroic act. This wasn't just a primitive idea, however; we still have heist movies in the modern day such as "Oceans 11." To a certain extent the need to be cunning is one of the morals of fairy tales, and indeed thieves and bandits were often glorified in England. During the Victorian Era a thief named Jack Sheppard came to be so famous that the greatest boxer of the time shared a drink with him and priests even used stories of his exploits in their sermons. Much of this comes from the fact that theft of various forms was important to the survival of many villages and peasants, which is perhaps why so many house hold deities, such as the domovoi of Russia and the tomte of Sweden, help their chosen families by stealing from the neighbors. The importance of stealing from neighbors in general can be seen in one of the most wide spread Indo-European mythological motifs is that of the cattle raid:

> In early Ireland the Tana cattle raids were a recognized narrative category and in
> a society where wealth was reckoned in cattle, cattle-rustling was regarded as the
> most appropriate activity for young male warriors. (Adams)

It's true of course that in the tale of "Jack and the Beanstalk" Jack is stealing gold rather than cattle, but as the definition of wealth changed one would expect the items stolen by these heroes to transform as well. For example, early Indo-European Cattle raiding myths included the well-known theme of slaying a dragon or giant, a combination which exists in the myths of India, Germany, Rome, Greece, Slavic, and Baltic mythology (Lincoln); while later Germanic tales of heroes slaying dragons had the beasts as guardians of gold.

The different morality of past cultures often makes it difficult to understand the message behind fairy tales, because in the modern world we frequently consider certain behaviors as immoral which were once celebrated. What's important to keep in mind is that the moralities of folk religions are primarily concerned with the harsh realities of daily life. Thus, I would argue that folk religion is the religion of people who must constantly worry about whether they will have enough food to eat, if their children will survive the long cold winter, and about the potentially disastrous effects of getting sick. This means that, while the religion of the nobility and priests of a nation, aka, the official religion, might influence the folk religion, and the folk religion might influence the official religion, the two were separate. What's more, many of the ideas within folk religions were more stable, because the needs of the people who followed them were less likely to change than the philosophical ideas which drove the nobility.

Still, the fact that religions, and especially folk religions, are centered on human survival means that they will adapt to new situations. Thus new religions come into being when there are significant changes to the political, environmental, social, or economic environment in which people have to live. Often during this process of transformation, many new religions will form and many new myths will be developed, but only a few of the existing religions will survive (Bulbulia and Slingerland, 2012). The myths, however, can continue on even after the religion which believed it has faded away. Everyone loves a good story after all. What we see then is that the things people of the past believed in were made up of many ideas, both from their own past and from neighboring peoples. Indeed any idea which allowed people to maintain their unique relationship with each other, other peoples, and the spirit world could be adopted.

The building of a network of support, both spiritual and human, was critical to people's survival, and so it is one of the primary focuses of folk religions. This can be seen in the pre-Christian belief system of the Sami, for whom balance has been maintained "through rituals, by following normative patterns of behavior, and established practices, by showing respect, and through a dialogue on both an individual and collective level." For them normative patterns of behavior was more than social morality, such patterns of behavior were essentially magico-religious ideas, which impacted their chances of survival in the world. Similarly, the Sami's relationship with the spirit world could be said to have been based on a similar set of social behaviors:

> The relationship with nature and its forces is not submissive but active. Humans can, when necessary, influence the powers of nature by giving, offering, sharing, asking, promising, taking care of, showing respect to, or assuming the shapes of animals. Offerings were made to the natural spirits only when necessary: for example, when a spirit was known to be angry because people had broken some rule. One did not ask spirits for help, but for goodwill and patience while one stayed in their area. Every geographical place was considered an entity in which the physical dimension was in balance with the spiritual one. (Delos Initiative)

People could plead with nature and its spirits throughout Europe, asking them for help. Consider, for example, the Romanian who would call out to the moon:

> "O luminous moon, luminous moon, come and take away the spell and the desolation, and the hatred from the world, and from my house, and from my table, and from my garden, and from my vineyard, and from my craft, and from my trade, and from my purse, and drive it away to wild mountains and forests , and us and our children and those who shall be born unto us hereafter, leave us clean and pure like refined gold and like the sun that shines brilliantly in the skies!"

As with many such chants there is a lot more going on here, than is readily apparent. Certainly it's quickly obvious that this prayer to the moon is asking it to drive away unclean forces. It's interesting to note, however, that this chant doesn't ask the moon to destroy unclean forces, and that it specifically asked to drive those unclean forces into the "wild mountains and forests." It was common in Slavic lore, for shamanistic figures, such as the "Living Saints" to drive evil to distant wildernesses, strange places without sound, without humanity. It was also common in lore, to view the forest as an otherworld, as a dark place filled with strange beings. The wilderness was also, however, the place where shaman figures, from saints to cunning went to receive their training. This duality of thinking about things as being both a pure and impure, as we'll see further, was extremely important to myth and fairy tales.

Perhaps, more important than the behaviors necessary to achieve a positive outcome, in so far as a discussion on fairy tales is concerned, are the behaviors required to avoid a negative outcome, in other words the taboos, the violation of which often carried serious consequences. For example, in Russian lore an angered spirit known as the bunnik might flay the flesh from someone's bones for entering the bathhouse at night. Further, those who whistled in the home would offend the domovoi, the house spirit which kept them safe and blessed their house. To offend him was to risk having one's household lose its prosperity. Thus many fairy tales include certain prohibitions, about not complaining, about not throwing ones sewage immediately out ones door where the house fairy might be standing, etc. These taboos very often end up in horror stories, in which the violator is punished by the magical being.

Perhaps, the most important and common taboo however, was that one should never directly talk about or discuss certain sacred things. This is the reason the Finnish people would avoid directly saying the name of bears, the Celts and English avoided calling fairies by their real name and instead called them by names such as; Good Folk, Greencoaties, the Strangers, The Tiddy Ones, and more. Further, people were often forbidden from directly discussing their relationship with the spirit world, or the metaphysical nature of the spirit world. Indeed, there are a number of Celtic Fairy Tales in which this need for secrecy about the fairy world is clearly spelled out. In "Kaddy's Luck," for example, the fairies come into Kaddy's home through the keyhole in order to dance the night away, and they always leave her a little money. After getting married she eventually tells her husband the secret origins of her money, and because of this violation of the taboo she soon "found her child had been changed in the night, and there was a very little baby in the cradle. And the child never grew big, for the fairies had changed her child for spite." The obvious message of this tale is that those who spoke of the magical world would be punished.

Cunning, witches, and shamans were also forbidden from sharing their secrets, according to Kira Van Deusen (2001), "It's dangerous to speak directly about the inner lives of shamans" which is why they discussed these using stories. Many of the pieces of fairy tales come from this need to discuss the spirit world in stories as well as from the magical beliefs people held about how the world functioned."

There were, of course, many other purposes to fairy tales which could serve as a form of entertainment, a way of bragging, teaching moral values, as warning tales, etc. According to Jean-Marie Déguignet people would often gossip about encounters they or people they knew had with the spirit world. For example, in one tale a young girl encounters a frisky little fairy in Dartmoor. In order to prevent the being from pixy leading her or causing her any misfortune she walks boldly on:

> The pixy had now reached the bridge, and remained jumping from side to side and performing a variety of antics upon it, as if to prevent her from crossing. But the dame's courage did not fail her, and having made up her mind not to be deterred from pursuing her way, she stepped fearlessly towards the spot where the pixy was, who continued his grotesque movements, leaping about with the greatest agility. As the stout-hearted women gained the bridge, the little fellow hopped towards her, when suddenly stooping down, she seized the pixy in her hand, popped him into the basket she was carrying, and secured the cover, resolving that instead of running any risk of being pixy-led she would turn the tables, and lead the pixy.

The fairy disappears before she can get home, but as the tale says "the good dame was always able to boast that she had had the courage to capture a pixy." In other tales people would beat boggarts with sticks, chase away witches, etc. People's inherent need to both brag and gossip in many cultures would explain how these stories got passed around Yet even stories which come from people bragging about encountering the spirit world are often based on previous folk religious ideas, such as the nature of fairies. People after all tend to get the ideas for their stories from their beliefs, or from the beliefs and stories of others.

"The Corpse Watchers" Analyzed.

One if my favorite examples of a fairy tale with many ancient origins is the Irish tale of "The Corpse Watchers;"

> There was once a poor woman that had three daughters, and one day the eldest said, "Mother, bake my cake and kill my cock, till I go seek my fortune." So she did, and when all was ready, says her mother to her, "Which will you have—half of these with my blessing, or the whole with my curse?" "Curse or no curse," says she, "the whole is little enough." So away she set, and if the mother didn't give her her curse, she didn't give her her blessing.

Poverty is often the greatest villain in fairy tales; it's poverty that causes children to cry with starvation, its poverty which left Europe desolate for over a thousand years. And as with "The Corpse Watches" it' is poverty which caused the mothers to fight with their children for food as happens in so many fairy tales. Consider for a moment the intense emotions involved in the opening to this fairy tale, emotions which the story doesn't explain, but which the people who lived with poverty knew all too well. The eldest daughter in this story is preparing to step out the door, to strike out on her own, leaving her family behind, and what happens? She and her mother begin to fight over a tiny amount of food. At the time of these fairy tales a person's greatest concern wasn't just that there were no guarantees that fortunes would be made, their greatest concern was that starvation was a very real possibility. Indeed many cities, and the countryside itself was filled with the starving and destitute. The danger of starvation is an important part of many fairy tales, for example, in the tale of the "The Two Travelers" a man runs out of bread so that:

> Hunger made itself felt again, and gnawed him almost to the heart. In the evening he fell down by a tree, and on the seventh morning he could not raise himself up for faintness, and death was close at hand.

This is why "The Corpse Watches," begins with a mother and her daughter fighting over food, with the mother essentially threatening to curse her daughter if she takes any more than a single meals worth of food for her long trip.

In addition to the social dimension of this tale, however, there is also an interesting magico-religious moral in the opening of this story as well: Which is that children need to seek after their parents blessing, for their relationship with their parents isn't just

9

important socially, it's supernaturally important as well. There was magic in a parents blessing as well as their curse. The magical nature of the mother's blessing is all the more clear in the Scottish fairy tale of "Maol a Chliobain," which like this tale begins with the eldest daughters taking the food rather than their mother's blessing, leaving only the youngest child to take the blessing. After this; "they went away, but the two eldest did not want the youngest to be with them, and they tied her to a rock of stone. They went on, but her mother's blessing came and freed her." In this story "the mother's blessing" seems to be a physical being, which has the power to help her children.

The elder sisters' failure to take their mother's supernatural blessing in place of material food is a clear sign that she is unprepared to enter the supernatural world people believed was all around them, a supernatural world that in fairy tales children were likely to encounter when they left home for the first time. Indeed, just as it is in "The Corpse Watchers" a child's first job in fairy tales was often with some supernatural being. For example, in the Cornish story "A Maiden from Zennor" the protagonist, a young girl, sets out on her own. At first she's optimistic about her future, but after she walks for some time the reality sets in that she is truly alone, that she may never see her family again. Overwhelmed with fear and sorrow, uncertain what to do she sits down and begins sobbing, that is until she encounters a fairy man willing to hire her to act as nanny for his child. In the case of the "Maiden of Zennor" the moral of the fairy tale is perhaps less mystical then it is in "The Corpse Bride," however, as the girl soon falls in love with her master who "steals kisses" from her on occasion, only to discover that he's cheating on her with another and is fired when she confronts him about it. The message here at least should be clear, that children leaving home were in a precarious situation and had to be cautious. The message of "The Corpse Watchers" as we'll see, however, is that one needs to be prepared to live in a supernatural world when they leave home.

"The Corpse Watchers" Continued...

> She (the eldest sister) walked and she walked till she was tired and hungry, and then she sat down to take her dinner. While she was eating it, a poor woman came up, and asked for a bit. "The dickens a bit you'll get from me," says she; "it's all too little for myself;" and the poor woman walked away very sorrowful. At nightfall she got lodging at a farmer's, and the woman of the house told her that she'd give her a spade-full of gold and a shovel-full of silver if she'd only sit up and watch her son's corpse that was waking in the next room. She said she'd do that; and so, when the family were in their bed, she sat by the fire, and cast an eye from time to time on the corpse that was lying under the table.
>
> All at once the dead man got up in his shroud, and stood before her, and said, "All alone, fair maid!" She gave him no answer, and when he said it the third time, he struck her with a switch, and she became a grey flag.

Here again, the eldest daughter's failure to share her food with an old woman is further evidence that she isn't ready to deal with the supernatural world, which prizes generosity and hospitality above nearly anything else. This is true throughout Eurasian lore. On the Steppes and in Siberia, for example, hospitality was so important that husbands would divorce their wives if they didn't show hospitality to everyone who came by (Siikala, Napolskikh, and Hoppal, 2007). Even hated enemies might at times be given a meal on the Steppes, although once the meal was over and the guest had left, they and the host would be enemies once more. Europe, at least Medieval Europe, might not have been so extreme, but hospitality was still very important to people who would often share their homes with travelers. In fairy tales the beggar or advice giver was often a deity[4] in disguise, as magical beings such as Odin often wandered the earth in human form, and those who failed to be generous with them were almost always punished. In one tale from Switzerland a young girl begs a wealthy man to help her sick mother, but is sent away empty handed. A dwarf appears and gives her both gold and a magical herb to cure her mother, while at the same time causing a rock slide which buries the home of the person who wouldn't help the young girl. Similarly, in East Prussia there was a village which mocked a sick beggar woman, so she cursed the village that the earth would swallow it up. and soon the village sank into a lake. In the story of "The Three Little Men in the Wood" a young girl is asked to share her meal with three fairy-like beings, and when she does so they bless her to grow beautiful, rich and marry well. However, her stepsister who is rude and refuses to share her food with the three men is cursed by them to suffer growing uglier, having frogs hop out of her mouth whenever she speaks, and to die badly.

Such stories are connected both to the moral imperative to give alms and the fact that in many lands it was believed that beggars had magical powers; that to refuse them alms was to risk being cursed. This isn't to say that people always gave alms, for just as people often go against their own moral and religious beliefs today, there were likely always people who weren't as generous as their culture said they should have been in the past. However, in the folk religious tales generosity is one of the most important moral lessons, and often times is the only real means of surviving the wrath of the supernatural.

The elder sister's lack of generosity in "The Corpse Watchers," is a sign that she's unprepared to deal with the magical world which she is now about to face. So it shouldn't be surprising that she's completely alone and unprepared when she finally does encounter the magical world in the form of the walking corpse. She should have been prepared, however, as the fact that the girls in this story were hired to 'watch' over a corpse that could still move around suggests that they were perhaps more than just ordinary girls, that they were a form of fairy doctor (which were a remnant of older shamanistic traditions). In other words, it was specifically their job to deal with the spirit world, and in order to do this they had to act in certain ways and undergo specific preparations. This means that the eldest sister failed not only as a moral person, but as a shaman as well.

"The Corpse Watchers" Continued...

About a week after, the second daughter went to seek her fortune, and she didn't care for her mother's blessing no more nor her sister, and the very same thing happened to her. She was left a grey flag by the side of the other.

At last the youngest went off in search of the other two, and she took care to carry her mother's blessing with her. She shared her dinner with the poor woman on the road, and she told her that she would watch over her.

---

[4] Deities – Deities are, loosely, those beings that dwell in the sky. In keeping with this idea, I will define deities as beings believed to live distantly from humans but which took an interest in our affairs and, in many cases, were the most important beings within the official religion.

Well, she got lodging in the same place as the others, and agreed to mind the corpse. She sat up by the fire with the dog and cat, and amused herself with some apples and nuts the mistress gave her. She thought it a pity that the man under the table was a corpse, he was so handsome.

But at last he got up, and says he, "All alone, fair maid!" and she wasn't long about an answer:–

"All alone I am not,
I've little dog Dog and Pussy, my cat;
I've apples to roast, and nuts to crack,
And all alone I am not."

The third and youngest daughter succeeds where her elder sisters failed, because she is kinder, cleverer, and perhaps braver than they are. She agrees to let her mother have half the food in return for her mother's blessing, then later shares some more food with the poor old lady she encounters on the road. She watches over the corpse with a cat, dog, nuts, and apples. The presence of each of these items is likely significant, as cats and dogs were the most common familiar spirits of witches in Great Britain and Ireland. Dogs especially seem to have some connection with death in Eurasian Lore, either as a Grimm Reaper figure, as a guardian to the realm of the dead, or as a companion to a deity of the dead.

It's well known that in Greece and Rome the dog Cerberus was the guardian to the underworld. Similarly,

> In India the path to the underworld is guarded by a pair of dogs,.. "In stanza 10 the two dogs are conceived as ill-disposed creatures, standing guard to keep the departed souls out of bliss. The soul on its way to heaven is addressed as follows: "Run past straight away the two four-eyed dogs, the spotted and (the dark), the brood of Sarama; enter in among the propitious fathers who hold high feast with Yama. (Bloomfield)

Yet in some stanza's the two dogs appear to act in a Grim Reaper type role in which they choose who is destined to become a companion of Yama.

In Britain spirit dogs would in various places; guard the graves of those who had died by violence, help hunt down the ghosts of wicked men, and act as a premonition of death. W. P. Witcutt claims that the black dogs of Britain, and presumably Ireland as well, are folk memories of a deity which appeared in the form of a dog. Further, the Celtic Deity Dispater, the Gaulish lord of the dead, appears with a small dog totem. On the Steppes, Erlik, the lord of the underworld, has dogs guarding his realm as well.

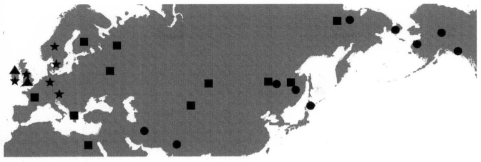

● Kind Grimm Reaper
★ Hunts down spirits of dead
■ Dog is a guardian or serves
▲ Death Omen

This map uses data collected by Berezkin

As you can see from the map, the dogs' connection to the spirits of the dead is one of the most pervasive ideas across Eurasia, and indeed in the America's as well; however, I decided not to include the Americas in this map, with the exception of Alaska because of size constraints.

It's interesting to note that throughout most of Eurasia the Dog is either a guardian to the realm of the dead, a companion to the deity of the dead, or else is a helpful spirit which farriers people across the river to the Realm of the Dead or guides them to it. Yet in Western Europe the dog has to hunt down the spirits of the dead, which given the danger of vampires isn't always a bad thing, and is a death omen. We can't be certain why Western Europe is different in this regard, however, the people of far Western Europe have a different genetic origin than the rest of the people in Europe, though there is some debate as to the exact nature of this origin which I'll discuss further in my chapter on "Migrations."

While the importance of dogs to the deity of the underworld may be an accident, given how common dogs were as pets, dogs were almost never found in the heavens or as companions to deities that have nothing to do with the underworld. So the fact that there's a dog watching a corpse with the youngest girl in "The Corpse Watchers" does seem to be significant.

The Cat

Cats are also a magical being, one which is still most often associated with witches, such as the youngest sister from "The Corpse Watchers." Cats, after all, as Briggs points out in "Fairies in Tradition and Literature," are often considered to be fairies in their own right, and they certainly have a strong connection with witches. Indeed in Ireland one of the most common familiar spirits for witches to have was in the form of a cat, something we are still aware of today. As familiar spirits they would act as mediators between the witch and the fairy world, though in this case the witch wasn't their master; the Queen or King of the Fairies or Underworld was. In Breton Lore a person would at times make a deal with a cat or their master in which the cat would make them wealthy for a number of years, after which the person would serve the fairies. (Fairies were always looking for servants to clean

13

for them, cook for them, play music, act as nursemaids for their children, watch their cattle, etc.). In this role the cat was often deceived by the cunning peasant, as there were tales of peasants making the deal with a cat, than waiting until their time of wealth was almost over, at which point they would have the priest or some witch banish the cat for them, so that they could keep the wealth and not have to work for it. In Germany, and Celtic lands it seems likely that many house fairies and spirits lived in the form of a cat. Indeed, Jacob Grimm believed that Puss in Boots was such a household family fairy.

Sometimes such household spirits were clearly related to the people whose home they shared, after all many people's spirits became fairies when they died. Yet other times the cat would live with a person because they had been banished from the fairy court. In one common Celtic tale a man discovers that his cat is the successor to the King of the Cats, when the current king of the cats dies.

In more modern times cats came to be thought of as more demonic than other fairies, but that doesn't seem to have been the case in ancient times. Certainly like all fairies there were good and evil ones, or the same one had both good and evil traits; meaning they could become vindictive and cruel at the drop of a hat. In one case, when a woman failed to feed a cat at the table because her friends were visiting, it ripped up her throat and eventually she died from the infection. (Wilde) Yet others, like Puss in Boots, could also be forgiving and helpful.

It's also interesting to note that some of the oldest enemies of the fairies/deities of Celtic lands were called dog heads and or cat heads. Other than the obvious, it's difficult to say what the exact nature of these beings was. Being enemies to the deities, however, doesn't make these beings evil per say. In Greek lore the enemies of the gods were often allies of humanity, and in Japanese lore many of the enemies of the Heavenly Kami (Kami is a term for any being which can supernaturally aid humans) became fertility spirits of the land. So it's hard to say what people thought of the god's enemies in ancient Ireland, given how few records we actually have of this.

Nuts

The nuts were also an important object for the girl to have, as in Ireland, as in other Celtic Lands, meals were given to the spirits of the dead in the form of nuts which were often placed in the burial coffin. So it would seem then that nuts may have been a way to placate the dead spirits. (MacCulloch) Hazel nuts specifically were considered magical. Callirisu was a deity whose name perhaps meant "hazel wood:"

> Hazel once had a powerful reputation for magic. In Ireland it was a tree of healing, in English folklore it was guarded by demons, in Scotland its nut was thrown at witches (Breeze).

So by having the nuts, the dog, and the cat, the youngest daughter in "The Corpse Watchers" is able to state that she was most certainly not alone, and so survive her initial encounter with the spirit world.

There is one more interesting tidbit about the girl's statement that she has a dog, cat and hazelnut, which is that another girl in Devonshire said it as well;

> A pixy looked into a house and said:
> All alone fair maid?

14

No, here am I with a dog and cat,
and Apples to eat and nuts to crack.' (Wentz)

Unfortunately the source for this bit of lore doesn't recall the story it comes from, so we have no way of knowing what lead to this or what happened next. Pixies are such strange and interesting little fairies it's difficult to know if this story of a pixie relates to something good or bad, a spirit of the dead or of nature. Because pixies were well known for causing mischief and at times even kidnapping women, this might be a good response to prevent spirits from doing bad things to people.

"The Corpse Watchers" Continued...

"Ho, ho!" says he, you're a girl of courage, though you wouldn't have enough to follow me. I am now going to cross the quaking bog, and go through the burning forest. I must then enter the cave of terror, and climb the hill of glass, and drop from the top of it into the Dead Sea." "I'll follow you," says she, "for I engaged to mind you." He thought to prevent her, but she was as stiff as he was stout.

Out he sprang through the window, and she followed him till they came to the "Green Hills," and then says he:—

Open, open, Green Hills, and let the Light of the Green Hills through;" Aye," says the girl, "and let the fair maid, too."

They opened, and the man and woman passed through, and there they were, on the edge of a bog.

Hills in Celtic, Scandinavian, and Germanic Lore are the gateway to fairy land, and the realm of the dead. According to the "Fairy Faith in the Celtic Countries;"

The Sidhe or Tuatha De Danann were a people like ourselves who inhabited the hills—not as a rule the highest and most salient eminences, but I think more usually the pleasant undulating slopes or gentle hill-sides—and who lived there a life of their own, marrying or giving in marriage, banqueting or making war, and leading there just as real a life as is our own...

Knock Ma, which you see over there, is said to contain excavated passages and a palace where the fairies live, and with them the people they have taken. And from the inside of the hill there is believed to be an entrance to an underground world. It is a common opinion that after consumptives die they are there with the fairies in good health.

What's more "sidhe," one of the Irish words for fairy, comes from the word 'sid', which is a term for hills or mounds, within which the old pagan gods were imagined to dwell (Patricia Monaghan). Within the Indo-European conception of the world there is a common division between the deities of the sky (divine beings) and the deities of the underworld (chthonian deities). The Rig Veda had a threefold division between earth, heaven and water (Griswold), an idea which was carried over into the primary deities of Greece (Zeus, Hades, and Poseidon). It's interesting to note at this point that in Europe deities which blessed the fertility of the field were often connected with the underworld,

15

with the spirits of the dead. This is something we see very clearly in Celtic lore where the existence of the fairies which dwell in the hills are often associated with the spirits of the dead, and create the fertility of the land. These spirits of the dead, and the agricultural deities who were connected to the earth, as this story has shown, could be very dangerous:

> Agricultural gods, too were easily roused to anger – for the crops often failed.... The Homeric Hymn dwells at length on the anger of Demeter. It is not the mild mother goddess who makes the whole world suffer because she feels she has been wronged. In fact, it would seem that the mildness which we attribute to Demeter was not her's in virtue of her being an agricultural goddess; it is a developed trait, due first to the fact that she was elevated from the position of a spirit of the grain to the rank of an Olympian divinity, and secondly to the striking development of the mother idea in connection with the story of the rape of Persephone. (Fairbanks)

The connection with fairies and hills in Ireland specifically means that after entering the hill the corpse and girl following him are in reality in the "otherworld" and that they remain there for most of the rest of the fairy tale. It also means that the protagonist is most likely a shaman, as one of the shaman's primary jobs was to bring back the souls of the sick and dying from the Underworld. Her journeying into the hills also means that she's in great danger, which is why it's a good thing she's already won favor with the supernatural world.

"The Corpse Watchers" Continued...

He trod lightly over the shaky bits of moss and sod; and while she was thinking of how she'd get across, the old beggar appeared to her, but much nicer dressed, touched her shoes with her stick, and the soles spread a foot on each side. So she easily got over the shaky marsh. The burning wood was at the edge of the bog, and there the good fairy flung a damp, thick cloak over her, and through the flames she went, and a hair of her head was not singed. Then they passed through the dark cavern of horrors, where she'd have heard the most horrible yells, only that the fairy stopped her ears with wax. She saw frightful things, with blue vapours round them, and felt the sharp rocks, and the slimy backs of frogs and snakes.

Here's where the youngest daughter's generosity truly pays off, for good fairies were far more likely to help the generous on their quests into the other world; and the help of spirits was important to a shaman's success and even their survival in the spirit world. This is because the spirit world was often made up of a series of horrors, as is highlighted in this tales "Cavern of Horrors," and flame filled lands.

"The Corpse Watchers" Continued...

When they got out of the cavern, they were at the mountain of glass; and then the fairy made her slippers so sticky with a tap of her rod, that she followed the young corpse easily to the top. There was the deep sea a quarter of a mile under them, and so the corpse said to her, "Go home to my mother, and tell her how far you came to do her bidding: farewell." He sprung head foremost down into the sea, and after him she plunged, without stopping a moment to think about it.

Like entering the hill, the glass mountain is a clear sign that the girl has entered the spirit world, as glass, crystal, or ice objects were a sign of the otherworld (Patch):

> In fact the glass mountain is oftentimes so far in the spirit realm that even the inhabitants of the otherworld don't know where it is. In the tale of "The Three Lemons" for example, a witch/fairy tells a prince that his wife is on the glass hill. After traveling over forests, deserts, and more the prince finds no sign of the glass hill. At last he comes to the home of winter (Jezibaba), who despite being the goddess of a major season hasn't ever heard of the glass hill, though she thinks that maybe her son, a cannibalistic monster has. Though even with his great knowledge, he also hasn't heard of the hill either, so he sends the prince on to see his brother, who also hasn't heard of the glass mountain and who, again, sends the prince on to his other brother. (Clara Vostrovsky Winlow)

The ocean too is often equated with the realm of the dead, as great bodies of water, such as the river Styx in Greek lore, were the barrier between the human realm and the realm of the dead.

"The Corpse Watchers" Continued...

> *She was stupefied at first, but when they reached the waters she recovered her thoughts. After piercing down a great depth, they saw a green light towards the bottom. At last they were below the sea, that seemed a green sky above them; and sitting in a beautiful meadow, she half asleep, and her head resting against his side. She couldn't keep her eyes open, and she couldn't tell how long she slept: but when she woke, she was in bed at his house, and he and his mother sitting by her bedside, and watching her.*
>
> *It was a witch that had a spite to the young man, because he wouldn't marry her, and so she got power to keep him in a state between life' and death till a young woman would rescue him by doing what she had just done. So at her request, her sisters got their own shape again, and were sent back to their mother, with their spades of gold and shovels of silver. Maybe they were better after that, but I doubt it much. The youngest got the young gentleman for her husband. I'm sure she deserved him, and, if they didn't live happy, THAT WE MAY*

Bringing peoples' souls back from the land of the dead was one of the most important jobs of the shaman. So within "The Corpse Watchers" are pieces of what are likely a shaman's journey to recover the spirit of a dying person from the realm of the dead, mixed with what are likely later motifs about happy marriages and children striking out to seek their fortunes. Part of the challenge to understanding supernatural fairy tales is that they are often populated by old shamans, witches, fairies, and deities whose names have been changed over time. Thus it's sometimes difficult to know who a story might have originally been about. Europe, after all, is filled with forgotten or nearly forgotten deities, for as each wave of people moved through Europe they often altered the religion of the place they moved into, or at times lost some of their own deities. This means that many of the pieces that make up fairy tales come from earlier ideas about ancient deities. In Russia for example;

17

Perun, the god of thunder and lightning, became Ilya the Prophet; Volos the guardian of herds and flocks became St Vlasia; Kupalnitsa, goddess of rivers and lakes became St Agrippina... Nevertheless, the memory of local gods persisted and the fear of them degenerated into superstition. At this stage of disorganization of local custom, the magic of folktales became half-fantastic, half-conventional; transmitted as they were, orally and under the ban of the Church, the tales became diluted with faint memories of real history, lost folk songs, and laments, Christian legend and superstitions dating back to earlier times. (Davidson and Chaudhri)

Stitching Tales Together

Perhaps the easiest place to see the transformation of gods into mere fairy tale characters, the piecing together of ancient divine myths with other tales is Greece, because here we know many (though not all) of the ancient myths about their deities. So when we see that God in Greek fairy tales uses lighting to smite the wicked and to battle a rebellion of giants who try to climb up a mountain to reach him, we are able to understand that this comes from myths about Zeus battling the titans to keep them from climbing up mount Olympus.

Perhaps even more interesting is the fairy tale about the Turk Magician who kidnaps the daughter of St. Demetra, a clear remnant of the Greek myth "The Rape of Persephone" in which Hades, the lord of the , kidnaps the daughter of the Greek fertility goddess, Demeter. In this story St. Demetra is a clear continuation of the goddess Demeter, with places in Greece even continuing the give offerings to the statue of the goddess Demeter while merely calling it an icon of St. Demetra, a saint who was never recognized by the Church and is unknown elsewhere. In tales St. Demetra was a kind and good old woman, devoted to feeding the poor. She had a daughter who was the most beautiful woman since Lady Aphrodite. A Turkish Lord of Souli (Souli is significant because it is a region with one of the mythological descents into the underworld, and is a place where one version of the "Rape of Persephone" by Hades took place), who was well versed in magic decided to kidnap her. One Christmas night, while St. Demetra was at church the Turkish lord seized the girl and carried her off on his black horse which breathed flames from his nostrils.

So far the story tracks fairly closely to the ancient Greek myth of Hades kidnapping the daughter of Demeter; with Hades and his black horses being replaced by a Turkish Magician with a black horse, and Demeter being replaced by a kindly saint. This, however, is where the stories begin to diverge, for in the ancient myth we know that the sun is the one who tells Demeter what happened to her daughter. In this later fairy tale however, St. Demetra asks the sun, but he tells her nothing, and so it's ultimately a stork, which is her friend, who tells her what happened to her daughter. The stork then offers to guide her on a journey to find her daughter. This element seems to come from some form of

18

shamanistic story which has pushed its way into the old myth, as birds were frequently guides of shamans into the spirit world. It gets more complicated however, for unlike the previous myth in which Zeus ordered Hades to free Demeter's daughter Persephone, St. Demetra must travel through the cold winter to find her daughter, all while being mocked by the people she encounters. At last she finds a kindly family which takes her in. In return for their kindness she blesses their fields with rich fertility. The son of this family then takes up St. Demetra's cause and travels in her stead to find her kidnapped daughter.

So once more we've switched the type of tale this is, and have moved from an ancient myth about a deity, to a story about a shaman, to a tale about a hero who must free the damsel in distress. In this story the young man encounters some dragons resting around a giant cauldron. The young man lifts this cauldron and the dragons are so impressed with his display of strength that they crowd around him and say;

> "You who can lift with one hand a cauldron which we by our united efforts can scarcely carry, you alone are capable of carrying off a maiden whom we have long been trying to lay our hands on, and whom we cannot seize because of the height of the tower wherein a magician keeps her shut up."

Not certain how to escape the, he opts to kill them one by one as they crawl through the window of the Turks tower after him. At last he finds St. Demetra's daughter when;

> Suddenly the magician appeared, and in a fury of anger threw himself upon the young man, who met him bravely. The former was of superhuman strength, but Nicolas' son was not inferior to him. The magician had the power to transform himself into anything he might choose; he changed successively into a lion, into a serpent, into a bird of prey, into fire — hoping under some one of these forms to wear his adversary out; but nothing could shake the courage of the young man. For three days the combat continued. The first day the magician seemed beaten, but the next he regained his advantage ; at the end of the day's struggle he killed his young opponent, and cut his body into four quarters, which he hung on the four sides of the tower. Then elated by his victory, he did violence to Demetra's daughter, whose chastity he had hitherto respected. But in the night the stork flew away to a great distance to fetch a magic herb which it knew, brought it back in its beak, and rubbed with it the young man's lips. At once the pieces of his body came together again and he revived. Great was his despair when he learnt what had taken place after his defeat; but he only threw himself upon the magician with the greater fury the third day, to punish him for his crime. (Cuthburt)

Here again we return to the notion of the stork as the shamanistic helper spirit, bringing the hero back to life so that he may continue his battle.

Like many fairy tales, this Greek fairy tale isn't a single story, rather it's potentially three different stories stitched together. It's common for fairy tales to be made up of many elements from other stories or superstitions which are placed into the plot but don't necessarily seem to fit with the original idea of the tale. So as you can see. the challenge to understanding the original meaning behind fairy tales isn't just that they have long complex histories, but that they are made up of various unrelated pieces which are often puzzled together over time. Each of these pieces may have its own meaning, its own history, and so when they are put together to make a single story, that story can become extremely confusing. Take "Hansel and Gretel" for example:

Analysis of "Hansel and Gretel"

Next to a great forest there lived a poor woodcutter with his wife and his two children. The boy's name was Hansel and the girl's name was Gretel. He had but little to eat, and once, when a great famine came to the land, he could no longer provide even their daily bread.
One evening as he was lying in bed worrying about his problems, he sighed and said to his wife, ""What is to become of us? How can we feed our children when we have nothing for ourselves?"
""Man, do you know what?" answered the woman. ""Early tomorrow morning we will take the two children out into the thickest part of the woods, make a fire for them, and give each of them a little piece of bread, then leave them by themselves and go off to our work. They will not find their way back home, and we will be rid of them."

This beginning likely comes from a cluster of Western European tales where children are abandoned by their parents, which may have originated with medieval famine. In addition to "Hansel and Gretel," these stories include "Mollie Whoopie" and "Little Thumb". Within these stories we see a much more shockingly horrifying picture of poverty than that portrayed in "The Corpse Watches." Indeed the poverty in "Hansel and Gretel" is so stunningly extreme that it's haunted the nightmares of people and delighted the pens of philosophers for two centuries. Poverty in general is likely one of the most important forces involved in shaping fairy tales. In the original version of "Hansel and Gretel," as with similar tales, it wasn't some step mother who banished Hansel and Gretel into the forest for want of food, it was their own mother. Unable to bear the thought that the children's own mother would send them off into the woods to die, the Grimm brothers changed the story. But in some ways Hansel and Gretel were lucky; in other lesser known stories, as well as one Biblical story, desperate parents seek to eat their children (and are punished for it).

Perhaps one of the harshest and most stunning tales of famine comes from Japan. This, however, isn't a fairy tale; instead it's part of a village record from little more than a hundred years ago. In this story a reed cutter was unable to sell his goods, so with no food to feed his starving family he made his way home. Unable to bear telling his children that he had no food for them, he snuck into the house and went to bed. When he awoke he was horrified to see his two little children sharpening his ax. When he asked them what they were doing, they told him that they wanted him to cut off their heads in order to end their hunger.

Starvation causes insanity. As the body begins searching desperately for a way to stay to keep the heart and lungs alive it breaks down a person's muscles. They begin to suffer anemia, rashes, and diarrhea, but without food what they are defecating is the broken down pieces of their own body. It gets worse, however, as those who are starving suffer depression and anxiety. They become unable to think and obsessed with food; all common elements found in fairy tale characters. The wish of many in fairy tales, it seems, is to eat their fill; to gain food, for which they will sacrifice nearly anything, even selling their soul to the devil in order to eat.

"Hansel and Gretel" Analysis continued...

Hansel and Gretel are too hungry to sleep while their parents are planning to leave them in the forest to die, so they overhear everything. Hansel, being clever, fills his pockets with white stones so that he can make a trail to lead him and his sister back home after their father abandons them in the forest. The Little Thumb does the same in his fairy tale. However, Molly Whuppie doesn't do this in her fairy tale, and neither do most characters in such abandonment tales, so this element seems to be German/French specific.

It's interesting to note that despite having been so desperate that they left their children in the woods to die, the parents are able to live with them for some time after they make it back home; until another famine strikes, when once again the children's mother gets their father to leave them in the forest. This may be due to later influence on the story, as the upper class people who got a hold of it may have viewed such abandonment as a result of the poor being wasteful whenever they got lucky enough to have plenty.

After being lead into the woods a number of times, Hansel and Gretel finally get lost as their mother wanted them to.

> They started walking again, but managed only to go deeper and deeper into the woods. If help did not come soon, they would perish. At midday they saw a little snow-white bird sitting on a branch. It sang so beautifully that they stopped to listen. When it was finished it stretched its wings and flew in front of them. They followed it until they came to a little house. The bird sat on the roof, and when they came closer, they saw that the little house was built entirely from bread with a roof made of cake, and the windows were made of clear sugar.

And here's where the second story enters in, for in "Molly Whuppie" and similar tales the journey in the woods is barely mentioned, the details of the forest being irrelevant to the story. This lack of information is fairly common in fairy tales where details, such as the journey across seven whole kingdoms, are suppressed into a single statement of fact, that the journey took place. Even in "Little Thumb," which mentions how scary the woods are, the children simply wander blindly through the darkness. In "Hansel and Gretel," however, the journey has an interesting element that isn't present in most other variations of this tale; that of following the little snow white bird from branch to branch. The bird is important because birds are often the guides of shamans into the spirit world, and were at times the form that the souls of the dead took (Schaefer). In an Irish tale a monk hears a bird singing so beautifully he follows it into the woods as it flies from tree to tree. Then when he returns home he finds that he's been gone for decades, as the bird had led him into the spirit world.

So the fact that Hansel and Gretel follow a bird is likely taken from an element which in the past had signaled that the characters are in the "Other World;" that they have reached the point in their starvation where they are on the verge of death and are now on their first shamanistic journey. In folk religion it was common for many shamans to starve themselves in the wilderness in order to enter the spirit world, bringing themselves to the edge of death in order to enter a liminal state between the world of the living and the world of the dead (Kelly and Thomas). Further, as I'll discuss later, such starvation can also lead people to have near death experiences, which are likely responsible for many of the shamanistic traditions and fairy tale elements humans had.

It is of course questionable if anyone at the time of the Grimm Brothers was aware of the shamans journey motifs inherent in the story, but the bird guiding the children into the spirit world isn't the only aspect of this tale that indicates the two children are in the spirit world. So it seems probable that the story of "Hansel and Gretel" was merged with a similar tale about children being taken captive by an otherworldly monster.

"Hansel And Gretel" Continued…

After gorging themselves on the house of bread for a while, Hansel and Gretel meet what at first seems to be the kindly old lady who lives inside it.

> She took them by the hand and led them into her house. Then she served them a good meal: milk and pancakes with sugar, apples, and nuts. Afterward she made two nice beds for them, decked in white. Hansel and Gretel went to bed, thinking they were in heaven. But the old woman had only pretended to be friendly. She was a wicked witch who was lying in wait there for children. She had built her house of bread only in order to lure them to her, and if she captured one, she would kill him, cook him, and eat him; and for her that was a day to celebrate.

The witch in this story seems to be similar in nature to Baba Yaga, who is a guardian to the realm of the dead. In "Baba Yaga: The Ambiguous Mother and Witch of the Russian Folktale" it's claimed that Baba Yaga herself is identical to the Germanic figures of Holda, Frau Holle, and Bertha. These figures cause the snow and the rain, but also care for the souls of unborn children until sending them to earth when they are ready. But perhaps most important for this story, they also receive the souls of dead children. (As an interesting side note, a connection is also made between Baba Yaga and mice who are the messengers of Death, and the Germanic tooth fairy, with the custom being that children will give their baby teeth to mice and ask for an iron tooth in return).

Like Baba Yaga, the witch in "Hansel and Gretel" can't really see the children, she can only smell or feel them. Propp saw this as further evidence that Baba Yaga was the guardian of the dead, for she couldn't see the living but only smell them. This idea is fairly common throughout Greek lore. The ghosts in the Odyssey, for example, had difficulty seeing the living, while the guardians to the realm of the dead in one Celtic tale of King Arthur couldn't see him very well either (Green, 2007). This is interesting because once again we have a symbol which places Hansel and Gretel in the realm of the dead.

"Hansel and Gretel" continued

After the witch captures them she stuffs Hansel with food and forces Gretel to work as a slave. This enslavement of the protagonist in the spirit world is such a common theme in fairy lore that it's even the subject of the film "Spirited Away." As with this film, it's very often a witch, such as Baba Yaga who does the enslaving, though some form of "forest king" will also buy peoples' souls to make them into slaves as well. In general the spirits of lore crave slaves, servants, or helpers to do their menial labor for them.

In the witches desire to fatten up Hansel we begin to truly see a completely different motif than is present in most of the other Western stories of this type. In stories such as "Molly Whuppie" the protagonist and her sisters are put to bed by a wicked giant who plans to murder them in their sleep. There is no cleaning the house, no caging the children to make them grow fatter, the story is fairly strait forward, with the giant simply planning to murder and eat the children in their sleep so that his kindly wife can't object. (This kindly wife of the lord of the dead will be the subject of a later study, however, suffice it to say that it's also a common theme in fairy tales). With Hansel locked away the witch begins waiting anxiously for the day that she can eat them.

> Every morning the old woman crept out to the stall and shouted,
> ""Hansel, stick out your finger, so I can feel if you are fat yet."
> But Hansel stuck out a little bone, and the old woman, who had bad
> eyes and could not see the bone, thought it was Hansel's finger, and
> she wondered why he didn't get fat.

The use of a bone to trick the witch into thinking the protagonist is too skinny to eat is interesting here, because this motif likely has its origin much further east, as there are a number of other places where this trick is used, including Mari-El (which is on the border between Europe and Asia in Russia), among the Sami to the North, and Poland.

Of these stories The Mari-El Tale is of special interest because it involves a witch called the Vuver, which also locks the children away in order to fatten them up for eating. According to Valery Petrov, Vuver spirits are serpent like witches that come from the souls of the dead or the souls of sleeping humans whose spirits have left their bodies to go on a spirit journey. The Vuver flies about at night in order to spread illness, spoil crops, and do many other things which are associated with witches. A witch based on the Vuver is an interesting enemy for Hansel and Gretel to face, because she could also explain why their mother is dead when they return home; because the Vuver were the spirits of astral travelers who sent their souls out of their bodies in their sleep. Thus the Vuver could have been the children's own mother seeking to devour them, and when they killed this witch, their mother died as well.

Here again we have sort of a conundrum: the Vuver is an evil spirit that dwelt in the folklore of a land which is nearly a thousand miles from Germany, where "Hansel and Gretel" was collected. Further, the tale of the Vuver in Mari-El that I know of doesn't have a Wicked Mother character, nor are the children abandoned by their parents, but instead are simply captured by the Vuver while they are gathering berries in the forest. This begs the question; could the witch in "Hansel and Gretel" be a witch who sends her soul out of her body? The answer is that it's certainly possible. as the German's believed in the idea of witches sending their souls from their bodies at one time. In fact there are stories of men capturing the souls of witches who had left their bodies, and forcing these souls to marry them. In one of these German tales, the witch herself was from England, and she eventually returned to her body there. Such stories show an obvious link to the idea that a witch, or other evil being could send their souls out of their body, an idea which exists all over Europe. Of course, whether the witch that Hansel and Gretel encounter is their own mother or not is entirely speculative, but often such beings would attack their family members first. A male Vuver, for example, is most likely to drain the life out of their wives before moving on to the rest of their family.

"Hansel and Gretel" continued

Frustrated by the fact that Hansel doesn't seem to be getting any fatter, and at last unable to wait any longe,r the witch decides to cook Hansel and Gretel despite how skinny they are;

> She pushed poor Gretel outside to the oven, from which fiery flames
> were leaping. " Climb in," said the witch, " and see if it is hot enough

> to put the bread in yet." And when Gretel was inside, she intended to
> close the oven, and bake her, and eat her as well.
> But Gretel saw what she had in mind, so she said, " I don't know how
> to do that. How can I get inside?"
> " Stupid goose," said the old woman. "The opening is big enough. See,
> I myself could get in." And she crawled up and stuck her head into the
> oven.
> Then Gretel gave her a shove, causing her to fall in. Then she closed
> the iron door and secured it with a bar. The old woman began to howl
> frightfully. But Gretel ran away, and the godless witch burned up
> miserably. Gretel ran straight to Hansel, unlocked his stall, and cried,
> " Hansel, we are saved. The old witch is dead."
> Then Hansel jumped out, like a bird from its cage when someone
> opens its door. How happy they were! They threw their arms around
> each other's necks, jumped with joy, and kissed one another. Because
> they now had nothing to fear, they went into the witch's house. In
> every corner were chests of pearls and precious stones.

With the witch killed and Hansel and Gretel as wealthy as kings you might think that the story is over, but it isn't quite yet. Remember that Hansel and Gretel were led into the spirit world by the bird and so defeating the witch wasn't enough; they now have to find their way out of this magical realm.

> " But now we must leave," said Hansel, " and get out of these witch-
> woods."
> After walking a few hours they arrived at a large body of water. " We
> cannot get across," said Hansel. " I cannot see a walkway or a
> bridge."
> " There are no boats here," answered Gretel, " but there is a white
> duck swimming. If I ask it, it will help us across."
> Then she called out:
>
> "Duckling, duckling,
> Here stand Gretel and Hansel.
> Neither a walkway nor a bridge,
> Take us onto your white back".
> The duckling came up to them, and Hansel climbed onto it, then asked
> his little sister to sit down next to him.

Despite having been able to walk to the witch's house, Hansel and Gretel are suddenly confronted with an uncrossable barrier of water on their way home. Water often acts as a barrier between the human and spirit world, a fact which is likely the reason characters such as the Headless Horsemen cannot cross it. In order to cross these barriers shamans had to pay a boatman, turn into an animal which could cross, or ride on a goose, swan or duck. Water fowl were often considered be travelers between the spirit world because that they could fly into the sky, or dive under the water, while nesting on the land, allowing them to exist in all three worlds.

The story of "Hansel and Gretel" then is made up of pieces from many different stories, containing both the Western elements of starvation and the defeat of a wicked being, and the Eastern element of a blind otherworldly guardian which is deceived through the use of a bone. It also potentially contains multiple elements involving witches, magical birds, and journeys into the land of the dead.

The Search for Meaning

In trying to understand fairy tales you must begin by defining your purpose for interpreting them. As you have seen, fairy tales are very often built up of multiple fragments of old ideas which may or may not fit together well. This still leaves the question, is this important? After all, as Karen Jolly (1996) rightly points out, in many respects interpreting each of these fractured meanings as I do can be meaningless for some purposes, because such interpretations don't tell us what the people who told the fairy tales when they were collected thought of them. So, just as most people now don't think of Arthur as a forgotten god, most people in the Industrial and Victorian Era's when these fairy tales were collected didn't realize many of the things I've mentioned in relation to fairy tales; therefor fairy tales had a different meaning for the people who they were collected from than they did for the people who first created them. So can anyone say that the meaning of the fairy tales comes from its origins, if no one is aware of these origins?

The answer depends on the purpose for interpreting fairy tales, as what ultimately matters is what you want to know about them. In my case, my purpose in reading fairy tales is to get as close to the root origins of the different pieces as possible, because I believe that doing so can give us some interesting insights into our history, helping us to better understand where we came from and the intimate connections between different peoples. Further, I like dreaming and imagining a more magical world, and so I believe that we can all benefit from thinking differently about the world's oldest fantasy stories, whether we are writers or just fans of the genre. More than this, understanding the transformation of fairy tales, understanding where they came from and how they changed over time gives us insight not only into who we once were, but how humanity has transformed from era to era and place to place. This is important because I believe that we can't fully understand what we have chosen to be without understanding what we gave up. More than this, however, seeing how stories differ from one culture to another can give us insights into the different ancient cultures.

Take, for example, the common stories about peasants outsmarting some powerful being which seeks to take half his crops.

"The Bear and the Peasant"

> Once upon a time a certain peasant lost his family and was left alone with no one to help him in his home or his fields. So he went to the Bear and said, "Look here, bear, let's keep house and plant our garden and sow our corn together." And bear asked, "But how shall we divide it afterwards?"
> "How shall we divide it?" said the peasant, "Well, you take all the tops and let me have all the roots."
> "All right," answered bear.
> So they sowed some turnips, and they grew beautifully. And bear worked hard, and gathered in all the turnips, and then they began to divide them.
> And the peasant said, "The tops are yours, aren't they, bear?"
> "Yes," he answered.
> So the peasant cut off all the turnip tops and gave them to bear, and then sat down to count the roots. And bear saw that the peasant had done him down. And he got huffy, lay down in his den, and started sucking his paws.

25

The next spring the peasant again came to see him, and said, " Look here, bear,
let's work together again, shall we?"
And bear answered, "Right-ho! Only this time mind! You can have the tops, but
I'm going to have the roots!"
"Very, well," said the peasant.
And they sowed some wheat, and when the ears grew up and ripened, you never
saw such a sight. Then they began to divide it, and the peasant took all the tops
with the grain, and gave bear the straw and the roots. So he didn't get anything
that time either.
And bear said to the peasant, "Well, good-bye! I'm not going to work with you
any more, you're too crafty!"
And with that he went off into the forest.

The Russian version of this story has both a bit of amusement and perhaps a moral as well; that one shouldn't try to cheat the forest spirit (deity) out of its fair share of one's harvest, for if one does the forest spirit will abandon them. I make this statement for two reasons. The first is that the bear in Russian lore is often believed to be one of the spirit owners of a location, one who in this case was willing to help the peasant during his time of need. In the end the peasant's greed, however, caused the bear to abandon him, leaving him with no one to help him the next year.

In the Grimm Brothers tale, however, the bear's role is replaced by that of a devil who rather than helping the peasant, wishes to buy food from a farmer who agrees to sell him the top half of the crops the first year and plants turnips, then plants wheat and gives the devil roots. The angry, cheated devil disappears into a chasm in a cliff at the end of this story and the peasant is able to become wealthy from his deal. So not only has the bear changed into a devil in the German version, but the moral has changed as well, to one in which cunning and cleverness, rather than honesty is the most important trait in dealing with the supernatural world.

Contrast these two stories with the one from Northampton shire, England where a Bogie (a form of mischievous fairy) doesn't make a deal with the farmer, but instead demands that the farmer give him half of the crop, and is tricked in the same way that the bear and devil had been. This is similar to a story from Lincolnshire in which a boggart in the form of a squat hairy man with long arms approaches a farmer who has just started plowing new lands and tells the farmer that he is the proper owner of the land and that the farmer must leave. Here again the farmer uses the same trick with potatoes and grain in order make a deal to purchase the land and trick the spirit in order to steal its land. This is interesting because among the English and the Celts there was an idea that they had taken the land from the fairy folk. In other words, this same story becomes a historical lesson about how people had tricked the fairies out of their land.

This is similar to the Danish version in which a farmer decides to begin plowing a little mound, and a troll comes up to demand that he stop plowing his roof. Again the farmer uses the next trick in order to gain the right to plow the land. Initially one might think that this tricking the spirit of the land is a Christian alteration, however, the use of deceit to take the land from the original owner is common in North East Asia, Korea, and Japan. Further, Irish, Welsh, and Cornish mythology all indicate that humans had to take the land from the previous magical inhabitants.

Finally, some versions of this story might be best explained by the tale of Prometheus and Zeus. Prometheus got Zeus to agree to choose which part of the animals would be offered to him in sacrifice forevermore. In order to help humanity, Prometheus wrapped the guts and bones in tasty looking fat so that Zeus would pick this. With Zeus thus tricked, humanity was free to eat the best portion of their food and leave the worst for the deities. So it seems possible that this story of a person tricking the deity into accepting the worst part of the plant as offering has a similar idea behind it.

Regardless of this tale's exact meaning however, what's important to understand is how easily morals and characters can change from place to place and time to time. Thus a popular story might spread from one land to another, but its nature would change. By looking at how the same stories differ from one culture to another we can begin to see differences in the way people thought from one land to another.

In addition to fairy tales, mythological figures and magical creatures can be a created through a synchronization of elements and ideas which vary from one culture to another. Take Baba Yaga for example, who is one of the most complex and confusing characters in Russian lore, with hundreds of stories told about her. Andreas Johns points out that;

> The complexity of Baba Yaga and other folktale characters derives in part from the fact that they are, on the one hand, the products of tradition, of collective history and psychology, a collective fantasy; on the other hand, they provide material for the fantasies of individuals. So it is clear that there can be no single correct interpretation or understanding of Baba Yaga. Potentially she can have a multiplicity of meanings for every individual tale-teller and listener. (Andreas Johns)

Thus our understanding of the fairy world is clouded by the fact that even within the same culture and era different people often believed so many different things about fairy tales and the spirit world. For example, the Celts of the Victorian Era had many differing individual beliefs about the fairies. Some thought of them as dead spirits of ancestors and neighbors, while others thought of them as fallen angels, or as the spirits of dead pagans. Some also thought of them as a previous people who'd been driven underground, as strange mystical beings, and on occasion as nature spirits. Finally there was an odd fairy tale in which;

> In our Savior's time there lived a woman whose fortune it was to be possessed of nearly a score of children, and as she saw our blessed Lord approach her dwelling, being ashamed of being so prolific, and that he might not see them all, she concealed about half of them closely, and after his departure, when she went in search of them, to her great surprise found they were all gone. They never afterwards could be discovered, for it was supposed that as a punishment from heaven for hiding what God had given her, she was deprived of them; and it is said these her offspring have generated the race called fairies.

It seems likely that very few people had all of these beliefs. More likely any individual only focused on a few ideas about the nature of fairies. However, at the same time a single individual could hold more than one belief about fairies which would, to an outsider, seem to have been incompatible with each other. As () points out, people have often held many incompatible ideas about a given subject. The number and complexity of beliefs that people held at the same time and in the same era makes it extremely difficult to make fast and certain statements about what people thought about fairy tales in general. Instead we can only say what one story or another says about fairies, or what common motifs existed at a specific time.

My final reason for my interest in interpreting fairy tales is that I find it frustrating that

27

human history is filled with so many vanished peoples, so many forgotten ideas, hopes and dreams which were never realized. However, bits and pieces of these cultures may live on in remnants which are found in fairy tales. For example, in Eastern China, one forgotten people was overrun by the growth of the Chinese Empire. Yet they are the geographical epicenter of the fox tales of Asia. So did they vanish, or do their ideas live on in some of the most famous and interesting tales of Asia? On the other end of Eurasia another people were over run as well, in Britain and Ireland, yet they too are the epicenter of the stories of small fairies, again begging the question, are these remnants of a culture which no longer exists? There is no certain way to answer these questions, just as there is no certain way to know what most archeological artifacts mean, but the exploration can still teach us a lot.

Understanding Fairy Tales as Folk Religion

To break down the meaning behind the many pieces of a fairy tales we must begin by understanding that the people who passed fairy tales on from person to person saw the world as filled with fairies, with spirits which controlled their fate, and that the stories within fairy tales are often about people's interaction with this spirit world. This means that as peoples' interactions with the spirit world changed, so too would many aspects of their stories. Thus while people don't necessarily believe that humans are the center of the universe, we do tend to tell stories centered on us. Still, as we've seen, remnants of previous ideas would remain no matter the social changes.

The first rule of folk religion is that it exists to serve the needs of the people. In other words, each idea within folk religion begins within people's needs, which are bound to change over time. Societies and people have many, many different needs, but perhaps the most important needs and changes which impacted folk religions are; 1-Food, 2-Social Political acceptance, and 3-Procreation

When reading through fairy tales then, one must think about them as more than just a story about a protagonist or event; they are the story of a series of cultures, the saga of human migration and survival.

Secondly, it's important to understand how fairy tales are passed on from person to person, generation to generation, and society to society, because the method and reason a story is transmitted has a huge impact on the story itself. For example, stories which were most likely to have been passed on by a shaman from a neighboring people likely had very different emotions attached to them, at least initially, than did stories which were passed down by a mother to their child in the middle of the night.

Think about folk tales in a different way

To understand the magical creatures in fairy tales and the folk religious and the elements within them, you must begin by trying to be aware of them. Fairy tales are filled with confusing plot twists, combs that turn into forests, girls who turn into lakes, and more. To try to understand these you have to begin by thinking of them in terms of the magical events which people often believed in, or which were symbolic of something else; rather than psychoanalytical fodder or meaningless story elements.

It's likely that only a very few things in fairy tales are repeated by accident. Most of the details in true folk tales have some meaning attached, which is why I think it was no accident; for example, that a bird was leading Hansel and Gretel into the woods. This is not to say that everything has a religious element. The bread house in other locales is a sausage house, while in other places children are lured to the witch with a duck stew. In this case, the food used is representative of what the children are dreaming of eating in the culture where the story takes place. Still, despite such differences, the meaning behind this food is the same in each of these places; it's bait to lure unsuspecting children.

Historic beliefs about the spirit world

Everything from ancestor worship to previous ideas about deities and the nature of the spirit world can all be guides to understanding the origins of characters within fairy tales. In Lithuania a one eyed figure, very much like Odin, would appear to give advice to would be heroes, while in Celtic and Germanic fairy tales it was dangerous to plow certain fields as this would anger the fairies. In order to fully understand these fairy tales we have to understand the nature of these fairies and deities, as well as humanities' relationship with them.

Shamanism and Post Shamanistic Ideas

Winkelman's (1990) survey of many different cultures shows that it's likely every people has a history of shamanism in the past, as shamanism is a series of responses to certain neurological activities. What's more, although they have been altered, many of the ideas within shamanism continued to survive into the modern day in many places in Europe; and as you saw in "The Corpse Watches," and "Hansel and Gretel," many elements from shamanism have made their way into fairy tales. More specifically, shamanistic elements show up in fairy tales in the following way:

- Journeys to the spirit world-Many of the journeys in fairy tales are based on journeys to the spirit world, such as journeys to the realm of the dead, to the realm in the sky, and even to distant lands which are often treated as a spirit world as well.

- Details from the spirit world-Even when characters aren't in the spirit world, many of the details from the spirit world will show up in their tales, such as glass objects.

- Helper spirits-The spirits who help shamans often feature fairly prominently in fairy tales, being represented by such characters and Puss and Boots, as well as other animals or humans figures which aid the character in their journey.

- Trickster characters-Shamans and many of the spirits they follow are natural trickster figures, or fools. I explain the reasons for this further in the chapter on shamans, but suffice it to say that the idea of the successful fool in fairy tales may have its root in shamanism.

- Astral characters and Dream Journeys-There are a number of fairy tales in which people leave their body in the form of a mouse, a horsefly, or some other animal in a dream. Similarly, characters like swan maidens, nightmare causing witches, even witches who turn into cats were likely astral characters, souls who'd left their bodies to wander the world.

- Theft of a soul -There are Greek and Eastern European tales in which a person's soul is taken by the fairies, while in Celtic and Germanic fairy tales the person is physically taken while a corpse made to look like them is left in their place. In both these cases the person often has to be saved from the spirit world in what is likely a remnant of a shaman's tale.

- Wise Characters-Shamanistic characters figure into many tales, as hen wives, as smiths, as people who tell the protagonists of the tales how they can succeed. Further many of the protagonists of stories are shamans as well. They are the ones who are seeking the water of life, who learn the language of the animals, who are learning secrets of divination from magical beings, etc.

Deities and Fairies

Fairies and deities show up many times in fairy tales as moral enforcers, as the cause of events, as advisers, occasionally as protagonists, and even as villains. Sometimes it's easy to spot them, such as in the case of ogres, who are partially, though not wholly based on the idea of the Roman deity Orcus. Other times it's exceedingly difficult to know for certain if a character is a deity or not.

Storytelling and Neuroscience
Although hugely variable from culture to culture, often to the point that blanket statements can't easily be made, human psychology still plays a big role not only in what stories people believe, but what they choose to tell and the stories they will remember.

Cultural needs
People tell stories based on their own social needs. Folk religion itself is based on a people's moral, social, and economic needs. For example, a large part of a people's culture is centered on what they eat; this is especially true when the majority of the population is engaged in trying to obtain food as it was during the time fairy tales were told. This is why so many folk tales, deities and fairies are centered on the idea of obtaining food.

Historical political situation
Politics has a substantial impact on people's beliefs, and on how willing they are to fight against the existing status quo.

Neighboring peoples
Neighboring people, both current and historical can have a huge impact on the fairy tales of a culture.

Related ideas
Many ideas, like the comb which turns into a forest or the already mentioned black dog, are present over vast areas. This means that either there is something in human nature which causes us to independently develop such similar ideas from one region to another, we passed these stories from one region to another, or they survived for thousands of years. Regardless, the differences and similarities between these tales form one culture to another can tell us a lot.

Living on the Edge of the Spirit World

The man's heart began to race, he'd traveled this path a thousand times before, he knew every blade of grass, every tree, every step of it, but suddenly he was lost, not more than a hundred feet from his door. He wandered round the field again but found nothing but sharp thorn covered brambles which had never been her before piled high over his head. He couldn't even find his way back out of the field. Panic set in as he paced around the edge of the field, quicker and quicker he went, his lungs starting to burn with the effort, his legs crying out for mercy, but it was no use; he couldn't find his way out. At last he collapsed too exhausted to go on. A moment later he heard thousands of tiny wings beating, heard the giggling of little voices, for with a single step he'd found himself outside of the human realm and in the realm of the spirits.

In Wales a man was bemoaning his troubles, wondering why he his cattle were always sick when he heard a voice answer him;

"I'll tell you," said a voice behind him. It (the voice) seemed half way between a squeak and a growl.

He turned round and there he saw a little, angry man. He was dressed in red, and stood hardly as high as the farmer's knee. The little old man glared at the big fellow and cried out in a high tone of voice, " You must change your habits of disposing of your garbage, for other people have chimneys besides you."

"What has that to do with sickness among my cows?"

"Much indeed. Your family is the cause of your troubles, for they throw all their slops down my chimney and put out my fire."

The farmer was puzzled beyond the telling, for he owned all the land within a mile, and knew of no house in sight.

"Put your foot on mine, and then you will have the power of vision, to see clearly."
The farmer's big boot was at once placed on the little man's slipper, and when he looked down he almost laughed at the contrast in size. What was his real surprise, when he saw that the slops thrown out of his house, did actually fall down; and, besides, the contents of the full bucket, when emptied, kept on dripping into the chimney of a house which stood far below, but which he had never seen before.

But as soon as he took his foot off that of the tiny little man, he saw nothing. Everything like a building vanished as in a dream.

"I see that my family have done wrong and injured yours. Pray forgive me. I'll do what I can to make amends for it."

"It's no matter now, if you only do as I ask you. Shut up your front door, build a wall in its place, and then my family will not suffer from yours." (Griffis, 2010)

Humans believed that they lived within the middle spirit realm, a place between the realms in the sky and the underground worlds. So while there were separate spirit worlds from our realm, people believed that we lived side by side with the magical beings, in a world where death, happiness, luck, illness and poverty were all real "living beings which could be pacified or overcome. In the story of "The Pale Maiden" for example, a poor farmer hears a grating behind his stove when he is getting ready to move to a new home, then;

> Out of the stove sprang a thin pale form, like a buried maiden. 'What the devil is this?' cried the father. 'For heaven's sake!' screamed the mother, and all the children after her. 'I am no devil,' said the thin pale maiden, but I am your Poverty. You are now taking yourselves off hence, and you are bound to take me with you to your new abode.' (Wratislaw)

This is the world of fairy tales, a world in which people believed that they could offend or befriend the spirits of fate, so it should come as no surprise that many of the fairy tales we know and love are in tales about how to survive in the magico-religous world people believed controlled their fates.

To get a better grasp on this concept it's perhaps best to begin in Siberia with peoples whose tales have clear roots in a time before civilization sterilized the world, when people were almost solely dependent upon the unpredictable forces of nature for their livelihood.

Into the Wild

A thousand dogs howled, turning their heads towards the red colored sky to sing out their primal song. As the sun sets, the night rises, for night is the time of the trolls, the fairies, and the other spirits or nature. So twilight is a magical time in Europe, it's a time that is neither fully day, nor night, a time in which fairies have their greatest power. Twilight the world of Once Upon a Time isn't simply a liminal world, for that would imply boundaries between humanity and the spirit world, but in this place such boundaries are never very clear, if they exist at all. Here people didn't live on the edge of the spirit world, they didn't live with 'batches' of wilderness. Instead they were surrounded by the wild. Whether in their little fish and hunting camps, herding animals over the grasslands, or in the villages, the wilderness was all about them. It stretched out for a seeming eternity, and given how long it might take to walk from one place to another, at times it might as well have gone on forever. Those who stepped away from their home could walk for days without seeing another person, another village, or any sign of humanity, which is likely why it's hard to make the distinction in stories when someone has stepped into the spirit world.

According to Siikala, Napolskikh, and Hoppal;

> Sometimes there is no clear-cut spatial localization in the description of the other world – one cannot say definitely if the matter concerns the space "underground", or "in the sky", or on the lower or the upper reaches of the river; the heroes find themselves in another world without it having any particular localization. In this case it is next to impossible to define the border between the real and the unreal worlds, and this fact is of fundamental importance not only in the mythology of the Selkups but also in many other West Siberian traditions.

The omnipresent wilderness is a mixed blessing, for on the one hand it's a place filled with food: the place of the hunt, and of wild vegetables and fruits to gather, of fodder for herd animals. On the other hand it's a place to be feared. So many people will go out into the wild and never return and often no one will ever know for certain what happened to them, they will just be gone; leaving behind only whispers, rumors of what might have happened.

This, perhaps, is why the spirits of the wild begin as a primal fear, for to those who set foot outside the small village or off the well-known routes, the eternal quiet stretches out before them. Sudden feelings of lonesomeness can wash over them, for there are no roads, no way to contact anyone for hours, or even days, if trouble should arise. Those out in the wilderness are truly alone, and they can die alone all too easily. Worse even than the feeling of loneliness however is oftentimes the feeling of being watched; the feeling that there is something in the trees, on the vast tundra, hiding among the rocks or in the water. Here in this lonely place witches clacked their claws in the long grass, waiting to devour children or other humans. Spirits snatched away peoples' souls dragging them into the "Other World," here one false step could send a person to a land of eternal torment.

One Nenet's tale, for example, begins:

> At the fork of a river was a chum (teepee) where a woman lived with her two sons. One day the woman went to gather food and never returned. What had become of her no one knew, perhaps a bear had eaten her or she drowned in the river. The only trace of her was her two little sons alone in the chum.

Even in the modern day, when I was growing up in Yupik villages, there were still occasionally people who would vanish, people who were out hunting or fishing and never returned. Because of this, it's actually very common for stories on the steppes and the tundra to begin with someone disappearing forever. A boy grows up alone and wonders why he's the only person in an Evanki tale, so he sets out to find other people. Eventually he meets a squirrel who is his sister, taken prisoner and transformed into an animal by the monsters that ate their people when the boy was too small to remember. In a similar story, a monster devours an entire village but for an old woman and a little boy. When the boy grows older, he wonders why there are so many yurts but no other people. From such stories, one certainly gets the sense that it wasn't uncommon in the distant past to come across empty chum, yurts or homes. Indeed a plague, an enemy or a storm while the people were away on the river could kill an entire village, leaving nothing but creepy, empty yurts and chum (teepee like structures). Going back to the story of the two brothers left alone by the riverside, they begin to live by gathering food and fishing until, years later, they decide there must be other people and that they should go and look for them. They set out and eventually find a girl picking cloudberries. The girl takes them back to her chum, and there the boys live with her and her parents where they have to learn how to herd reindeer and do similar tasks.

There is typically a lot more to these tales than simply a "Jungle Book"-like tale of a child who is the only survivor of his or her people, or one of ghost camps left by a people wiped out by some evil spirit. In many of these stories, the child must set out into the spirit world to seek revenge, to kill the monster that slew his or her family. These are also stories about people seeking to find someone to marry, to find a way to continue their people's legacy. These stories are about the death and rebirth of a people. They are about the constant struggle for life in the spirit world, which people believed always threatened to swallow them and their legacy.

In a Tatar tale, three brothers are out hunting when they come upon a girl who lives alone in a hut, so they adopt her as their sister. It is never said why a young girl was living alone, but presumably, like so many others, her family or her people are just gone, leaving her to try to get by on herself. Like her family, she is almost killed by the 'other world' all around them, for she and her new brothers have an Aeneas (a witch/vampire with long fangs and leopard claws who drains marrow from sleeping people) for a neighbor. The girl meets her neighbor when she goes out to try to find something to start a fire while her brothers are out hunting. Starting a fire was difficult without matches, so neighbors would often borrow hot coals from each other to make it easier. The girl sees some smoke rising in the distance and realizes that someone must have a hearth, so she goes through the woods and knocks on the Aeneas's door. The Aeneas greets her, saying, "We are neighbors. You should be my guest." At first, the Aeneas appears nice, even giving the girl some coals in a bucket to take back with her to start a fire. Later, the Aeneas comes for a visit and tells the girl that she is bored. The girl happily invites her in and eventually falls asleep. While she sleeps, the Aeneas drains some of her marrow and leaves her lying on the carpet. Realizing what has happened to their sister, the brothers wait to ambush the Aeneas when she comes back, but one by one, she drains them until the last brother overcomes her and beats her until she heals everyone. There are many similar tales of people with dangerous neighbors living in the wilderness, which was home to witches and vampires.

Interpretation of a Vampire Tale from Northern Romania

Once, vampires were as common as the grass or berries in a pail. They traveled among the people during the night, joining gatherings in villages. When many young people would gather together for a party, the vampire would do what they loved, causing great fear and suffering as well as the drinking of blood.

One evening, when some young people were having a party, a stranger entered—a vampire, although no one knew it. He seemed to be a handsome young man, one who was fun to have at a party. He joked so well with the girls that they couldn't stop laughing. There was, however, one particular girl to whom he paid the most attention, teasing her without mercy, although she'd told him to stop.

People's belief in vampires was a clear sign of how prevalent and dangerous they considered the spirit world around them. It was believed in many places that the land of the dead was in the hills, forests, and oceans near where they lived. However, there was more to it than this, for many souls refused to travel on to the other world. Instead, these souls continued to live near humanity in graveyards and haunted houses. These souls that remained behind almost always became bloodthirsty and dangerous.

What's important to understand here is that people believed that the realm of the dead wasn't necessarily some distant place; it could be all around them, and the spirits of the dead were as prevalent as berries in a bucket.

Vampire Tale Continued...

The vampire kept teasing the girl, pinching her until she was covered in bruises. Again, she tried to dissuade him, and as she was doing so, she dropped her distaff. When she bent to pick it up, she saw the vampire's tail and realized what he was.

She tried to warn her friends of the danger. However, they were laughing too hard to hear, so she eventually had to flee on her own, pretending to need to take some linin to storage. Once she got out, she ran as fast into the forest as she could.

There are two common ideas that likely merged together to form this vampire image. One is that of the dangerous forest spirits, and the other is that of the spirits of the dead. Often, these two beings were one and the same, with the spirits of the dead going into the wild and becoming the spirits of nature, trees, lakes, rocks, hills and more. However, they weren't always the same, so can be difficult to tell which is which. This vampire, given that he has a tail, appears to have been inspired by nature spirits.

Nature spirits often drank blood in lore. In Germanic lore for example, elves would sometimes drain the blood of people as fairies did in Celtic lore. Even among the pygmies, who viewed the wilds as a pure place, the spirits of nature loved the taste of blood. Thus, women would leave the blood from their menstruation in the woodlands for these spirits. Then, when a woman became pregnant, the spirits would often grow angry that she was no longer leaving them blood and would try to punish the men in her family by ruining their ability to hunt. In order to deal with this, the woman would cut herself and mix her blood with other red substances. Her husband and sons would put a bit of this on their foreheads as an offering to the spirits when they went out hunting.

Vampire Tale Continued…

Her friends waited for the girl to return, and at last the vampire began to freak out, demanding that they find her. They looked for a time, but when it was obvious that they would not find her, the vampire drained the blood, cut off their lips to make it appear they were smiling, and put their heads on stakes in the window. He then decorated the room with their intestines.

There are a number of other tales in which vampires or cruel nature spirits will decorate rooms with people's blood and body parts. Romania's vampires especially seemed to love to cut people's mouths so that it looked like they were smiling, then put their heads on stakes so that those coming across them would think they were laughing until they got close enough to see the truth.

Vampire Tale Continued…

He (the vampire) then ran into the forest where he found the girl hiding under a beech tree. "Why did you leave, girl? Why did you run from me?" the vampire asked her.
The girl was too afraid to speak to him, however.
"You are afraid. Come with me; you'll feel better in my home."
Then, against her will, the girl followed him.

Vampires often seem to have power over people's minds in lore. They are able to make them do things against their will. What's more, however, is that they often seek out special companions that they take home. This doesn't discount the possibility of their killing those who they bring home; indeed, this is often the end result of these tales when the girl doesn't escape. However, sometimes vampires were said to marry and live with someone, even having children with them.

Vampire Tale Continued…

They arrived at vampire's home, which was a cave in the forest. The vampire tried to get the girl to enter the hole. However, she managed to refuse, telling him to enter first. After he did this, she blocked the hole with the linen she'd brought with her. She then fled deeper into the forest until, at last, she came to house with a corpse in it. She hid behind the stove of the house and fell asleep. As she slept, the first vampire came. However, the corpse on the table was a vampire as well, and they began to fight. They fought until the cock's crow banished them both. With the sun up, the vampires were gone.

The girl awoke at last and found herself in a forest that was so beautiful, filled the sound of birds, that she thought herself in heaven. She wanted to bring her parents to that place, so she returned home and told them the story. On hearing the tale of a vampire, the parents crossed themselves, and the girl began to sink into the ground, for she had been bewitched by the vampire and by the beauty of the forest and so had become a vampire herself.

Here again, the hut in the forest seems to point to nature spirits, who would often fight each other in Slavic lore. Further, the girl's love of the forest seems to have transformed her, making her an outsider, a strange other creature. This makes it clear that the forest was a spirit world, a place for those who did not belong within the human realm.

Fate

In this land, as well as in Europe right up into the modern era, many people believed that nothing happened by chance; everything was caused by the spirits. If a person went hungry, vanished, or became sick or injured, some evil influence was at work. One Votian man tells the story of a water spirit that kept stealing people's animals:

In ancient times there was a place in a little valley of our village where cows and sheep used to sink and drown. No spring passed without a cow or a sheep or a horse drowning in this place. The place was called 'the eyes of springs'. They had poked a stake three fathoms long there and couldn't reach the bottom. Old people all gathered together and discussed what to do if this spring eye was going to take a horse or a cow or a sheep every single year. And so they thought that we would promise a ram to the spring. Every spring the village people would buy a ram, when the earth softens. Then the ram's head is cut off and the whole ram is cast into the spring, saying: "Here's the whole summer's food for you." (Ergo-Hart Västrik 1998)

Spirit World Within Our Homes

In Hattifedrr Marsch near a dike. There was a Frisian named Harro Harrsen. When he was planning on building a home he saw a hole in a log, he realized that it would make the perfect place for a little Niskepuk to live. So he built a home, and when it was finished he nailed a board as wide as his hand to act as a trim beneath the hole. He put a bowl filled with gruel and plenty of butter on the trim and in a friendly way called, "Come, loving Niskepuk!" He didn't have to wait long for the Niskepuk's came to look over his new home, which they danced through. Only one of them – who was three inches tall – stayed, living in the hole in the pillar in Harro Harrsen's home.

Harro would continue to give the Niskepuk butter for years. In return for this butter, the Niskepuk cleaned and swept his house, and "from that day on the cattle thrived, giving abundant milk. And the sheep had many lambs, so Harro Harrfen became a wealthy man." (Müllenhoff, 1845)

This story likely wasn't a rare one as the Niskepuk (also known as the Isebok, Pulter Claas, Puk, Niss Puk) share many features with the prototypical European house fairies and may even be the origin of the famous Puck's name. Like the underground people or Oennereeskc, they wear pointed red hats, long gray or green jackets, and slippers on their feet. Jacob Grimm stated that this hat gave house spirits and other fairies the power of invisibility while the slippers gave them the power to run at supernatural speeds. (Thoms, 1865)

A more feral domestic fairy is to be found in Croatia. Here, a forest spirit known as the *vedi*, which could grow to be as tall as trees, lived deep in the forest, where they enjoyed the suffering of people, whom they might kidnap and torture. Oddly enough, these same forest spirits would adopt human families that they would care for, though they were still dangerous to their neighbors (Conrad, 2001). This idea that household fairies are kind to their own family and dangerous to everyone else is a common one, with fairies often stealing from a family's neighbors to give to them. This act of stealing from neighbors while also protecting one's own family means that these spirits could, on occasion, come into conflict with each other. In Scandinavia, for example, there is a common story about two neighboring house fairies running into each other after each was stealing from the others home, at which point they got into a fight.

Despite the house fairies' importance to a family, people felt a certain amount of trepidation about their presence, as they could anger quickly and would punish those who they found in their spots or who didn't provide them with their payment of porridge and butter. As the story of the Niskepuk shows, though:

> These spirits are on the whole well disposed towards mankind, and anxious to be on good terms with them. For, like the Oennereeske, the Puks are of themselves neither decidedly malicious nor beneficent. When pleased with the master of the house in which they reside, they take upon themselves at night the performance of all the household duties, — wash and cleanse the rooms and furniture, bring in fodder, tend the cattle, and take care that everything thrives. Nay, so anxious are they that it should be so, that rather than fail they do not scruple to rob the neighbors. They are oftentimes heard in the middle of the night bustling over their work and going up and down about the house; and sometimes they amuse themselves by playing tricks upon the maids and servants, tickling them under the nose to make them sneeze in their sleep, pulling off the bed-clothes. (Thams, 1865)

Sometimes such spirits would start out as harmful and dangerous but could be made to be helpful. For example, in parts of Italy one could leave a home without paying rent if it was believed that there was a fairy in the home. Because of this, one student was able to rent a home with a *munaciello* (a house fairy) in it for very cheap. This munaciello quickly went about the business of causing trouble, stealing things, making noises, etc, but the young man blamed mice for all of this and so bought a cat. Annoyed that he was being ignored, the munaciello escalated to breaking things, but the young man blamed shifting houses, old nails, and more or slept through the munaciello's rampages. Finally, the munaciello introduced himself to the young man, but the young man shrugged the event off as a dream. At last, unable to think of any other way to get the human to acknowledge him, the munaciello helped the young man become wealthy (with the promise that the young man would never reveal the source of his wealth). Once again, we see support that many fairies desired to be acknowledge by humans and to partner with them in some way.

Because of their importance to the success of a home and the danger of the fairies' wrath, people often planned to build their homes around the desires of the fairies or, more specifically, the desires of the spirits of nature, the spirits of the dead, household deities, the soul of the house itself, and perhaps a few other strange beings of whose connection to the household we can't be certain.

There were potentially thousands of little rituals used in order to determine if it was acceptable to build in one place or another, to determine where a house or other building could be constructed. What's important to understand about these rituals in general was that every place had a spirit owner, and the wishes of this land's owner had to be taken into account—even if this was only to trick them out of their land (as happened in fairy tales from Southern England, Korea, North East Asia, and Japan) or drive them away. More often, people would try to look for a sign that it was okay to build in an area, which could be anything from finding a coin on the land to finding an ant mound - specifically black ants on the land, or at the place where animals laid down. Others would spend the night in the place in which they intended to build. If the spirits didn't disturb them, then it was okay to build there. If, however, their sleep was disturbed or they had problems on the site, they would go somewhere else. They would also avoid building in border regions, as these were the exclusive home of the spirits, and in some places large rocks needed to be avoided as these also were the exclusive home of the fairies. There were, of course, many other signs for determining where it was acceptable to build a home, but they are too extensive to all fit into this book.

Once a site was determined for a new building, it needed to be purchased, or, at the very least, the spirits on it had to be made friendly. In one case:

> When Christianity was introduced to Rugen, it was decided that a church should be built in Vilmintz. But try as the people might they could not build the child, because every night the devil would tear down what they had built in the day. So they bought a child, gave him a roll and a light, after which they put him in a cavity of the buildings foundation which was walled up. Now the devil could no longer interfere with the construction. (Haas, 1903)

This is a fairly gruesome but common story, though it was more common for people to sacrifice some food or an animal to the fairies. Horses were one of the most commonly sacrificed animals, and their skulls have been found buried in the foundations of a number of buildings. In Flintshire (Wales), some people needing to repair their floor discovered the skulls of two horses underneath it, with a dark one used to "propitiate the spirit of the soul, disturbed by the displacement of the soil for the foundation, and the white was set there to protect the house and its inhabitants against evil spirits." (Brown, 1966)

The Irish believed that these horse skulls were buried in order to possess a good echo, and that fields with such an echo had a horse's head buried within them as well (Johnson, 1867). This is interesting because it has also been found that the caves with good acoustic properties were also the most likely to have cave paintings of animals within them. (Waller and Kolar, 2014) believes that Stonehenge was also built in such a way as to create better acoustics, as such echoes could resemble the' thunder deities' when a series of people clapped loudly.

In addition to placating the spirits within the foundation, sacrifice was at times intended to give the building a soul, a spirit of its own, which could protect the inhabitants. Many of the spirits of the dead watching over a household, though, were old family patriarchs, founders of a farm, first farmhands to die on the farm, etc. In addition, a building could obtain a soul through a large cross placed inside it during its construction, a tree used in its construction, or a tree planted beside or within it.

There were many other spirits that sought to serve humans for their own reasons or which chose to live in homes. Some of these were refugees from various otherworldly courts. In one case, there was a troll who had to flee from the troll court because of an affair he'd had with the wife of a larger troll named Knurremurre. In order to hide, the young troll turned himself into a cat and lived in a human home. (Keightley, 1850)

In another story, a house fairy living within a castle was asked where he came from and why he was in the castle and responded that:

> He was come from the Bohemian mountains, and that his companions were in the Bohemian Forest—that they would not tolerate him, and that he was in consequence obliged to retire and take refuge with good people till his affairs should be in a better condition. He added that his name was Hinzelmann, but that he was also called Lüring; and that he had a wife whose name was Hille Bingels. (Keightley, 1850)

Perhaps more interesting are the stories of fairies that disguise themselves to enter the service of a human. Sometimes, they would disguise themselves as a desirable object, which the person would bring home, or an animal. In one case, a spirit assumed the form of a handsome young man and went to a knight to offer his services. The young man was a diligent and devoted worker, so much so that the knight was amazed by his skills. One day, when they had reached a river, some enemies were chasing them, but the young man was able to show his lord a ford which had never before existed. Startled that they had managed to cross the fordless river, their enemies ran away in fear, thinking the devil himself was aiding the knight. In addition, the young man was able to get milk from a lioness in order to treat the knight's wife. He did all this because he wanted to be in the company of and serve humanity.

If Lecouteux (2013) is correct in presuming that the young man in the previously discussed story was really a house fairy, then this would indicate that many of the characters who help protagonists in fairy tales may also be house fairies. It is possible that the old man who gives someone advice, the mouse who steal from them, and other such characters could all be house fairies.

In addition to all of these, there were deities who took on the role of house spirits. Zeus, for example, also known as Zeus Herkeios (for the fence around people's homes), had an altar in people's courtyards and protected their homes from intrusion. In a more interesting case, Zeus Ktesios appeared in the form of a snake, which would live in and protect people's homes. House snakes were of the utmost importance throughout much of Europe and, interestingly enough, Japan as well. Still, what's important to understand here is that, in addition to all the other spirits of the home, there were also major deities in charge of the home. (Nilsson and Nock, 1972)

Finally, the fire in the hearth had a sacred spirit in it as well. This is especially well attested to in Eastern Europe where the Mari-El would abstain from cursing in the home in order to avoid offending the spirit of the flame. Rome, too, seems to have believed in sacred fires, and it probably isn't a coincidence that many of the fairies in Britain lived in the fireplace.

In other words, there are a number of different sources for house fairies, including ancestral spirits, spirits of sacrificed beings, the soul of the house itself, spirits of nature who have moved into the home, owners of the land who now accept the house, deities of the home, and fire spirits. All of this leads to some confusion as to the exact origins of any one house fairy. Indeed, despite tales that indicate that the Roman house spirit and the Votyak house spirit were eventually believed to be spirits of the dead, Wissowa and Paulson, respectively, believe that they couldn't always have been. Paulson (1965) specifically states:

> The close relationship between the building and its protecting spirit indicates that the figure of the house spirit originally cannot have belonged so exclusively to the death cult as different researchers formerly believed, but that it must represent a supernatural concept of its own in the house and family cult.

Such confusion can make it nearly impossible to fully interpret any tale with what may or may not be a house fairy in it. Nevertheless, there are certain things that house spirits tended to share in common, regardless of their origins.

- Morality-Nearly all fairies are concerned with human morality, but perhaps none are more concerned than those of the household, for they have to live with people. It could be said that their actions and personality are a reflection of the people with whom they live. If these people are good and decent and follow the cultural norms, then the fairy will be kind and helpful; if they break with the cultural norms, then so will the fairies. The cultural norms that they concern themselves with can include women not going outside with their heads uncovered or people staying up to work too late. This prohibition against staying up late cuts two ways. On the one hand, it prevents people from staying up as late as they might want; on the other hand, it has the potential of preventing husbands from forcing their wives to stay up late working. As I'll discuss further, it is common for fairies to force people to take vacations and breaks.

- Mischievous/Childlike Characteristics-As with many fairies, these spirits have a mischievous streak to them and seem very childish at times, not only in their prank playing but also in the way they enforce morality, their attachement to children, and their way of becoming easily offended by every little thing. I discuss this further in my section on the "Childlike nature of fairies." However, it's worth noting here that house fairy mischief has a close connection to horses, either helping or causing them mischief. In France, one of the fairies' favorite things to do was to tie horses' tails together, though they would also tangle up people's weaving or tickle the legs of women and flip their skirts up. ("The Traditional Savoie" by Marie - Therese Hermann)

- Easily angered-As some of their tales on morality enforcement show, house spirits can be easily angered, and they are often able to hold a grudge for a long, long time.

41

- Desire to be in the company of humans-House fairies often want to be around people and will try to trick or cohorce their way into a person's home. Even when a person tries to get rid of them, they persist in staying.

- Protective-House fairies protect their chosen family from supernatural dangers, fire, and even vermin. In one tale in particular, a *bunnik* (spirit of the bathhouse) protects a girl from a vampire that is chasing her.

- Act as a bridge between families and the spirit world-House fairies were commonly the bridge between the family and the spirit world.

- Steal from the neighbors.-Despite their push for humans to act in a moral way; it was commonly believed that house spirits would steal milk, money, etc. from the neighbors.

Pixies and Humanity

A farmer in Dartmoor was working in his fields when one of his workers came to tell him that someone was in his barn. The farmer went to the barn and, hearing a "merry chatter" and the sounds of flails, realized that it must be pixies inside. He hurried away from the structure and told his farmhand to stay away from the barn while the pixies were at work. From then on, he left cheese and bread in the barn every morning. In the evening, a pile of corn would be threshed. Eventually, he ran out of corn to thresh, but the pixies continued to come, leaving him new piles of corn in his barn so that his fortune began to grow and grow. (Crossing, 1890)

What makes this story so interesting is that pixies are generally believed to be mischievous members of the fairy court. One man from Cornwall believed that the pixies were a previous people who'd been forced into hiding by the coming of humanity. Others believed that they were the spirits of the dead, fallen angels, and the other typical ideas about fairy folk. However, in all cases, they aren't specifically house fairies, yet in many tales, they go out of their way to help people. In John Lloyd Warden Page's book on pixies, he states:

> Pixieland is a shadowy realm somewhere beneath the bogs, down which the pixies vanish at the approach of dawn, or when weary of dancing on the smoother pieces of turf... Their tricks are endless. They will turn the good wife's milk and steal her butter, blow out the candles and kiss the maids. But the lonely wayfarer is more especially the object of their machinations; and if he have spoken of them with scan respect their malevolence knows know end. They cause him to wander from his path hour after hour, and only at sunrise will they vanish along the crevices of the tors or disappear in the morasses. There is but one way for the pixy-led traveler to retain his path; he must turn some article of clothing or part of it, inside out. (Page, 1892)

Here, we see that pixies are clearly spirits of the wilds, of the bogs and the moors. They might, in some accounts, enter people's homes, but they tend to do the bulk of their mischief in the wilderness. This is also where they eventually go when they are finished with their business in people's homes and on their farms. In other words, pixies are rarely ever fairies that choose to live with humanity; rather, they are fairies that choose to come out of their homes to aid humanity.

There are two other items of interest here The first is that pixies will actively attack those who speak ill of them. As already mentioned, it is in the nature of fairies to become easily offended, so it seems possible that many of the tales of pixies attacking people originate from this idea, mixed with the general fact that people would get lost in the wilderness, especially in the treacherous bogs where pixies were often believed to make their homes. The second point of interest is that people could protect themselves by turning their shirts inside out. Fairies exist in a topsy-turvy world, where everything isn't quite right and where they act as their own opposites, allowing people to pass safely if they do something ridiculous. This strange aspect of fairies shows up in many fairy tales, which describe them as "funny" men, so it's worth bearing in mind.

Ancestor Worship

Perhaps nothing connected people to the spirit world more than the commonly held belief that their ancestors were a part of it. The exact nature of this involvement is highly variable, for just as today, even the same country or, at times, the same person can hold multiple ideas about the afterlife that, to an outside observer, might seem to conflict with each other. The modern-day belief in ghosts alongside the belief in heaven/hell would be a good example of this. Further rituals, such as speaking to the dead, specifically at graves, shows that people entertain slight ideas about death which, if questioned, they would likely say they don't have. While people will go to graves to speak to their dead loved ones, they don't necessarily believe the spirits of those they love are trapped in the graveyard. Instead, they believe that the spirits of those they love are in heaven, that they are ghosts in their home, etc. Such complexity of ideas makes it hard to say for certain what people believe exactly. However, even if people don't explicitly believe that their ancestors' spirits wander the graveyard for eternity, our stories still speak of ghosts as if they are there, as if they haunt houses built on their graves, and at the same time our stories speak of the spirits of the dead as being in heaven and hell. Thus, from a folkloric perspective, all these ideas matter.

Fairies are very often the souls of the dead. Indeed, the fairy world could often be thought of as being a bit like heaven, a place of endless parties and beauty, or of hell, where people are forced to live as slaves to the other fairies. From fairyland and heaven, the spirits of the dead often seek to help their decedents, as shown by the Grimm Brothers' version of the "Cinderella" story in which a girl named Aschenputtel is forced to live with a wicked stepmother and stepsisters:

> One day, the gentleman visited a fair, promising his stepdaughters
> gifts of luxury. The eldest asked for beautiful dresses, while the
> younger for pearls and diamonds. His own daughter merely asked for
> the first twig to knock his hat off on the way. The gentleman went on
> his way, and acquires presents for his stepdaughters. While passing a
> forest he got a hazel twig, and gave it to his daughter. She planted the
> twig over her mother's grave, watered it with her tears and over the
> years, it grew into a glowing hazel tree. The girl would pray under it

43

three times a day, and a white bird would always come to comfort her.

Later, when Aschenputtel wishes to go the ball:

The girl retreated to the graveyard to ask for help. The white bird dropped a white gown and silk shoes. She went to the ball, with the warning that she must leave before midnight. The prince danced with her, but she eluded him before midnight struck. The next evening, the girl appeared in a much grander gown of silver and silver shoes. The prince fell in love with her and danced with her for the whole evening, but when midnight came, she left again. The third evening, she appeared dressed in spun gold with slippers of gold. Now the prince was determined to keep her, and had the entire stairway smeared with pitch. Aschenputtel lost track of time, and when she ran away one of her golden slippers got stuck on that pitch. The prince proclaimed that he would marry the maiden whose foot would fit the golden slipper.

There are two things that are apparent from this story. The first is that it is the spirit of Aschenputtel's mother, possibly dwelling originally in the tree as a nature spirit, who is Aschenputtel's "fairy godmother," as it were. The second is that Aschenputtel is much more than an ordinary girl; she is a cunning, one who clearly has knowledge of magical rituals that allow her to communicate with the spirit of her mother.

With regard to the first of these, it wasn't atypical for people to believe that the spirits of the dead continued to live in natural features. Many people believed that the spirits of the dead became tree spirits, especially if those trees were growing in graves. Others believed that the spirits of the dead would travel into rocks or hills around their home. Often, these souls of those who had passed on would appear as white moths, or white birds, though other forms, including mice, snakes, crows, and more, were also possible depending on the region and the person telling the tale. In Estonian Lore:

The dead continue their lives somatically on earth as there is no exactly determinable idea of the beyond, the killed at the spot where they died, and those that died naturally – in trees, on shelf-boards, or on stones in a hilltop wood. (Loorits, 1998)

This Estonian point of view is interesting because, outside of the Sami people, they are the most genetically similar to the original hunter-gatherers of Europe. The Sami also hold a similar idea about the spirits of the dead—that they travel into the hills around their homes. Other places in Europe have similar ideas, alongside their belief in a location for the afterlife, yet they clearly still have tales and beliefs which indicate that the afterlife is all around them.

As for the second point, it is obvious that Aschenputtel isn't just some poor girl who gets lucky, as she is in the French version of this story. Rather, she is clearly a cunning, a decedent of Europe's shamanistic traditions who knows how to get help from the spirit of her deceased mother and speaks with white birds, which in this case are likely the souls of the dead. This, however, is one of the only versions in which the Cinderella character takes such an active role in helping herself by using her cunning arts. In most of the other versions, the fairy godmother figure is some form of spirit, which simply chooses to help her. In Portugal, it's a cow that gives her aid, while in the Irish version of this tale, "Fair,

44

Brown, and Trembling," the Cinderella character gets help from a hen wife, which often plays the witch role in Irish and British folklore. In the Scottish version of the tale, the Cinderella character gets help from a gray sheep, while her wicked step-mother employs a hen wife to try to counteract the sheep's magical aid.

There are other times, however, when the Cinderella character takes an active role in her own success. In the Greek tale of "Little Saddleslut," the Cinderella character gathers up her mother's bones, buries them under the grate, and smokes them with incense for forty days in order to get help from her spirit.

These girls who take an active role in their own success are interesting characters in fairy tales, not only because they exhibit remnants of shamanism. but also because they potentially give us the back story of the fates who were once mortal. The writer of "The Golden Bough" and Jacob Grimm both believed that women could not only obtain greater status than men through their shamanistic powers, but also do so in the afterlife, where they could essentially become powerful beings that even controlled the fates of the gods themselves. In other words, people once believed that characters like Aschenputtel would become one of the deities that helped to control the fate of everyone.

Another tale in which an ancestral spirit may help a cunning is "Jack and the Beanstalk." In this tale, a young boy in desperate need encounters a magical man, one who trades him beans that allow him to enter the realm of the sky in exchange for a cow. This man may very well have been an ancestral spirit; it was common, after all, for shamans to encounter such ancestral spirits when they were at their most desperate, and cows were a common sacrifice to them. The beans, themselves, however, are what point me to the idea that this man might be an ancestral spirit.

There are a number of tales throughout Eurasia in which a person receives magical seeds that grow up to the sky. In the Philippines, a woman obtains magical rice seeds, which grow up to the sky, allowing her to ask St. Peter for a magical wand. In Russia, an old man gets magic cabbage seeds, which grow to the sky. Beans, however, are fairly common for this use, such as with another old man in Russia who receives beans that grow up to the sky. However his tale, as with the Russian tale about the giant cabbage, ends badly with his wife dying and leaving him alone in his poverty. In a French fairy tale, a man gets a bean from Christ that grows up to heaven. Excited to pick the beans at the top, the man climbs and climbs until he reaches St. Peter's house. He eats and drinks and then returns home. His wife, however, demands that he go up and ask for a new house. Then, unsatisfied by this, she demands that he ask to be king and his wife to be queen. Eventually, his wife gets him to demand too much, so St. Peter makes him poor again.

Beans, Beans, the Magic Fruit

Jack's story is clearly different, for he succeeds in stealing from the upper world. This makes him a clear shamanic character, and, in his case, the beans may actually be significant to that role. Beans of various sorts are the food of the spirits of the dead across Eurasia. In Japan, Azuki beans are eaten during Obon, a festival to honor ancestral spirits. And, interestingly enough, broad beans were also used as a food for the dead in Rome and Greece during the Lemuria festival. In Suffolk, a pair of green children would only eat beans that were given to them. These children came from St. Martin's land in which the sun never rose, but where a bright country could be seen across a broad river. In other words, these green children came from the land of the dead. (Keightley, 2012)

The nature of beans as a food of the dead, and the fact that others in a similar situation to

Jack encounter spirits of the dead offering them aid, begs the question, 'is the funny little man Jack encounters a spirit of the dead?' As with many such questions in fairy tales, there is no certain way to answer this. However, the elements of this type of encounter are all present.

Beans played a role in magic rites conducted in connection with Taita or Uta, a goddess of the dead. The Priest of Jupiter was forbidden to touch a bean or even to mention its name. The Egyptians had a taboo against eating beans, but they left them as offerings for the dead in tombs. All of these rules existed:

> Beans were conceived to be the abodes of the souls of the dead, but we must be careful not to think of these souls in terms of Christian theology as eternal entities possessing the attributes of the physical beings in which they once lodged. We must rather visualize them as modicums of the life principle, vague and intangible, released from the body at the moment of death. This packet of force, if we may so term it, was both beneficent and maleficent. (Andrews, 2009)

Shamanism

The fact that people believed the spirit world was all around them explains the importance of those believed to bridge the gap between the spirit and mortal realms. These people in folk religion are generally shamans or those who fill roles based on shamanistic traditions. Shamanism is the act of falling into a state of ecstasy (an altered state of consciousness) in order to communicate with the spirit world and/or send one's soul outside the body in order to travel through the spirit world. Historically, shamans have used a number of methods to enter this state of exstasy. Although mos tmethods involve singing and dancing, some also involve drugs. Other methods for falling into a state of ecstasy involve tribulations such as starvation, exposure to extreme temperatures, and other hardships. Finally, and perhaps most commonly, falling into a state of ecstasy was a skill that involved meditation or rhythms without the use of drugs or hardships. Additionally, there were many reasons a shaman might undertake a spirit journey, whether it be to divine the future, to learn secrets from the deities, or to bring back the soul of someone who was sick.

A good example of some of the ideas behind shamanism that survived in Europe at least until the 19th century comes from Oberstdorf in the high mountains. Here, a herdsman engaged in an intense, months-long period of prayer and piety after which an angel appeared to him. From then on:

> Whenever his guide appeared, Stoeckhlin would fall into a kind of trance. His body would remain motionless whenever he had been, while his soul separated itself from his body and followed his psychopomp, the angel. He evidently had no choice about participating in these travles, and they were not always pleasant. They traveled long distances and for many hours, in groups that included both men and women. And Stoeckhlin had a precise notion of this group and a specific name for it that he strubbornly held on to : "the phantoms of the night." (die Nachtschar) (Behringer, 2000)

Shamans would travel with the spirits of the dead and dance in the mountains and meadows. This spirit journey was primarily about dealing with the fear of death and understanding the afterlife—though, as I'll discuss later, it is closely related to similar spirit journeys that were about defending crops from evil spirits.

Shamanism has been a part of humanity for a long time and was, at one time, the most widespread religious phenomenon outside of the belief in spirits and deities. Indeed, I haven't found a people who didn't have some form of ecstasy-based ritual for communicating with the spirits at one time in their history. Of course, even if the worldwide distribution of shamanism had come from a single origin and diffused to every land, the idea would not have persisted in nearly every culture in the world if it wasn't so well ingrained into our way of thinking (Winkelman, 1990). In many cases, shamans told of their journeys into the spirit world as metaphorical tales—tales which, like all other stories and ideas, were likely fragmented and inserted into other stories.

Folktales about heroes are often filled with fragments from the stories of shamans entering the other world. Indeed, witches and many of the deities of European lore are the shaman's religious descendants. Often, the claim is made that these shamanistic ideas were borrowed from Siberia. However, I believe that, while this might be true sometimes, shamanism doesn't have to be borrowed from anyone. This is because many religious ideas, from shamanism to polytheism, are fairly similar from one culture to another across the whole world. Robert Kaplan (1994) argues that this is because "shamanism is a cultural adaptation of hunter-gathering societies to the biological potential for altered states of consciousness." In other words, things like near death experiences, altered states of mind, and hallucination are all interpreted in similar ways by people based on their survival strategy, and for hunter-atherers, this interpretation forms the basis for shamanism. As a result, people the world over have a history of shamanism in one form or another.

The idea behind shamanism is fairly simple: it is the process of negotiating with and, ultimately, building a close personal relationship with the spirit world. There are three primary methods that shamans use to work with the spirit world in order to achieve their ends. The most important of these, as far as fairy tales are concerned, is the ability to send their souls out of their bodies to enter the spirit world and go on adventures, fragments of which often enter the fairy tales of later societies. The second is the practice of becoming possessed by spirits and allowing the spirits to work through them. Finally, shamans will utilize helping spirits in order to achieve their goals. In magico-religious terms, what this means is that, while shamans have power and often need strength to fulfill their roles, they don't necessarily use their own knowledge or strength to achieve their goals. Rather, shamans primarily use their relationship with the spirit world to get the spirits to perform tasks for them. Ultimately, a shaman can be said to be someone who has a special relationship with the spirit world and can often be considered a religious leader, though this isn't always the case.

The idea that shamanism and religion itself come from a biological part of our brains shouldn't be too surprising as 20%–40% of the population will have some form of mystical experience, be it a feeling, a quick vision, or an encounter with the spirit world. The commonality of these experiences leads Kaplan to conclude:

> There is every reason to believe that the majority of shamanic individuals are normal and do not have neuropsychiatric disorders. He even points to some studies that showed that Bhutanese shamans had no more psychiatric disorders than non-shamans, and they had less anxiety disorders than other people. (Kaplan, 2006)

On the other hand, Joseph Polimen (2003) believes that mental illness may have evolved in people in order to further enhance shamanistic traits. Schizophrenia, for example, is characterized not only by delusions, hallucinations, and disjointed thoughts but also can include an inability to connect with other people and causes such extreme impairments in one's ability to hold a normal job that the unemployment rate among people with schizophenia is nearly 90%. Despite the problems it causes, schizophrenia is a genetic trait that is nearly ubiquitous throughout the world, so perhaps there is something to Polimen's idea that it was evolutionarily selected, at least in part. Further:

> The association between madness and creative genius has been surmised since antiquity. Aristotle said, "No Great genius has ever existed without a touch of madness."

> Novel insights require being "off" from conventional thoughts – but not by too much, or thinking becomes disorganized and ineffective. ... Insanity, toned down, could result in cognitive fluidity suitable for creativity.

Mild psychiatric conditions can include certain symptoms such as hypomania or nonconformity which seem to be especially useful for creative endeavors. Hupomania, for example, boosts energy while enhancing effective attainment – a mental state particularly useful in creative writing and music compositions.

In one study, non-paranoid schizophrenics came up with more creative uses for objects than other study groups. Schizophrenics' tend to have higher marks in art, language and religion classes.

Other studies imply that the nonconforming disposition of schizophrenic patients as a potential contributor to ingenious creativity.

What we see, then, is that madness prevents people from working traditional jobs so that they seem to appear lazy, foolish, and unsocial. At the same time, it also makes them more creative and, if Polimen's hypothesis is to be believed, more likely to be the shamans.

Michael Winkelman, too, believes that shamanism has persisted worldwide because it is "based on innate brain structures and reflects an evolved psychology of humans." Winkelman further goes on to discuss these brain structures in relation to modern mental illnesses, indicating that shamanism can, indeed, be tied to mental illness and certain social problems.

With this in mind, consider the tales of the fool who turns out to be a heroic, almost shamanistic character, such as the tale of "Little Thumb."

> They (Little Thumb's Parents) were especially concerned, because the youngest was very sickly. He scarcely ever spoke a word, which they considered to be a sign of stupidity, although it was in truth a mark of good sense. He was very little, and when born no bigger than one's thumb, for which reason they called him Little Thumb.

> The poor child bore the blame of everything that went wrong in the house. Guilty or not, he was always held to be at fault. He was, notwithstanding, more cunning and had a far greater share of wisdom than all his brothers put together. And although he spoke little, he listened well.

In another tale, "The Fool and the Birch Tree," the fool sets out to sell his cow when he thinks he hears a birch tree talking to him. The birch tree offers him gold in return for the cow, so he ties the cow to the birch tree for the wild animals to eat. This is interesting because people once believed that wind in the tree branches was the spirits talking to them, and, indeed, when the boy leaves his cow for the tree, his luck improves such that he becomes wealthy. What seems foolish to others is perhaps his own ability to understand the spirit world better than they. Indeed, even after he becomes rich, his brothers still make fun of him for being silly and foolish, for thinking that he can speak with trees. In another Russian tale, that of "The Norka," a simpleton brother sets out to defeat the evil Norka and succeeds in entering the spirit world by climbing down a deep pit—succeeding where his elder brothers failed.

Shamans in fairy tales are often bizarre, and frequently seem foolish to those around them. Jack, in his tale, was willing to trade a cow for a couple of beans. Characters like Cinderella are rejected by their stepmothers and, in many ways, their actual fathers. Even the shamans in history seem to act is bizarre ways that are difficult for people of their own cultures to understand. In describing one man who would have been a shaman if not for

49

the Soviet laws against this, an anthropologist says:

> Meeting Tokoyeu's grandson had been one of the most jolting and significant experiences of my fieldwork. He was a downcast and disheveled young man, with long straggly hair and black leather jacket... When he had been a teenager, he had had all the signs of shamanic sickness... a torturing test by the spirits... in the Soviet period, "shamanic sickness" in a young man was taken to be extreme mental illness, both politically and socially dangerous. And indeed, the grandson admitted with a wry half-grin, it was probably a little scary for his fellow villagers when he rode a motorcycle around the graveyard and came down the hill toward the village with no hands on the handlebar. (Balzer, 1996)

Other shamans would run screaming into the woods, refuse to bathe for years, talk to things no one else could see, weep for what seemed to be no reason, withdraw from society, or refuse to get out of bed, so it is easy to see how some researchers consider shamanism a healthy way to deal with insanity.

The shaman's sickness was caused by the spirits possessing the shaman for the first time. Among the Yakut, the guardian spirit of a shaman who had died would possess one of the shaman's kinfolk. This person would begin raging like a madman.

> Suddenly he gabbles, falls into unconsciousness, runs about the woods, lives on the bark of trees, throws himself into the fire and water, lays hold of weapons and injures himself, so that he has to be watched by his family. (Wardrop, 1895)

While among the Buryat, those in the process of becoming shamans would have wild dreams, swoon, and fall into fits of ecstasy as they wandered from village to village. Among the Altai, the shaman would become very sick and fall into frenzies. (Wardrop, 1895)

In Russia, girls would be taken into the woods by the Leshii (forest kings) and return a few years later wild and covered in moss. Most often, these girls would use the knowledge they'd gained about the wilderness spirits to become witches. Indeed, it was common in tales for those who were approached by the spirits to become shamans to emerge from the woods looking wild and filthy. With this in mind, consider the story of "Bearskin" in which a poor man is certain he'll starve to death until the devil (a forest spirit called Greenjacket in the tale) appears to him and makes the following offer:

> *For the next seven years you are neither to wash yourself, nor comb your beard and hair, nor cut your nails, nor say the Lord's Prayer. I will give you a jacket and a cloak, which you must wear during this time. If you die during these seven years, you are mine. If you stay alive, you are free, and rich as well, for all the rest of your life.*

With the exception of the ownership of the soul should the soldier die, this story tracks fairly closely to the common European witch experience, with the spirit appearing to someone during a time of need and, of course, the person needing to go through a period of being wild and feral before becoming a shaman. Later, as Bearskin goes unwashed for some time, he begins to look like a monster.

> *For the next seven years you are neither to wash yourself, nor comb your beard and hair, nor cut your nails, nor say the Lord's Prayer. I will give you a jacket and a cloak, which you must wear during this time. If you die during these seven years, you are mine. If you stay alive, you are free, and rich as well, for*

all the rest of your life.

His hair covered nearly his entire face. His beard looked like a piece of coarse felt cloth. His fingers had claws, and his face was so covered with dirt that if someone had planted cress on it, it would have grown. Everyone who saw him ran away.

Shamans often seemed to be wild, otherworldly beings in their own right, and like otherworldly beings, they were often required by the spirits for whom they worked to be kind to the poor. Ultimately, what we see is that, whether or not shamanism is a healthy way to deal with insanity, shamans and their representatives in fairy tales certainly fail to conform to social norms and so seem to be insane. This begs the question of why. Why should religious leaders fail to conform to the society of which they are leaders?

The answer may be that the shaman's lack of conformity helps to create diversity within what would normally be a fairly homogeneous community. Leung, Maddux, Galinsky, and Chiu found that multicultural experiences helped to enhance the creativity of everyone within an educational or business setting. Similarly, in their research on brainstorming, Wang, Fussel, and Cosley found that:

> An important issue for supporting group brainstorming is to consider ways of supplying sufficient diversity of concepts. These sources of diversity may be either internal or external to the group. Internal diversity refers to background differences between group members that originate from long-term learning and socialization, such as knowledge, experiences, and cultural background.

There are many other studies showing that diversity helps groups to be more innovative and creative and to make better decisions. However, hunter-gatherers of any given region tend to have similar traditions and ideas, having intermarried and communicated with each other for centuries if not millennia. This means that much if not all of the diverse thinking that happens within ancient hunter-gatherer cultures must come from within the group itself. Shamans, with their different way of looking at things, may provide the diversity in thinking necessary for a group to make better decisions. As a consequence, shamanism is primarily a mental and charismatic exercise geared towards building a relationship with the beings people believed controlled their fate. Given, however, that this is a discussion of fairy tales rather than of psychology or sociology, perhaps the best way to understand the shaman's journey is to examine the journeys themselves.

Among the Kam, a shaman sending his or her soul into the realm of the dead in order to free a sick person would travel south and climb over the Altai Mountains, enter China, and ride over a yellow steppe so large and desolate not even a magpie could fly over it. This desolate, long journey is a common feature of spirit journeys, as are the mountains made of strange materials; such as the iron mountain the shaman would climb to reach the heavens known as Temir Shaikha. As they climbed, the shamans would see the many bones of those shamans who had been too weak to climb the mountain. Here, then, we see that a shaman did, at times, need strength to survive the challenges of the role. In other tales, shamans needed strength to get across the river into the land of the dead, and so a stronger shaman would encounter weaker ones who had been unable to cross into the realm of the dead or get home again.

After climbing the mountain, the Kam would go down a hole that would lead to the underworld sea. In order to cross this, the shaman would have to cross an extremely thin bridge. Those who had sinful souls would be unable to cross and would fall off, their corpses added to the pile of impure shaman bones at the bottom of the sea. On the other side of the bridge, the shamans would witness the suffering of sinners whose punishments corresponded to their guilt. This portion of the journey holds an important purpose for many shamans, as it allows them to warn people to behave morally. Finally, the shamans enter the castle of Erlik, the Lord of the Realm of the Dead, where they get Erlik drunk and negotiate with him on the price for returning the soul of a dying person. When they are finished, the Kam cannot return on their own but must, instead, ride on the back of a goose. (Mikhailovski, 1895)

We have already seen some of these elements in the stories of "The Corpse Watchers," in which the shamanistic character must climb over a mystical mountain and then plunge down into a land with a sea; and in "Hansel and Gretel," in which those returning from the spirit world can only do so by riding a water fowl.

In another interesting shamanistic remnant tale, "The Drummer," the shaman is wandering from town to town as shamans often did.

The Drummer

> *A young drummer went out quite alone one evening into the country, and came to a lake on the shore of which he perceived lying there three pieces of white linen. "What fine linen," said he, and put one piece in his pocket. He returned home, thought no more of what he had found, and went to bed. Just as he was going to sleep, it seemed to him as if someone was calling his name. He listened, and was aware of a soft voice which cried to him, drummer, drummer, wake up. As it was a dark night he could see no one, but it appeared to him that a figure was hovering about his bed. "What do you want," he asked. "Give me back my shift," answered the voice, "that you took away from me last evening by the lake." "You shall have it back again," said the drummer, "if you will tell me who you are." "Ah" replied the voice, "I am the daughter of a mighty king. But I have fallen into the power of a witch, and am shut up on the glass-mountain. I have to bathe in the lake every day with my two sisters, but I cannot fly back again without my shift. My sisters have gone away, but I have been forced to stay behind. I entreat you to give me my shift back." "Don't worry, poor child," said the drummer. "I will willingly give it back to you" He took it out of his pocket, and reached it to her in the dark. She snatched it in haste, and wanted to go away with it. "Stop a moment, perhaps I can help you. You can only help me by ascending the glass-mountain, and indeed if you were quite close to it you could not ascend it."*

One can't help but see similarities between "The Drummer" and "Swan Maiden Tales" in which someone steals a magical piece of clothing from a female heavenly or fairy being. However, the man in these stories typically steals the Swan Maiden's clothing as a way of forcing the beautiful woman to marry him. For example, in a Swedish tale, a hunter follows the advice of his mother and steals the clothes of a swan maiden while she's enjoying swimming in the water.

> *Soon thereafter two of the swans were heard to fly away, but the third, in search of her clothes, discovered the young man and, believing him responsible for their (her clothes) disappearance, she fell upon her knees and prayed that her swan attire might be returned to her. The hunter was, however, unwilling to yield the beautiful prize, and, casting a cloak around her shoulders, carried her home. (Hofberg, 1890)*

Such Swan/Heavenly Maiden tales are scattered throughout Eurasia and often are examples of the suffering of spirit beings at the hands of humanity. For example, in one Greek fairy tale, a man named Kapetanakis sees three beautiful heavenly maidens:

He could not let them go. Madly he plunged after them and seized the veil of the one nearest. There was a shriek. The two others darted with the speed of a kite straight to the sea and vanished while the third swayed, her face unveiled, gazing after them in terror and dismay.

Kapetanakis stood amazed. He saw before him a maiden whose beauty rivaled that of Aphrodite. What was she? What were the two who had fled? He wanted to ask, but he feared his voice would make her fly away after the others. At the end of a long moment she turned slowly toward him and the look in her eyes was of such hopeless sadness that he instinctively dropped to his knees.

"Oh, do not be sad,"" he begged. "Only stay with me and I shall make you happy!"

The maiden was silent.

""Speak!"" he pleaded. ""Speak to me and tell me that you will stay and be happy!"

Still the maiden did not answer. For three days it continued, his pleading and her silence. Finally she looked at him, her eyes full of grief and reproach, and said,"
Why did you do this?"

Kapetanakis had never heard a voice so angelic. The love that had been stirred by her beauty at the first moment he saw it was now awakened into life.

""Speak again!" He cried. ""I am happy only when I hear your voice. I love you, Agnoste. I want you for my wife."

She whom he called Agnoste, Unknown One, was thoughtfully silent for a time. Then she said, ""I shall marry you on one condition."

"Only one!" he exclaimed joyously. "What is it?"

"I am a fairy. You have me in your power. The condition is that I shall never speak again." (Gianakoulis and MacPherson, 1930)

In most of these tales, the fairy maiden, after years of suffering through a forced marriage, eventually escapes the grip of the man who has captured her. There are only a few very interesting and sometimes odd exceptions to this. One such exception comes from Japan; the man who captures a heavenly maiden that leaves him eventually builds a pile of sandals up to heaven so he can once again be with his wife forever.

Among the Oroqen, a young girl kidnaps the swan maidens in order to save her brother.

A brother and sister lived deep in the mountains, one day while the brother was out hunting he was having ill luck, so he decided to try fishing instead. Soon he caught a beautiful red fish which cried and begged for its life. Feeling bad for the fish he let it go, as it happened the fish was the son of a Dragon King, and in gratitude for the life of his son the Dragon King sent a magical horse to the boy. This horse brought the boy great luck while he was hunting, so that once while out hunting during mating season he saw three stags fighting over a doe. With his new found abilities he was able to quickly kill all three stags, unfortunately, one of these stags wasn't quite dead when he approached and was able to gore the boy when he got close, killing the him.

On seeing that the boy had died the horse put him up on her back and took him back to his sister. The girl wept when she saw her dead brother, for her father and mother had both died when she was very young, and now her elder brother had left her alone. After some, time, however, she was able to work with the horse to come up with a plan. She put on her brother's clothes, and changed herself to appear to be a more handsome version of her brother. Then she rode the horse to the three star-ponds. One beautiful heavenly (fairy) maiden was bathing in each pool.

"Steal the maidens' clothes," the horse told her. "Without these they can't return to heaven."

So the woman took the fairies clothes and then called out to the fairies who ducked down to avoid being seen, but it was too late.

"I've seen you naked, so now you must marry me as is the custom," the girl told them. "What's more your clothes are with me, and I'll only let you have them back if you agree to marry me."

The fairies did like the look of the one they thought was a young man and agreed softly. "I need more than a simple agreement. You must leave your footprints on the ground and put your fingerprint to a contract," the sister told them.

The fairies agreed to all of these, and when they had left their fingerprints and footprints the sister returned their clothes, and they went up to heaven to inform their parents of their agreement.

The sister waited by the pools of water for some time until at last the fairies called her up to meet their Father and Mother.

The sister mounted the horse and flew up into the sky, where she was given a feast as a guest. After paying her respects, the sister displayed the contract of marriage. The fairies parents were upset; they didn't want their daughters to marry a human. They could not oppose the union directly however because of the contract. So they told the sister that she must jump onto the stone threshold so hard that it would break, shoot an egg from 30 paces, and the eye of a needle from 100 paces.

The sister had no choice but to agree, though she was nervous that she wouldn't be able to achieve all of this. The fairies were upset, for they liked the young 'man,' they flew off.

The sister shot the egg and the eye of the needle. Then she went to the threshold

54

and as she leaped up into the air three bees landed on her and pushed her down with a great force causing her to shatter the threshold. The three bees, as it turned out, were really the three fairies, but they flew of before their parents learned what they had done. So the parents how had to agree to the marriage.

The young woman rushed ahead of the fairy girls as they returned back to her house. When she got there she stripped down, put her own clothes on again and put her brothers on him. When the fairies had arrived, the girl called out to them, weeping that her brother had died on entering the house. The fairies rushed forward with waters of life which they used to bring the girls brother back to life. Soon after the fairies married the sister's brother and lived happily with their new sister-in-law. When these fairies died they became the goddesses who help to cure illness, the eldest was Egeduge who protects against smallpox, second is Nichikun who protects against measles, and the youngest is Ehu who protects against typhoid fever.

Swan Maidens themselves are interesting figures, for many of them are deities in their own right, while others are servants of the lord of the dead. In Siberia, Swan Maidens serve Erlik, the lord of the dead, as Grimm Reaper-type figures. In Scandinavian mythology, they serve Odin by gathering up the souls of the dead to bring to his realm. Odin and Erlik themselves seem to exist on opposite ends of the spectrum, as deities go. Erlik is a cruel cannibal in many tales, whereas Odin, though often wild and unruly, seems to be trying to help the living. In both cases, however, it seems that the Swan Maidens are willing servants of the lord of the dead. According to Briggs, it was common for Swan Maidens to have an evil father such as a wicked magician or ogre-like monster. In "The Drummer," the swan maiden wishes to be freed from a witch who lives upon a Glass Mountain.

Regardless, as you can see, "The Drummer" is fairly unique among European tales about men who meet a heavenly maiden in that he didn't actually steal her clothes, and he returns them when asked. This begs the question, is this an original part of the story? Many of the fairy tales the Grimm Brothers collected, after all, were told by educated women in literary circles, which makes one wonder if perhaps this story was changed from its original form to avoid the rape theme inherent in the original. Another possibility is that the story comes from Asia, where Swan Maidens and mortals seem to get along better than in many of the European tales. One such tale comes from the Kalmyk, a people from Mongolia who settled in the West to become the only Buddhist nation in Europe (now part of Russia). In this story, the young man steals the shift from the swan maiden but feels bad when she starts to panic and so returns it to her. It is only after she is free that this swan maiden agrees to marry the young man and help him on his spirit journey to cure the Khan. In this case, the swan maiden gives the young man a yellow spotted silk scarf to show a magical tigress so that the tigress will know that he is friends with the swan maiden and so will allow him to milk her.

Given their propensity to work for the lord of the dead and to act as psychopomp, as well as the fact that they can only travel to the spirit world with the help of special clothing, one has to wonder if swan maidens themselves were originally shamans astrally projecting from the spirit world. This would mean that these swan maidens would eventually have to return to their bodies or risk dying, whether they wanted to or not. As previously mentioned, there are tales about people who kidnap astrally traveling witches to be their wives in German lore. In one of these cases, two farm workers were living together in a room, and every night a *mahrt* (nightmare) came to ride one of them. Finally, tired of being attacked by the mahrt, he asked his comrade to wake him the next time he was groaning in his sleep. His friend did so, and he reached out and grabbed a piece of straw, which began twisting and turning in his hand (the straw was the witch). He managed to hold it tightly until his friend had stopped up the knothole that the witch had come through (witches have to return the way they came).

The next day, they discovered that the witch was very beautiful, and so they argued for a while about who was going to marry her. At last, the one she had been tormenting with nightmares won and married her. Together, they had three children and lived happily... or so it seemed. The witch, however, would constantly beg her husband to show her the knothole she'd entered the room through, saying that she could hear her mother in England calling the pigs, and she wished to see her one more time. At last, the man gave in, and she flew off, never to be seen again (Brockhaus, 1848).

Drums of the North

Another interesting aspect of this tale is that the Drummer is, in fact, a drummer. In Northern Europe, The Sami *noaidi* (shaman) uses a drum as an aid for going into a trance to enter the underworld and retrieve lost souls. In this case, the shaman's soul was no longer in his or her body but journeying out with the aid of several helping spirits. This is true in many places throughout central Asia and the Americas as well. Although it is less well attested to in Central Europe, there is a case in Northern Italy in which shamanistic figures were called by a drummer to the spirit world to do battle.

Still, the lack of evidence for such drummers in Germany itself means that this element is likely merely a job description to indicate the wandering status of the character. The tale may be ancient enough to recall a time when the shamans of Germany used drums, or the drum element may have been borrowed from elsewhere.

"The Drummer" Continued...

Getting back to the drummer's spirit journey, he must travel out into the forest where he finds a giant sleeping. He wakes the giant with a drum roll and tricks the giant into thinking he's leading an army to slay him. Afraid of the imaginary army the giant agrees to carry he drummer to the Glass Mountain. Such deceit is an important part of the success of many shamanistic figures in lore. Indeed, trickster spirits are the creators or heroes of many peoples, and the drummer isn't done tricking the creatures of the spirit world, for, on reaching the Glass Mountain, he realizes that it is too smooth for him to climb.

> *Whilst he was standing thus, not knowing what to do, he saw, not far from him, two men who were struggling fiercely together. He went up to them and saw that they were disputing about a saddle which was lying on the ground before them, and which both of them wanted to have. "What fools you are" said he, "to quarrel about a saddle, when you have not a horse for it." "The saddle is worth fighting about," answered one of the men. "Whosoever sits on it, and wishes himself in any place, even if it should be the very end of the earth, gets there the instant he has uttered the wish. The saddle belongs to us in common. It is my turn to ride on it, but that other man will not let me do it." " I will soon decide the quarrel", said the drummer, and he went to a short distance and stuck a white rod in the ground. Then he came back and said, "now run to the goal, and whoever gets there first, shall ride first." Both set out at a trot, but hardly had they gone a couple of steps before the drummer swung himself on the saddle,*

wished himself on the glass-mountain and before anyone could turn round, he was there.

On the top of this glass mountain, he meets an old witch who is keeping the Heavenly Maiden prisoner. As with many such stories, the witch demands that the protagonist work in order to be allowed to live. However, she gives him impossible tasks, such as emptying out a lake with a thimble. Here, again, we see a fairly common idea in fairy tales that those in the spirit world must work to survive, with good spirits giving people tasks they can complete and rewarding them handsomely for it, and wicked spirits giving them impossible tasks so that they must rely on good spirits for help.

In many ways, this story is similar to "Nicht Nought Nothing," which Briggs compares to the Swan Maiden tale. Similar to the "Drummer," the protagonist of "Nicht Nought Nothing" finds himself in the clutches of a giant— but in this tale, the giant kidnaps him and takes him back to his palace.

> *The giant had a bonny dochter, and she and the lad grew very fond of each other. The giant said one day to Nicht Nought Nothing, "I've work for you tomorrow. There is a stable seven miles long and seven miles broad, and it has not been cleaned for seven years, and you must clean it -to-morrow, or I will have you for my supper."*
>
> *The giant's dochter went out next morning with the lad's breakfast, and found him in a terrible state, for aye as he cleaned out a bit, it aye fell in again. The giant's dochter said she would help him, and she cried a' the beasts o' the field, and a' the fowls o' the air, and in a minute they a' came, and carried awa' everything that was in the stable, and made a' clean before the giant came home. He said, "Shame for the wit that helped you; but I have a worse job for you to-morrow." Then he told Nicht Nought Nothing that there was a loch seven miles long, and seven miles deep, and seven miles broad, and he must drain it the next day, or else he would have him for supper. Nicht Nought Nothing began early next morning, and tried to lave the water with his paii, but the loch was never getting any less, and he did no ken what to do ; but the giant's dochter called on all the fish in the sea to come and drink the water, and very soon they drank it dry. When the giant saw the work done, he was in a rage, and said: "I've a worse job for you tomorrow. There is a tree seven miles high, and no branch on it, till you get to the top, and there is a nest; and you must bring down the eggs without breaking one, or else I will have you for my supper." At first the giant's dochter did not know how to help Nicht Nought Nothing; but she cut off first her fingers and then her toes, and made steps of them; and he clamb the tree, and got all the eggs safe till he came to the bottom, and then one was broken. The giant's dochter advised him to run away, and she would follow him. So he travelled until he came to a king's palace; and the king and queen took him in, and were very kind to him.*

This tale is related to a number of others from those of the Oroqen to the Japanese. and even the Zulu, who tell of a young man brought to the home of a monster. The daughter of this monster, however, helps him survive so that they can be married. This story motif may be related to the idea of bride service, a common practice among hunter-gatherers and early agriculturalists in which a man must serve his potential bride's father for a number of years in order to be able to marry her.

Perhaps more interesting than the idea of bride service, however, is how common it is for a kindly female spirit to live with an evil one. For example, in the tale of "Jack and the Beanstalk," a woman answers the door to the giant's home.

> *"Good morning, mum," says Jack, quite polite-like. " Could you be so kind as to give me some breakfast." For he hadn't had anything to eat, you know, the night before and was as hungry as a hunter.*
> *"It's breakfast you want, is it?" says the great big tall woman, " It's breakfast you'll be if you don't move off from here. My man is an ogre and there's nothing he likes better than boys broiled on toast. You'd better be moving on or he'll soon be coming."*
> *" Oh! please mum, do give me something to eat, mum. I've had nothing to eat since yesterday morning, really and truly, mum," says Jack. " I may as well be broiled, as die of hunger."*
> *Well, the ogre's wife wasn't such a bad sort, after all. So she took Jack into the kitchen, and gave him a junk of bread and cheese and a jug of milk. But Jack hadn't half finished these when thump! thump! thump! the whole house began to tremble with the noise of someone coming.*
> *" Goodness gracious me! It's my old man," said the ogre's wife, " what on earth shall I do? Here, come quick and jump in here." And she bundled Jack into the oven just as the ogre came in.*

Similarly, when Molly Whuppie is lost in the woods with her sisters, they come to a house.

> *They knocked at the door, and a woman came to it, who said: " What do you want?" They said: " Please let us in and give us something to eat." The woman said: " I can't do that, as my man is a giant, and he would kill you if he comes home." They begged hard. " Let us stop for a little while," said they, " and we will go away before he comes." So she took them in, and set them down before the fire, and gave them milk and bread.*

This is similar to a tale of two sisters from the Amur River who are being chased by a cannibalistic monster. These sisters are rescued by a kindly old woman whose son is also a man-eating monster. In the tale of "The Dragon and his Grandmother," some soldiers are forced to sell their souls to a dragon in order to avoid starving to death. The dragon tells the soldiers that, if they can solve a riddle, he'll let them free. Unable to figure out the riddle on his own, one of the soldiers manages to find the dragon's home in the forest.

> *A very aged woman was sitting, who was the Devil's (Dragon's) grandmother, and asked the soldier where he came from, and what he wanted there? He told her everything that had happened, and as he pleased her well, she had pity on him, and said she would help him. She lifted up a great stone which lay above a cellar, and said, "Conceal thyself there, thou canst hear everything that is said here; only sit still, and do not stir. When the dragon comes, I will question him about the riddle, he tells everything to me, so listen carefully to his answer."*

In Greek mythology, Persephone was the queen of the underworld and wife of Hades, the lord of the underworld. She, however, was kind and part of the Agrarian and mystery cults that gave hope to people both in life and in death.

There seems to be no connection between all of these stories, however, as the exact purpose and origin of the monster's wife, grandmother, daughter, etc. seems to be different from place to place—as is the relationship between the monster and the grandmother, wife, daughter. This would seem to indicate that the idea of having a powerful evil being living with a kindly female is deeply rooted in our psychology as so many people developed stories and their spirit world around this idea.

Near-Death and Out of Body Experience

People's historic beliefs that the spirit world existed all around them and that their fate was in the hands of supernatural entities gave encounters with the supernatural huge impact on their stories and thinking. Consider the story of Veronkia Barthel, who, after being struck by lightning, found herself in what can only be described as hell, a place filled with demons torturing screaming victims where it was difficult to breath because of the stench. Her journey into hell even included a lake of lava. After spending some time in this hell, her soul was finally transported back to her body. (Frater, 2014)

Veronika's experience with demons and dark forces during a near-death experience is not uncommon, so it should come as no surprise that, in lore, many people who went on spirit journeys found themselves in hell, oftentimes in order to receive a warning about living moral lives. Most near-death experiences, however, are peaceful and serene, although they are all dramatic, and they all speak to something humans naturally fear: death and the afterlife. All living organisms try to avoid death; after all, if we weren't naturally averse to death, we wouldn't survive. As with anything we fear, we often ponder and try to understand death as well as how we might overcome it. For many people, near-death experiences give some explanation about the most mysterious aspect of life, so it makes sense that the elements within them made their way into folk religion and fairy tales.

It's important to understand that it's not necessary for someone to die to have a near-death experience. Serious illness and pain can result in similar experiences. What is interesting is that so many of these experiences have similar elements and that they can be fairly commonplace. In a number of studies from Australia to Germany, anywhere from 4 to 9% of the population reported having near-death experiences (Horizon Research, 2007). This is a large portion of the population, and it does not include the number of people who had these experiences just before dying and were able to report them before ultimately passing away. With such a high frequency of experiences along with people's longing to understand death, near-death stories cry out for explanation. Near-death experiences commonly share a number of features (Parnia, Spearpoint, Vos, et al, 2014):

- Tunnels –a common feature of the near-death experience, which may be one reason so many otherworldly beings exist in an underworld.

- Out-of-body experience – the sensation of having left one's body and even the ability to see one's body lying lifelessly. This leaving of the body is an important part of the lore of everything from shaman spirit journeys to vampires, which were often said to be souls who left their bodies in order to drain the living of their blood.

- Seeing spirits of loved ones who have died – may explain why so many people believe that the spirits of their loved ones will meet them when they die.

- Encountering a strange spirit being for the first time – Who or what this being is varies greatly from one culture to another. In India, for example, people often

59

encountered Yamraj, the Hindu King of the Dead, while Christians tended to encounter Christ, God, or an angel. This may be due to personal interpretations of the encounter rather than its actual nature. What's important for our purposes, however, is that an encounter with an otherworldly being will often take place, prompting people to ask, "Who did I encounter, and what is their nature?" Such questions need to be answered and likely often lead to the creation and/or alteration of the deities a people believes in.

- Bright light – Although this is common in modern thinking about near-death experiences, it isn't as important in fairy tales or even mythology as the other features mentioned so far.

- A border between earthly life and the next – From vast rivers to mountains to a massive wasteland, fairy tales are rife with borders between the human realm and the otherworld.

Some few also encounter a hellish place filled with demons and darkness, which likely explains why journeys to hell were such a common feature in the spirit journeys of folklore. Still,

> although it does seem that the central features of near death experiences have been recorded throughout history and across numerous cultures, the actual interpretation of what people claim to have observed, of the experience they claim to have lived through, may reflect personal religious or cultural views. In other words, during a close encounter with death, people from different parts of the world may feel peaceful, see a tunnel, a bright light and a being of light, and have a sensation of detaching from their bodies, but they may identify the being of light according to their own cultural and religious backgrounds. Furthermore the overall interpretation of someone's experience, as with any experience, depends on their own background. For example, an atheist with a NDE may simply believe they had experienced a hallucination, while someone who believes in Jesus may believe they had met Christ. (Horizon, 2007)

Hero Tales and Royal Bloodlines as Remnants of Shamanism

Just like shamans, heroes in tles embark on epic journeys into the otherworld, battle strange beings, and meet gods.It shouldn't be surprising, then, that many of the ideas from shamanistic tales make their way into the stories of heroes. For example, Hercules' descent into the underworld to defeat Cerberus has ties with many shamanistic tales. This does not mean that Hercules was a shaman or was ever understoood to be one. What it means is that, because shamans were considered heroic and because so many myths were pieced together from many different places, many of the ideas in shaman's tales found their way into mythology among other places. Often, shamanistic elements even found their way into the tales of the founders of a civilization and the leaders of a society. Sometimes, the transfer of the elements from shamans' tales to heroic tales of founding leaders was purposeful, as many the elements in shamans' tales gave one the right to rule and allowed kings to pass on the supernatural favor of the gods to their decedents. After all, in most ancient societies, the right to rule came from people's perception of a person, which could be improved by divine tales.

In determining one's status image and perception, have always been important as more tangible reality. A reputation of being successful and successful qualities reinforced each other. Successful qualities had to be advertised. Thus, overt or subtler display of worth is a constant human activity, as it is with animals. It is limited by the balancing consideration of avoiding the provocation of a negative social response because other people as well jealously guard their honor in the social competition for esteem. In traditional society in particular, people were predisposed to go to great lengths in defense of their honor. The slightest offense could provoke violence. Where no strong centralized authority existed, one's honor was a social commodity of vital significance, affecting both somatic and reproductive chances. (Gat, 2000)

In other words, especially among early peoples, the ruler's grasp on power was often tenuous at best. According to Tacitus, ancient Germanic tribes had leaders whose only power base came from the respect that they could violently command. Those leaders who lost respect would often be "unelected" by their warriors in a bloody coup or simply by having their troops desert them. We also see this in later Germanic societies, such as the Holy Roman Empire. What's important to understand here is that respect and the right to rule were based not only on strength but also on the abstract notion of it. On top of this, in some cultures, people have an interesting need to justify their actions, to explain why they deserve and have the right to live on a land while driving others off. Both these ends can be served by claiming descent from a deity or shamanistic figure. Thus, the tales of the founders of a culture often took on these elements.

Indeed, many of the earliest societies, from Ur to Egypt, had rulers who claimed to be not only descended from the divine but divine themselves, and often this divinity was claimed through stories reminiscent of shaman's tales. Early Rome also had an origin story that resembles a shaman's origin story: that of Romulus and Remus. In this tale, two children are born to Rhea Silvia, who had been forced to remain celibate for life as a priestess but was seduced by Mars (or Hercules, in some tales). Once these two boys were born, the king tried to kill them by setting them adrift in the Tiber River, a common beginning for a number of shaman-like characters in fairy tales. The two brothers were rescued by the river deity Tiberinus, then found and suckled by a she-wolf and fed by a woodpecker. Eventually, however, they were raised by a simple shepherd and his wife.

This notion of being descended from sacred animals or divine parents was an important signifier in ancient times of the right to rule—just as it had been an important signifier of the right to become a shaman at one time. In societies where power was centralized within a king and shamanism had lost much of its significance, leaders took on this divine mantle.

Alexander the Great's mother claimed that she had been with Zeus in the form of a white snake, and it was he, this god, and not her husband who was Alexander's father. Such a claim of divine parenthood likely helped to give Alexander status during his vulnerable first years before he had fully proven himself and may have given him and his men a moral boost. They had to believe that, because he was Zeus's son, the god must be with him. Similar notions are prevalent throughout the world, with people using a birth from a deity, a gift from a fairy, etc. to boost their status and claim the right to rule. Such stories, however, require more than just a statement of birth; they may, at times, require a statement as to why descent from such a spirit is impressive, a statement which can be fulfilled through stories about the deity and his children's great deeds. These stories, like so many others, are likely eventually altered or broken into remnants that become pieces of other fairy tales.

The spirit journeys of shamanistic figures themselves also have a number of impressive and often strange features, which likely made their way into fairy tales. In the tale of "The Three Hairs of The Devil," for example, a man seeking magical knowledge must cross into the realm of the devil with the help of a boatmen who is cursed to row people across the river until someone takes the oar from him, which is likely a version of a tale in which a man takes a shaman to the realm of the dead.

In Greek mythology, Psyche's journey to Hades takes a lot of themes from spirit journeys. In this tale, she must travel with two honey cakes and two coins in order to bribe the guardians of the spirit world (the dog and the boatmen). Bribing the guards of the otherworld is a typical part of any shaman's journeys and is the reason that sacrifices of paper, food, animals, etc. were made during and before their ceremonies—so that they would have these available in the spirit world to offer the spirits as they passed.

When Odin worried about the life of his son Baldar, he rode his horse Sleipner over the Bifrost:

> Towards the north, and descended unto darksome Nifelhel, where dwelt the spirits of the great giants who were crushed in the World-mill. On the borders of Hela, as he rode speedily, a great and fierce hel-dog came after him. There was blood on its breast, and in the darkness it barked loudly. When it could go no farther, it howled long with gaping jaws. (Mackenzie, 2011)

Despite being a deity, Odin must seek answers in the spirit world as any other shaman would. He rides out on his spirit helper, an eight-legged horse given to him by a strange trickster character (Loki). He rides to the North, the direction of the Sami lands (it is fairly typical of Scandinavian lore for people to ride north or east in order to enter the spirit world or the realm of the trolls). As I'll discuss further in the chapter on "Influence from Neighboring Peoples," people often thought of their neighboring kingdoms as spirit worlds. More important than this, however, is that Odin clearly had to travel a long way to enter the spirit world, and he even had to flee from the hel-dog guarding the realm of the dead. It is also interesting to note that the gods in Germanic lore also entered this realm of the dead when they died, as Odin's son Balder did later in this tale.

When Balder died, the god Hermod made his own trip into Hel in order to try to free Balder's soul. His journey was far longer than Odin's—or at least more detailed:

> Meanwhile, Hermod made his darksome way through Nifel-hel towards Hela's glittering plains. Nine days and nine nights he rode on Sleipner through misty blackness and in bitter cold over high mountains and along ridges where chasms yawn vast and bottomless. On Hela's borders the terrible wolf dog of the giant Offotes followed him, barking in the black mist. . . . Then Hermod reached the rivers. Over Slid, full of daggers, he went, and over Kormet and Ormet, and the two rivers Kerlogar, through which Thor wades when he goes to the Lower Thingstead of the gods. He crossed shining Leipter, by whose holy waters men swear oaths that bind. At length he came to the River Gjoll and its golden bridge
>
> Modgud, the elf maid who watches the bridge, cried aloud: " Whence cometh thou who hath not yet died?" (Mackenzie, 2011)

Hermod's journey may be longer because he isn't as experienced as Odin, who is better equipped to travel into the spirit realm. While in the realm of the dead, Hermod encounters an elf maid who doesn't recognize him as a god. Instead, she demands to know why someone who isn't dead has entered this realm. People often saw many similarities between the divine beings they worshipped and the shamans who helped them negotiate with the divine to the extent that the tales of shamans and deities entering the spirit world were often the same.

Hemod reaches his destination in the underworld (Heljar-ran), which is home to those who would repopulate the world after Ragnarok.

> Over a long green plain went Odin, while the hoofs of Sleipner rang fast and cleat-, until he came to a high dwelling, the name of which is Heljar-ran, of which the keeper is Delling, the Red Elf of Dawn. Therein have their Hela-home the fair Asmegir--Lif and Lifthraser and their descendants who shall come at Time's new dawn that shall follow Ragnarok to regenerate the world of men.

> To the eastern gate went Odin, where he knew there was the grave of a Vala (prophetess). Dismounting from Sleipner, he chanted over her death chamber strange magic songs. He looked towards the north; he uttered runes; he pronounced a spell, and demanded sure response. Then rose the Vala, and from the grave chamber her ghostly voice spake forth and said:

> "What unknown man cometh to disturb my rest? Snow has covered me in its deeps; by cold rains have I been beaten and by many dews made wet. . . . Long indeed have I lain dead."

> Odin answered: "My name is Vegtam and my sire was Valtam. Tell me, O Vala," he cried, "for whom are the benches of Delling's hall strewn with rings, and for whom are the rooms decked with fine gold?"

> The Vala answered and said: "Here stands for Balder mead prepared, pure drink indeed. Over the cup shields are laid. Impatiently do the Asmegir await him and to make merry . . . . Alas! by compulsion hast thou made me to speak . . . . Now must I be silent."

> Odin said: "Silent thou must not be until I know who shall slay Balder--who shall bereave Odin's son of life." ((Mackenzie, 2011)

Here, it becomes all the clearer that Odin's tale is likely either influenced by or is an influence of shaman tales. Odin must use his magic formulas to raise the spirit of the dead and ask her for knowledge that he doesn't have, for those in the realm of the dead, it seems, know that they are preparing to receive the spirit of Balder within their own mead hall.

Again, when Balder dies, Hermod travels down to this same hall to try to bring Balder back:

> There in a golden hall he saw Balder seated on a throne of gold. Wan was his face and careworn, for the gloom of death had not yet passed from him. On his brow was a wreath of faded flowers, and on his breast the ring Draupner. He sat listening, as if he still heard the voice of Odin whispering in his ear. Before

him stood a goblet of mead, which he had touched not. Nanna sat by his side, and her cheeks were pale.

Hermod beheld nigh unto them Urd, the queen of Hela. In cold grandeur she stood, silent and alone. Deathly white was her face, and hard and stern, and she looked downward. On her dark robe gleamed great diamonds and ornaments of fine gold. . . .

To Balder spoke Hermod, and said: "For thee have I been sent hither, O my brother. In Asgard there is deep mourning for thee, and thy queen mother beseecheth thy speedy return."

That Balder's mead cup has been untouched gives hope that he could be returned from the underworld, for to accept hospitality in the land of the dead is to give it ultimate power over you. This is especially true of eating and drinking, although allowing a spirit to comb one's hair is also noted to be dangerous. When a shaman is unable to cure someone, he or she would sometimes explain that the person had already tasted of the food in the realm of the dead or started making a life there. It is not the gods who can return Balder to Asgard; only Urd may do that, so Hermod begs:

"In Asgard," Hermod said, "the gods sorrow for Balder, and on earth is he also mourned. All who have being and all things with life weep for Balder, and beseech thee that he may return again."

Urd made answer coldly: " If all who have being and all things with life weep for Balder and beseech his return, then must he be restored again. . . . But if one eye is without tears, then must he remain in Hela forever."

Bargaining for the release of souls from the land of the dead was one of the shaman's primary jobs. In most cases, people believed that many illnesses could be explained by a person's soul being taken to the realm of the dead. What's interesting about this instance is that Hermod is a god trying to bargain for the release of another god from the realm of the dead. Gods in lore were very much like humans; they could die and needed to use shamanistic powers.

How Fairy Tales Are Passed On

All it takes to completely transform our understanding of Grimm's Fairy Tales is to learn that they were primarily collected from educated upper- and middle-class women, some of whom got these stories from French books. These women told the fairy tales in literary sitting circles. Yes, the fairy tales still, for the most part, had their origins in "peasant's" tales, but it is also true that any story will change according to who tells it and why. Therefore, understanding the way fairy tales are passed on can give us some insight into the development and evolution of fairy tales and the magical creatures that inhabit them.

Because they have lasted for so long and traveled so far, some fairy tales were likely passed on by dozens, even hundreds of people before being written down. With so many tellers, it is impossible to know every way that any given fairy tale was told. There are, however, a few storytelling settings and types of storytellers that are likely particularly important to understanding the evolution of fairy tales.

It is commonly presumed that fairy tales were passed on from mothers to their children across many generations. These "Old Wives Tales" were a way for women to entertain the young and each other. More specifically, Karen E. Rowe (1986) states that these stories gave voice to the voiceless, helping the women of the past overcome the social censorship they faced, allowing them tell of the evils of being sold off by their fathers, of rape, of abusive husbands, and of the harshness of life. Marina Warner (1995) speaks of nurses, of seamstresses, of mothers and grandmothers who passed on stories, while Jacob Grimm collected his own stories from women. The notion of children snuggled around a fire with their mother- of children tucked away in bed listening to their nursemaid, listening to ancient stories, to an ancient heritage—is certainly romantic. It is only a small part of the story and likely not even the most important part.

Olly Wiessner (2014), in his studies of the !Kung, found that stories were more likely to be told at night by the light of the fire than during the day. Further, conversations at night around the fire were more likely to be about thoughts on the spirit world and how it influences the human world. At night, healers would go into trances and travel to the gods' village in order to speak with the spirits of deceased loved ones trying to take sick people away. Thus, according to Wiessner:

> There is something about fire in the middle of darkness that bonds, mellows and also excites people. It's intimate. Nighttime around a fire is universally a time for bonding for telling social information, for entertaining, for a lot of shared emotions.

It was also found, however, that the !Kung had extended communities—that is far-flung networks of mutual support. It wasn't only mothers and families sharing fairy tales with children; it could also be people from other villages sharing stories with each other.

During the Medieval era, people would travel to church towns and hang around after services to buy and sell crafts, animals, and more. In addition to local people, these markets would attract peddlers and minstrels from long distances. Also during the Medieval era, girls would be married to men a few villages over, thus becoming mothers to children far away while their own daughters would often be married to people a few more villages over, and so forth. Further, travelers would often stay together in rooms where they would also share stories and gossip or else stay the night with a family with whom they might also share stories. In addition, however, among some Siberian tribes, there were fairy tales that had to be told while fishing and those that could be told at night, while along the Amur River women would share fairy tales as a means of distracting the spirits of the earth so that they wouldn't notice the men out hunting. There are folklorists who also think that folktales were used in a similar way in Russia (Johns, 2004).

Fairy tales were told in many places and for many purposes, but perhaps most interesting of all were the traveling professionals who told stories. In Russia, the Sokolov brothers described the following scene:

> In the winter, in the depths of the forest, far from any habitation, there is often a whole village gathered together -peasants, their wives and children. By day there is heavy toil, but when it begins to grow dark, there is a well-deserved repose beside a blazing hearth. In the forest they build a camp – that is, a spacious mud hut with a hearth in the middle. The people are packed in and they warm their chilled limbs and satisfy their hunger and thirst. They then begin to while away the long winter evening...

> What a valuable person, then, does the storyteller prove to be. In the midst of the dense forest, with trees crackling from the frost, to the accompaniment of the howling of wolves, beside the blazing fire – what an apt setting, what a wonderful atmosphere for a folk tale full of every imaginable kind of terror. (Davidson and Chaudhri, 2006)

Story tellers would often travel from village to village, getting hired to tell stories not only to villages of people at night but also to fishermen who had long days on the boats. Similarly, J. F. Campbell (1891) said that, in the Western Highlands, people would:

> ...gather in crowds at the houses of those who are reputed to be good tale-tellers. Their stories frequently relate to the exploits of the Ossianic heroes, of whose existence they are as much convinced as ordinary English folk are of the existence and deeds of the British army in its most recent wars. During the tales "the emotions of the reciters are occasionally very strongly excited, and so also are those of the listeners, almost shedding tears at one time, and giving way to loud laughter at another. A good many of them firmly believe in all the extravagance of these stories."

Another collector of fairy tales said that, fifty years before Campbell's experiences, around Loch Lomond, the old and young people would gather separately and amuse themselves with games and stories. Thus, both men and women would share stories in a community setting.

> But the chief story-tellers appear to have been the tailors and shoemakers, who were literally journeymen, going from house to house in search of work. As they traveled about, they picked up great numbers of tales, which they repeated; "and as the country people made the telling of these tales, and listening to hear them, their winter night's amusement, scarcely any part of them would be lost." In these tales Gaelic words were often used which had dropped out of ordinary parlance, giving proof of careful adherence to the ancient forms; and the writer records that the previous year he had heard a story told identical with one he had heard forty years before from a different man thirty miles away; and this story contained old

66

Gaelic words the meaning of which the teller did not know. A gamekeeper from Ross-shire also testified to similar customs at his native place: the assemblies of the young to hear their elders repeat, on winter nights, the tales they had learned from their fathers before them, and the renown of the travelling tailor and shoemaker. When a stranger came to the village it was the signal for a general gathering at the house where he stayed, to listen to his tales. The goodman of the house usually began with some favorite tale, and the stranger was expected to do the rest. It was a common saying: "The first tale by the goodman and tales to daylight by the guest," (Campbell, 1891)

While it's true that fairy tales were frequently shared around the fire, they were very often village based experiences carried to others by travelers, which can help to explain the similarities of fairy tales from one place to another. There is another point to this, however: the best stories got their tellers more work. On the one hand, a storyteller might follow old traditions, but at the same time, the ones who were able to add a little something more to their tales earned more money, making the temptation to do so all the greater. Moreover, it is these popular stories that would be remembered the most.

Further, being told by a few skilled storytellers to communities, as well as parental figures, means that fairy tales had an important social element; they were altered to fit the needs of society and to communicate moral messages. These messages could evolve based on the desires of a few skilled people trying to create the society they wanted. After all, even when storytellers tell "true" stories or stories about real people, they are likely to alter them to fit their audience and, at times, their social agenda or, at the very least, focus on the elements that match their ideas.

What's most important to understand, however, is that the fairy tales and fairy tale elements we know are the ones that survived the process of being told and which people remembered or chose to retell.

A tale becomes traditional not by virtue of being created, but by being retold and accepted; transmission means interaction, and this process is not explained by isolating just one side. A tale created, that is, invented by an individual author – may somehow become "myth" if it becomes traditional, to be used as a means of communication in subsequent generations. (Zipes, 2012)

What this means is that, while there were likely many tales told, the ones that survived were the ones that people liked the most in a sort of winner-take-all competition between stories. Certain elements that resonated with people culturally and psychologically were more likely to survive. For example, research has shown that people are more likely to recall stories with supernatural elements in them but that still fit with basic human thinking (Atran and Norenzayan, 2006). This, in turn, helps to explain why stories about magical beings with what amounts to a human psychology are so prevalent, notwithstanding any beliefs people might have had about a deity's omnipotence or the odd behavior of magical beings.

I would further argue that the winner-take-all model of storytelling also helps to explain why many of the fairy creatures seem to have taken on darker, scarier elements; after all, there are many reasons why scary stories and creatures might become more prevalent when passed from person to person for generations.

The Importance of Horror Stories

Research has shown that people tend to focus on the negative aspects of stories, and even negative stories themselves, such that these tend to be remembered longer than positive stories (Baumeister and Bratslavsky, 2001). Further, Kathellen Vohs (2014) found that negative events had a bigger impact on a person than positive ones, and because of this, bad impressions and stereotypes take root faster and soon become resistant to improvement by positive events. On top of this, in their research, they found that people tend to prefer to tell stories with a negative slant rather than a positive one.

What this means is that the more negative aspects of any creature from stories, such as fairies, can easily move to the forefront, but only as long as people aren't specifically pushing to keep positive stories in focus. In other words, as long as there is an organized religious structure built around a fairy, people will actively try to tell positive stories about it. For example, in ancient Greece, people worshiped nymphs as the founders of cities, so for a while, positive stories basically balanced out negative ones. However, once the nymph cults decreased in importance, stories about nymphs drowning people, turning them into animals, kidnapping children, possessing people, etc. became the focus of people's storytelling. This is not always the case, of course, as shown by the stories of the Greek deity Pan, who became Panus in modern fairy tales; a kind-hearted being despite previous negative stories about him (Lawson, 1910). Still, despite exceptions, many of the beings that were both good and bad likely shifted to become worse and worse as time went on.

This negative slant on stories would be further pushed by the fact that many people are attracted to scary situations and stories (Zillmann and Vordere, 2010). In the modern day, we see how people who love scary stories can subvert innocent images and turn them on their heads by making dolls, children, and clowns creepy. Anyone who was to watch the horror movies of today might presume that we find childlike images horrifying. We see something similar in some fairy tales in which bread houses can be the homes of witches, cats are vampires, and handsome men or beautiful women in the wilderness are likely to drain away a person's life. In other words, there is a frequent theme in fairy tales that what is desirable has a monstrous core.

Horror and monsters violate cultural norms, and because of this, a paradox emerges. Normally, people would be unlikely to seek out what they find disgusting and scary, but they do. In one theory, horrors attract people "because anomalies command attention and elicit curiosity." In other words, we find the monsters of horror fascinating because we are curious; we want to discover and think about something unusual (Grossberg and Polloc, 1997). In support of this notion, "various studies have found that sensation seeking is an important variable in the enjoyment of horror films" (Beth and Sanders, 2004).

Hence, people will seek out scary situations in order to discover new and interesting monsters. There is even a scary fairytale about this in which a bored smith says:

> *"They say there's evil in the world. I'll go and seek me out evil." So he went and had a goodish drink, and then started in search of evil. On the way he met a tailor.*

"Good day," says the Tailor.

"Good day."

"Where are you going?" asks the Tailor.

"Well, brother, everybody says there is evil on earth. But I've never seen any, so I'm going to look for it."

"Let's go together. I'm a thriving man, too, and have seen no evil; let's go and have a hunt for some."

Well, they walked and walked till they reached a dark, dense forest....

After a while, the smith and the tailor meet an old woman (secretly a monster known as a lihko) who terrifies them, but they agree to eat dinner with her. After they have finished eating, the old woman slits the tailor's throat and tosses him in the oven. She then demands that the smith forge her an eye. After he does this, the smith manages to tie the witch up under the pretense that he has to hold her still to put the eye into her socket. With the lihko tied up, he attempts to flee but is recaptured and made a prisoner (being stored for food). However, he manages to figure out another way to escape.

By-and-by the sheep came home from a field, and she drove them into her cottage for the night. Well, the Smith spent the night there, too. In the morning she got up to let the sheep out. He took his sheep-skin pelisse and turned it inside out so that the wool was outside, passed his arms through its sleeves, and pulled it well over him, and crept up to her as he had been a sheep. She let the flock go out one at a time, catching hold of each by the wool on its back, and shoving it out. Well, he came creeping up like the rest. She caught hold of the wool on his back and shoved him out.

This story of a man escaping from a blind one-eyed monster is similar to the story of Odysseus escaping the Cyclops Polyphemus in the Odyssey, which likely isn't an accident. There is a plethora of similarities between Slavic and Greek lore, including their ideas about nymphs and dead spirits' frequent desire for blood. It seems likely then that these two peoples passed a number of stories back and forth over the years, and it is often pointless to try to speculate on which ideas came from where.

Even after escaping, the smith in this tale isn't out of the woods (literally; he's still in the forest, the lihko's domain). As he runs through the forest, his hand gets caught by a magical trap that the lihko set for him. After being trapped for a grizzly amount of time in which the lihko draws closer and closer to him, he must at last make the horrifying decision to cut off his own hand.

Such twisted suspense is not uncommon in fairy tales. Consider the buildup of horror in the story of "Little Red Riding Hood," in which a young girl visits her grandmother's house where a wolf is pretending to be her grandmother:

It seemed strange to her that the door was wide open, and when she entered the room everything seemed to her so peculiar, that she thought, "Ah! My God! How strange I feel today, and yet at other times I am so glad to be with granny!"

She said, "Good-day!" But received no answer.

Thereupon she went to the bed and undrew the curtains. There lay granny, with her cap drawn down to her eyes, and looking so queer!

"Ah, granny! Why have you such long ears?"

"The better to hear you."

"Ah, granny! Why have you such large eyes?"

"The better to see you."

"Ah, granny! Why have you such large hands?"

"The better to take hold of you."

"But, granny! Why have you such a terribly large mouth?"

"The better to eat you up!"

And there with the wolf sprang out of bed at once on poor little Red Hood, and ate her up.

Anyone telling this story to children will likely see how the anticipation builds as it becomes more and more obvious that Little Red Riding Hood isn't going to realize the wolf's true nature in time to escape. This anticipation likely leaves those in the audience wanting to scream, "It's the wolf, you idiot! It's the wolf!" We do the same thing in our modern horror stories, commonly with a young girl who is home alone when she hears a strange noise in the attic or basement and goes to investigate. Given that there is a psychological basis for horror stories, which are present in nearly every culture, it seems likely that these spooky fairy tales served the same purpose as our spooky campfire stories and horror movies.

There is perhaps more to these stories than simply the odd desire to share scary stories, however, as the magical beings within these stories were thought to control people's lives. At the same time people couldn't help but have noticed all the bad things that happened to them, bad things they thought the fairies weere responsible for. In this way, spirits that are normally or often considered good can at least sometimes be transformed into evil beings in fairy tales. We see this transformation even in the modern day transformation of the clown. Because of their makeup, Stott says of them, "Where there is mystery, it's supposed there must be evil, so we think, 'What are you hiding?'" (McRobbie, 2013).

To some extent...

> Clowns have always had a dark side, says David Kiser, director of talent for Ringling Bros. and Barnum & Bailey Circus. After all, these were characters who reflected a funhouse mirror back on society; academics note that their comedy was often derived from their voracious appetites for food, sex, and drink, and their manic behavior. "So in one way, the clown has always been an impish spirit... as he's kind of grown up, he's always been about fun, but part of that fun has been a bit of mischief," says Kiser. (McRobbie, 2013)

For a short period of time, people viewed clowns in the domain of children's entertainment. They were thought of as purely whimsical characters. Then John Wayne Gacy, a Chicago clown, murdered over 35 young men between 1972 and 1978. What ultimately turned clowns into icons of horror, however, were Spielberg's film "Poltergeist" and Steven King's novel "It." Soon, horror stories of clowns were popping up everywhere so that now, rather than funny, most children find them scary (McRobbie, 2013).

The fear that grew up around ancestral spirits is a good example of such a transformation. While people would often pray to and honor their ancestral spirits, there seems to have been a close to universal fear that these could turn evil at the drop of a hat. Chagnon (1992) says of one South American tribe:

> The Yanomamo have an almost morbid fear of becoming cannibals, almost as though humans are precariously close to an inherent predisposition to devour members of their own specious.

Similarly, in "The Odyssey," the ghosts of the dead had a strong desire to drink blood, an idea that existed in Eastern Europe and among Siberian peoples who believed that, if a soul remained behind after death, it would essentially become a vampire. It's very easy, then, for magical beings to go from kind to demonic as stories progress, given our propensity to tell horror stories and the mystery that perpetually shrouds spirits.

A Monkey on the Porch

Kipnuk is a Yupik Village in the Kuskokwim Delta, Alaska that was still fairly traditional in the early 1980s, with many people getting most of their calories from hunting and fishing. It was here that a mother told her child a scary story about a monkey that lived on the porch in order to keep him from going outside without her, where he would be vulnerable to the frigid winter and rabid animals. The tradition of telling children scary stories to keep them from going places they shouldn't is fairly common, which is why so many monsters target children in places they shouldn't be. What's interesting in the story of the monkey on the porch, however, is the woman's choice of a monkey to scare her child. Monkeys are typically used as a fun, albeit mischievous creature in Western culture and would likely attract most children in the rest of America onto the porch. But to the Yupik mother and her child, the monkey was a foreign entity, and she needed something foreign to scare him.

Many people used foreign gods and even other peoples as the monsters in their tales. In this way, what was otherwise good could be perceived as bad. Now, consider what would happen when two neighboring cultures that had used each other's fairies in odd ways began to merge over time, as happened not only through invasion but also through simple marriage between neighboring peoples many times throughout European history. During such marriages, the beings that one culture knew of as good and the other knew of as evil would also merge, becoming a single dualistic spirit.

Scary images aren't only a means of controlling children. However, they can be used as a way to control nearly every sort of moral behavior. For example:

> Horror films could function as a way of discouraging "rebellious" adolescent behaviors such as sexual promiscuous or experimentation with drugs has received a fair amount of critical attention. For example, Dika argued that the rise in the popularity of the slasher film can be partially explained by a societal shift

toward more conservative social, sexual, and political values, culminating in the election of Ronald Reagan to the presidency. (Oliver and Sanders)

This use of horror stories becomes fairly obvious when reading many tales about vampires. In one such tale, the young people of a village sneak into abandoned houses outside the village to holhold a party. Then some vampires show up and slaughter one of the girls, strewing her guts about the house. In a Scottish tale, some boys are lured into dancing with some beautiful girls who turn out to be vampiric women who use their long claws to drain and drink the blood of the victims. In another Russian story, two girls agree to sneak out and meet some boys by the river, but as you can guess by now, the boys turn out to be vampires.

It's not just sexual behavior that horror stories aim to prevent. There are many, many moral and even semi-religious behaviors that people would try to reinforce using scary stories. In the story of "Frau Trude," an obstinate girl seems interested in learning witchcraft. However, when she approaches a known witch, she is turned into a piece of wood and tossed into the fire (Grimm and Grimm). In an Irish fairy tale, a vampire is unable to enter any home with clean water but is free to enter homes with unclean water and drain the inhabitants of their blood. This need to leave clean water is related to the offerings of bread and water, which the Celts would leave for fairies; those who failed to do this would also have their blood drained or would receive some punishment. Other fairies would punish messiness, laziness, greed, cruelty, drunkenness, and other undesirable traits.

In other words, fairies often existed to act as authority figures and enforce morality. As part of this, they often determined people's fates. Many people have a natural inclination to dislike authority figures. Whether or not they are doing anything wrong, they feel uncomfortable having authority figures watching over them. Fairies were authority figures that people believed controlled the weather, illness, and other seemingly random events. Thus, fairies used their authority in unpredictable and often cruel ways. The neoroscientist David Rock, in his interview with the New York Times, stated:

> People react to a performance review as if someone is saying your life is in danger. And the pushback is real. People will push back so intensely because they experience a strong unconscious threat response. It's the same mechanism that makes people argue to be right even when they know they're wrong. Certainty is a constant drive for the brain. We saw this with Hurricane Sandy. The feeling of uncertainty feels like pain, when you can't predict when the lights will come back on and you're holding multiple possible futures in your head. That turns out to be cognitively exhausting. And the more we can predict the future, the more rewarded we feel. The less we can predict the future, the more threatened we feel. (Bryant, 2013)

While David Rock's example of how authority figures can make us nervous is related to workers in the modern day, I would point out that fairies are often very closely connected to people's attempts to get food. In agricultural societies, they are tied to the fertility of the fields, and in hunting societies, they are involved in the hunt. A person's success or failure at anything was believed to rest on them. However, no one can ever be certain where they stand with the fairies. This uncertainty "feels like pain."

Imagine how much more intense the problems created by authority figures would be when those believed to be in authority were invisible beings watching over eveyone, threatening to cause them to sicken and die if they did something wrong. Further, as new peoples or

72

religions moved into an area—especially if they came to dominate it—the local people would tell them not to do certain things or else they would be punished, not by an evil being, but by good enforcers of morality. The new culture or religion wouldn't see it that way, however, as all they would know is that the new being was threatening to kill them.

Consider, for example, the story of a woman who went out onto her porch without covering her head in order to look at the stars. When she went inside, the domovoi (a spirit that normally protects the people of the house) seized her by the hair and pulled her into the attic. Luckily, before he could do something worse to her, she managed to utter a prayer, causing him to vanish.

Changing Faiths

The religion practiced by various peoples has changed many times in history. It's probable that, at one time, the Germanic people worshiped Tyr as the head deity rather than Odin and then later became Christian. The Irish had a faith before they spoke the Celtic language, which also changed again when they became Christian. Often, a new faith will alter people's perception of the older one both by chance and through a purposeful campaign to demonize old ideas. Take, for example, the story of St. Collen, who is invited to dine with Gwyn ap Nudd (i.e., the King of the fairies) on a hilltop. After refusing the invitation many times, Collen finally goes with a bottle of holy water to protect himself against the devils. Here, Collen uses the power of god to reveal that the beauty and happiness of fairyland is nothing but a devilish illusion and uses his holy water to drive the hell-bound spirits away (Thomas, 1908).

Liars, Liars

Finally, it's also worth noting that Tamborini, Stiff, and Zillmann found in their research that higher levels of the Machiavellian trait of deceit were positively associated with greater preference for graphic horror. They interpreted this finding as suggesting that horror film enjoyment may reflect a desire to engage in social norm violation. Further studies found that people with lower levels of empathy were more likely to find horror stories enjoyable. In addition to the normal healthy people who find horror stories interesting, then, dishonest people and people who are more likely to violate cultural norms often find horror appealing. This begs the question, what kind of stories would they tell during a time when tale swapping was part of the social fabric of life?

A Natural Goodness

There is a flip side to scary stories, however: humans, in general, naturally care about each other to a certain extent and so assume that others will care about them as well. What's more, humans are capable of forming relationships with fictional characters, imaginary friends, deceased relatives, unseen heroes and fantasized mates (Boyes, 2008). What this means is that, while people often imagine horrors, they are perhaps more likely to give names to the magical beings they believe care about them. People very often believe in an inherent goodness—loving beings that care about them.

In addition, people can and do build emotional attachments to beings that they should be afraid of, especially during times of turmoil and change. In the past century, fairies have quickly become symbols of childhood—as have vampires, to some extent. Even Polyphemus, the cannibalistic cyclops of the Odyssey, was later portrayed in a romantic light. The poet Theocritus, for example, paints Polyphemus as a herdsman who is in love with a sea nymph, even though he cannot swim and she cannot come onto land.

A few centuries ago, the Tengu (anthropomorphic raven/humans that later becomes red-faced men with long noses) were typically believed to be horrifying monsters. However, as time went on, they came to be beloved. The Kami, who protects children from being burned by the stove and prevents house fires, for example, is a Tengu king who originally sought to destroy humanity but became a good and kindly household deity. In the modern day, we have even turned vampires into romantic beings. Indeed, it could be argued that the scary, dark element to the vampire's nature is what has made them so attractive. We are naturally drawn to what scares us, even as it drives us away. Thus, things that were traditionally thought of as evil are often romanticized and made good.

More than this, people will often love the beings they feel a spiritual connection with.

Folk Memory

In trying to understand fairy tales, I have spoken a lot about events that are in the far distant past, which begs the question: how long can people remember an event or idea? How long will remnants of different fairy tales last?

It's difficult to answer this question for certain. We can't know for sure how long any story existed before it was written down. However, at the same time, there isn't any real time limit on how far folk memory extends. The Alonquin tribe, for example, still recalls a strange creature that wandered their land, leaving big round footprints, with massive ears and a long nose. Over 10,000 years after mammoths disappeared from their land, the Natives of Labrador Island still remember them, along with giant beavers, which also went extinct at least 10,000 years ago (Strong, 2009).

> For centuries the Battle of Bodsworth (Fought in 1485) was thought to have taken place at one particular place which fitted the landscape described in contemporary chronicles. All the books and all the maps and tourist signs followed accordingly, despite local people always insisting that it was fought some several miles away from that point. Then detractors discovered the debris of battle, armor, arrowheads, even cannon balls, exactly where local people said they would be. The history books had to be rewritten. (Phelps, 2013)

Another folklorist found that folk memory extended back to a 15th century battle in which some Welshmen brought French soldiers with them into Worcestershire (Phelps, 2013). Beyond remembering a battle from so far back, however, what's interesting about this story is that the French in it used guns instead of the bows they would have used, and the man who told the tale thought the event had perhaps occurred during his grandfather's time. In other words, the story was passed down through the family, but the exact timing of certain details were brought closer to the current teller's life experience.

In another example, the Irish seem to recall in their mythology that they migrated to Ireland from Spain thousands of years ago. Ideas from stories—the notion of a dangerous spirit of the lake, a kind forest fairy with a beard of twigs, that the grave mounds can have dancing spirits within them—could all last for thousands, even tens of thousands of years. It's unlikely in such cases, though, that any story told to a folklorist would be the same as the original. Jamshid J. Tehrani (2013) has pointed out that, like biological species, folktales evolve by descent and modification from one generation to the next. While they are altered slightly as they are passed down, one can use phylogenetics to trace their origins.

Phylogenetics is the method of creating the evolutionary history/family tree of different organizations. The idea is that any species will resemble its parents in some way and that, through these resemblances, family trees can be built. The same is true of fairy tales; any given tale will likely resemble its parent tales in some way. The one caveat I would add to this is that, while an animal species likely evolves in a more or less straight line (in other words, a horse never breeds with a lizard), fairy tales, religion and myths will intermingle all the time to create entirely new stories. Nevertheless, these stories will resemble their "parents" enough that "it is possible to establish coherent narrative traditions over large geographical distances and historical periods."

Culture and Cultural Transformations

It's undeniable that people's beliefs and ideas about the spirit world have changed over time and that, to some extent, many of these changes are semi-predictable—or, at the very least, traceable. Nevertheless, one shouldn't make the mistake of thinking that there is a specific religious evolution followed by all cultures. Many of the ideas which people once thought of as primitive, from totemism to mana, aren't found everywhere and so may very well have been ideas that developed long after the advent of religion. It's impossible to say what the first religion was or that there was a single progression in thinking from one type of religion to another. What we can say, however, is that any religion will slowly adapt to fit the needs of the people who follow it.

Means of Obtaining Food

It has been said that people once lived according to the rhythms of the earth, their activities dictated by the seasons and the environment in which they lived. However, it would be more accurate to say that people once lived in rhythm with the food that they ate, for what people were focused on wasn't the earth or the weather themselves but how these things impacted their food supply. Perhaps more than anything else, food mattered to the peasants during the once-upon-a-time. When most people were farmers, hunters, or fishermen, cultures were defined in large part by what tactics they used to get food. For example, many Europeans were dependent on cow's milk for cheese and butter to survive (Curry, 2013). Cows had to be milked and fed every day. As a result, people's daily schedules were defined by their cows. Further, their lives hinged on their cows producing enough milk. For them, the greatest nightmare was having vampires come to kill their cows, elves that drained their cattle of their milk, or witches who prevented them from churning butter and cheese. This meant that these people's destiny wasn't in their own hands; it was in the hands of their cow's health. In Irish lore, *piseogs* (spells and mystical beliefs and magical actions)...

> Were often associated with certain families and certain parishes, with the piseog being passed from mother to daughter. The female connection was due to women being in charge of butter making and butter was a source of wealth in the old days.
>
> "If the butter failed, you couldn't pay rent so you were out on the road," Eddie says. "It's no wonder the women were always watching each other's butter and their success."
>
> Protecting the milking cows from piseogs was absolutely imperative on May Eve, when it was believed piseogs were even more powerful. To ward off bad luck, a red ribbon would be tied to the cow's tail or around her neck. (Murphy, 2011)

The importance of milk and food in general also explains why so many fairies in Northern Europe were connected with both the wilderness and herding animals, for here it seems that the hunting deities eventually transferred to those of dairy. Thus, fairies would keep and milk deer as if they were their cattle and help humans with their own cattle. There were a number of prayers to nature deities to watch and care for people's cattle. For example, in Finland, they had the following:

> Distinguished woman, Suvetar, Nature's old wife, Etelätär, that art a watcher of

76

the herd, a keeper of the mistress's flock, arise to cleanse the byre, to watch the cattle of the byre, bring hither luck to calves, toss in to the oxen luck...

Ukko, the golden king, the god that in the sky abides, come watch my herd beautifully all summer-time; as thou hast watched them 'neath a shed, watch them among the heather too, as thou didst tend them in the house, so tend them in the clumps of fir, tend them among the firs, rule over them near boughs of pine.

Or

King of the forest, Kuitua, Hongas, the mistress benevolent, daughter of Tapio, Tellervo, thou tiny little forest lass, when I send out my cows to the delightful Metsola, set a shepherd of willow wood, tall lassies of mountain-ash, cow-watchers of alder wood, of wild bird-cherry to drive them home, without a shepherd's driving them, without a herding-lassie's care. (Aercromby, 1898)

In the first of these prayers, the Finnish people ask a nature goddess, the god of lightning (Ukko), to watch over their cattle while they were out in the forest. In the third, they ask the daughter of Tapio, the forest king, to set the tree spirits to watching the cattle. These poems asking the wilderness deities to watch over the cattle are paralleled by the poems to deities of the forest to help with hunting, such as: "O lovely being of the heath! Show me the path, open the door, proceed to indicate the path, to give instructions for the way, to set up posts along the road and landmarks make." In other cases, their request for help in the hunt is more direct, such as: "O forest-daughter, delightful girl, O Tapio's daughter, Tuulikki, chase the wild creatures out to run from the forest-castle slopes, make them to scamper, make them scud for my good luck." From this, it's easy to see how the forest spirits went from helping people to hunt to helping them herd cattle.

The importance of food is also why heaven/fairyland itself was a place of milk, butter, cheese, and, yes, honey—though it might also be depicted as a land of rice, of sausage, or of many other foods, depending on the culture telling the story. Wishes themselves often involved food. As Maria Tatar (1999) puts it:

It is not at all uncommon for a peasant hero, faced with three wishes, to ask first for a plate of meat and potatoes, or to be so distracted by hunger that he yearns out loud for a sausage while contemplating the limitless possibilities before him.... Wish-fulfillment in fairy tales often has more to do with the stomach than the heart.

Hence, it's more common for the heroes of fairy tales to have a magical caldron or tablecloth that provides food than to have a magical sword.

Regardless of the strategy that ancient peoples employed to get food, starvation could be a constant concern. Indeed, "famines have claimed more lives across human history than all the wars ever fought" (Dando, 2012). Food was more than just flavors or nostalgia; it defined people's hopes and dreams as well as their fears. People lived and died according to what they ate or failed to get enough of.

Food also defined the psychology of a culture. For example, researchers found that, in China, people who grow rice are more collectivist than people who grow wheat. What's more, these differences are stable over time even after the former farmers' decedents have long since moved to the city (Tahlhelm, et al., 2014). The stability of cultural psychology associated with food production is important, as it indicates that, at least for a time, people retain their cultural values, even after massive shifts in the way they live. Similarly, Joseph Vandello and Dov Cohen found that individualism and collectivism varied across the United States based on the types of farming that had been performed in each region. Here, too, farming systems that required many workers, like those in the South, led to collectivism, and those requiring only a few workers, like small-group pastoralism (cowboys), led to individualism.

It should come as no surprise, then, that food, at first, was what defined human thinking about folk religion and fairies. It was the fairies who helped the crops to grow, who helped the cattle to be fertile, who ensured that children would have enough to eat... or who withheld their blessings and caused famine. Right into the 20th century, people in Eastern Europe were still making offerings to water fairies for a good harvest. From fertility goddesses to foxes that protect the crops, people had the deepest connection with the spirits that helped them get food. This is one reason Zeus as a weather god was so important in Ancient Greece as the peasants "needed rain, and sometimes cool weather" (Nilsson and Nock, 1972). Zeus lived on the highest mountain in each region (not just Mount Olympus) and became the king of the deities within the Greek world because he brought the weather that the farmers prayed for and needed. Because of this need, one of the most important rituals in Greek life involved climbing up to the mountain with its cool, moist weather and praying for rain and cooler weather below. This same thing is true in Japan, though oftentimes they would also perform rituals to attract the mountain kami down to them.

People who fished for their food also knew that their destiny was not in their hands. Instead, it rested in the movement of the fish from one place to another, a movement that was largely unpredictable. For many of the early tribes of Europe and Northern Asia who subsisted largely on fish (Richards, 2002) (Richards, Pittit, et al, 2001) their lives were largely dependent on water spirits. This, in turn, could explain why water spirits were considered the deities of the native inhabitants in places as far flung as Greece and Japan.

Witches and shamans were also defined by the food that people ate; in addition to helping to cure illness, the purpose of shamanism Was to help people obtain food. Thus, as a culture changed the means by which they obtained food, the nature of the religious leaders changed as well. In his study, Kaplan found that shamanism tends to share certain characteristics across many different hunter-gathering cultures, which he reasons is because people tend to interpret certain common mental experiences the same way, depending on their means of obtaining food. Further, Kaplan states that the religious leaders of a community will change in semi-predictable ways with the method for obtaining food. Thus, what he defines as shamans will transition to priests, then to mediums as hunter-gatherer societies progress to agricultural societies. This is not the full picture, however; as we'll see the peasants had their own magico-religious practitioners separate from their culture's priests. Thus, shamans would continue to exist among the peasants long after the priest class had formed. Even so, the shaman's job would change as a culture went from one means of obtaining food to another. Just as most religious ideas and fairy tales are based on fragments of previous ideas, much of the magico-religious culture would likely be similar to that of previous eras. Ultimately, this means that it is possible, at times, to unravel the origin of fairy tales by looking at the beginnings of people's attempts to gather food.

Because the first people were hunter-gatherers, they worried about the spirit guardians of forests and other hunting grounds, or of the guardians of waterways, as fish provided a large portion and often the majority of what the ancient peoples of Europe ate. At their root, many of the tales we have of fairies were adapted from the stories of hunter-gatherers—from the people who lived off the land and water.

We see remnants of these in a number of fairy tales, such as the Scottish tale in which two men out hunting encountered a fairy known as the Brown Man of the Muir;, a guardian spirit of the wild beasts who caused the hunters to sicken and die. The Leshii of Russia are considered to be the owners of the forest, and one needed to make offerings to them in order to pass safely through the woods.

Interestingly enough, further west, the Leshii had started to transition into spirits of agriculture and even people's homes in addition to the forest. Thus, what was once a wilderness spirit involved in hunting very clearly became an agricultural spirit. In Northern Russia, the Leshii transitioned into spirits that aided herdsmen in the woods.

The fact that so many fairy tales and fairy beings start as the stories of hunter-gatherers means that there is something feral in their nature. The wilderness, after all, is both cruel and kind; it is a meditative and beautiful place that sometimes provides food, but it can also withhold this sustenance. Further, underneath the surface of its beauty is a danger, for as previously discussed, many people would go into the wilderness and vanish without a trace. Even when it was obvious what happened—that their boat had sunk, that the child was carried off by a wolf, that a rabid animal had infected someone, etc.—the reason for these bad things still had to be explained by examining the spirit world. After all, most peoples believed nothing happened by chance. The fairies were involved in everything, both good and bad. The dependence of people on the natural world and their fear of it are one possible explanation for the multiple natures so many people believed applied to any given supernatural being.

Dark Forests and Sacred Water

You only manage to see it for a split second: a deer shimmering in the sunlight before it vanishes into the thick underbrush, and then it's gone—along with your hopes of capturing food for the day. Your stomach burns with hunger, and your thoughts go fuzzy. It's too early in the year for the bounty of fruits and nuts to spring forth from the trees. Overhead, squirrels and tiny birds chitter, mocking you. Catching enough of them to feed your family is difficult. A few snares may very well bring in some tough, unsatisfying meat, but that can't last long, and success in catching enough small game to survive will quickly deplete the forest, leaving you starving once more.

As you pick your way through the thick brush, the sudden sense that you're being watched washes over you. You glance nervously at the bushes, searching for the eyes you are certain are looking at you, listening carefully for the crack of twigs. A branch falls from the trees, startling you, and everything goes quite. Then a primal sound echoes through the forest, and though you've lived your whole life in the wilderness, you've never heard anything like it. Your heart races, and you grip your bow tightly as you wait nervously, not for food, but for whatever strange spirit is stalking you.

The later part of this story happened to me and some of my friends while hunting in the vast wilderness of Alaska. Many people have similar stories of being watched, of having mud flung at them seemingly from nowhere, of strange events and sightings in the wild. Perhaps this is why, among many cultures, the forest is considered a dark and foreboding place, an idea that likely had its start even among the hunter-gatherers. For example, while the Ket, the last group of hunter-gatherers in Central Siberia to survive the spread of pastoralism, saw the forest as a source of food during the wintertime, they also saw it as a place of danger and lack. It was the rivers that provided the summer's bounty, the fish that made up the majority of northern hunter-gatherer diets. (Vajda. 2011)

Hunting for enough food in the forest is hard. It's difficult to see game animals through the thick trees, and the games animals themselves are often too few and far between to provide much sustenance anyway. Even for animals, the forest can be a hard place, which is why most big game or herd animals lived in larger numbers on the open plains. Over half the year, the forests of the north provide no plants that can be gathered for food. Berries, nuts, watercress, etc. don't grow in abundance until mid-summer and late fall. But it's not just the north where forests fail to provide ready diets; even in tropical rainforests, it's difficult for humans to make a living as pure hunter-gatherers. According to Terese and John Hart (1986), who carefully studied the Mbuti pygmies of the Ituri forest in Zaire (now Congo):

> For five months of the year, essentially none of the calorically important fruits and seeds are available. Honey is not abundant during this season of scarcity. Wild game meat is available year round, but the main animals caught have low fat content. This makes them a poor substitute for the starch dense agricultural foods.

Similarly, Headland (1989), who studied people in the rain forests in Asia, stated:

> For some of us who have left the movie theater and actually gone out and lived with human foragers in a tropical forest, sooner or later we come to realize just how difficult it is for native peoples to live and to find wild foods in such environments. After I had lived for most of a quarter century in the Sierra Madre, the largest rain forest in the Philippines, I wrote an essay to dispel this myth of such forests being a cornucopia of foods. In fact, I argued, it would have been impossible for any human group to have survived for long in tropical rain forests without at least some access to cultivated starch foods.

He goes on to point out that, while there is some archeological evidence for hunter-gathers living in forests in small groups, there were none in the interior of the forests.

There is, of course, some disagreement on this point; hunting-gathering, after all, is an important philosophical notion, and we reserve a certain sacredness for forests in postindustrial cultures. What's important to understand, however, is that, regardless of whether or not tribes can survive in the forest, it's still difficult to do so. Large clusters of people need large, open spaces to survive. Compare, for example, the number and size of the buffalo of the great plains of America's past to the number and size of deer in the forests. Thus, the most successful pure hunter-gatherers tended to live near open spaces with fish-filled water or open grasslands on which they can hunt large herd animals.

The earliest Europeans lived in much the same way as the plains Indians, hunting large game on vast grasslands, but then the environment began to change, and forests began to grow on the boreal grasslands that had once been filled with mammoths and other plentiful large game. This forced the tribes to move into smaller and smaller spaces or risk

80

starvation. As the hunter-gatherers grew more desperate, Neolithic farming was able to move in and dominate. Still, there were hunter-gatherers who resisted the coming of farming for a long time. The early people of Britain and Ireland, for example, managed to build extensive civilizations by gaining a lot of food from fishing (Oppenheimer, 2012).

It is perhaps the fact that only a few people can live within the forest that leads to the fear of the forest. Among the Tlingit, and Haida Tribes of Alaska/Canada, the forest was believed to be a scary place filled with evil spirits, a sort of hell-like realm, whereas the ocean was filled with good spirits and the heavens. This same idea seems to have been present to a limited extent in Ireland, where heaven—the spirit world—was on islands far out at sea.

This is not to say that people didn't worship the spirits of the forest and trees, for the forest was a mysterious and magical place, and trees inspired a certain awe in people. Further, even those few people who were the most afraid of forests could still respect them, as people often worship and even love what they fear. In one case, a folklorist in 19th-century Russia was shocked to see a woman placing an offering before an image of the devil. When the folklorist asked the women about this, she said that she had no way of knowing what would happen, so it was good to have friends everywhere.

Tacitus wrote one of the most telling passages on the relationship between the Germanic tribes of his time (98 A.D.) and the forest:

> They possess a wood which fear has haunted since the days of old, And rites ancestral make a holy place...

> There is another superstitious observance also connected with the wood. Every man who enters it must do so bound with a fetter, as a mark of humility and an avowal of the power of the divinity. If he happens to fall down, he may not lift himself up and rise to his feet, but must roll himself out along the ground. This wood is the center of their whole superstition, being looked upon as the cradle of the race, and the god of it as the universal ruler to whom all other things are subject and obedient.

This forest grove was both worshiped and feared Germanic people. Even among the Selkup of Siberia, the forest was a place for outsiders and the spirit world (Napolskikh and Hoppál, 2007).

In fairy tales, the forest is very often the home of the "others." It's a spirit world, a land of the dead, a strange realm. It's where people encounter witches, wolves, ogres, vampires and more. Those who lived in the forest could be considered outsiders, supernatural beings, and this wasn't only true in Europe. In an article on the folk tales of Tono Japan, she says that people feared those who lived in the wilderness—those who existed outside their society—often considering these outsiders to be demons, witches, and dangerous spirits. Consider the already discussed tale of the Romanian girl fleeing from a vampire in the forest who manages to find a place to sleep. When morning comes, she finds herself in a beautiful forest with birds singing and beautiful landscape, and because she falls in love with the forest, she becomes a vampire herself—an outsider.

I don't mean to suggest that the forest was frightening for everyone. Many peoples, such as those of Finland and Northern Russia, depended on the forest for resources, and to this day, the people of Mari-El still worship in sacred groves as the Celts, Germans, and others once did. Further, in places that still have hunter-gatherers, such as Africa and Malaysia,

81

there are people who think of the forest as a place of cool peacefulness, and joy. Specifically, the Aka of the Congo consider the forest a place to dance, play and be happy and the land outside as filled with evil spirits; in the villages, there are graveyards filled with the wicked spirits of the village people's ancestors (Lewis 2002).

In Malaysia, the...

> Orang Rimba believe that the forests were the creators' first and favorite creation. Life within them is still believed to run according to the oldest customs and laws (adat) of the forests, and, according to the creators' wish, should remain separate from customs in the village. The Orang Rimba often stress that if they were to not follow adat in the forests, or in any way confuse or mix life in the forests with life in the village (mer'uba adat or mer'uba halom), the gods would ignore or abandon them, and life in the forests would become impossible. (Sager, 2008)

Worse, they believe that the creator might destroy the world if they left the forest. In their belief system, the forest is purity, and the outside world causes illness and death. Even eating domesticated animals causes one to become unclean.

What's important to understand is that people tie a certain sacredness to the place that provides them with most of what they eat and fear the places that provide them with the smallest amount of food. Thus, the farmers, plains hunters, and fishermen of Europe likely saw the forest as a place of fear from the very beginning—though, even among agricultural peoples, hunting is often a meditative, emotional experience. Many people view hunting as a means of communing with the deities, which is why sacred hunt tales were so popular. Arthur participated in many of these sacred hunt stories when he followed the white boar, and the Finnish have an epic that is, in essence, a sacred hunt story in which a hero must catch a magical reindeer in order to marry.

The Sacred Hunt

Hunting is a sacred and magical act, for, as previously mentioned, the wilderness is an otherworld—a magical place. The hunting grounds were considered to be of both the human world and the realm of the spirits. This was the realm of forest masters and spirits. The hunting ground, in truth, was a gateway to the otherworlds. Similarly, the fishing grounds along rivers and the bottoms of lakes were gateways, places where a person could be carried off into the spirit world by the waters.

The trees themselves were often believed to be connections between the earth and the sky. Thus people would hang offerings from the trees in the forest in order to appease the gods of the heavens, for the two were closely connected. The Uakut would also stretch ropes between trees from which they would hang offerings of woodpecker feathers and animal pelts. They would then pray for a successful hunt. The Komi would preserve sacred groves of pine trees outside each village on which women would place candles in order to pray. The Celts and Germanic peoples would place the skins and heads of dead animals in the trees or tie strips of cloth to them as a sign of respect for the spirits within.

These deities and spirits of the forest could be generous. For example, among the Selkup, Ilinta Kota, a heavenly spirit, depicted as an old woman, would throw down feathers, which would become ducks for hunters. Yet, as with all supernatural beings, there are many conflicting reports about her. She is said in some tales to rule over both birth and death, famine and plenty.

In Selkup lore, each important place within the forest has a tutelary spirit known as a Maci Yula. This spirit helps hunters and fishermen, but will also punish or harm them if they dare to violate acceptable conventions. Thus, the hunters leave him strips of cloth and coins in trees. The Maci Yula themselves seem to live much like solitary herders, moving their animals from one region of the woods to another based on agreements and trades between them. This means not only that humans must ask the Maci Yula for permission to hunt, but also that they must continually try to get the ones in their region to buy up more animals for them to hunt. The Russians have a similar spirit lord of the forest, known as the Leshii, who, like the Muci Yula, is a satyr-like being (animal legs and horns) to whom people had to leave offerings for the right to hunt.

Even the animal spirits that people would hunt were considered to be magical and were often a part of the "fairy court." Among most hunter-gatherers, this meant that no one was skilled enough to obtain a successful hunt on their own; they could do so only through the wills of the animals they were hunting. In other words, these animals were often believed to willingly sacrifice themselves to the hunters, knowing that their spirits would be reincarnated. This animal spirit had to be given veneration and respect so that it would continue to give the tribe its blessing, for without this blessing, there would be no food.

Sometimes, of course, it was the animals' spirit owner who would order them to sacrifice themselves. For example, the Kalasha people believed that the fairies would tell an ibex (mountain goat) to go to this or that specific hunter so that he might shoot the animal. Later, after the hunter and his family had eaten, the fairy would bring the ibex back to life. The danger in hunting these spirits came from the fact that they could curse people with illness and cause any number of other problems.

So sacred were the animal spirits that it was at times considered bad luck to use the actual name of the animals. To deal with this, sacred animals were often given honorific names. Bears might be called "honey eaters," "tsars of the forest," "forest grandfathers", "old men of the mountains," the "fur men," etc. This use of an alternative name for the bear spirit has two very interesting connotations. The first is that, while people believed that animal spirits would at times sacrifice themselves to the hunters, it was also clear that one had to be quiet to capture an animal, which meant that there were dual beliefs in this regard. The hunters avoided using the animals' names to avoid letting the animals know whom they were hunting.

It's obvious that animal spirits are easily offended; they don't like to have people gossip about or discuss them too openly. Similarly, forest tsars and similar spirits live deep in the wilderness for solitude, so they despise noise and will punish those disrespectful enough to make it. Whistling or acting boisterous can bring down the punishment of the spirits of the forest, as can smelling strongly of the human world. Emotional sensitivity is a hallmark of the spirit world and of the animals on which people's lives depend, which is why bragging about one's skill is so often forbidden.

In the Kalevala, the hero Lemminkainen seeks to marry the daughter of Louhi, Mistress of Pohyola. At first, Louhi refuses his request:

> *Answered thus the wild magician:*
> *"I shall never give my daughter,*

Never give my fairest maiden,
Not the best one, nor the worst one,
Not the largest, nor the smallest;

However, in the end, Louhi concedes, telling Lemminkainen that he can woo her daughter "[w]hen thou bringest me the wild-moose From the Hisi fields and forests."

The reference to this forest as "hiisi" is significant. Hiisi could refer to either a sacred location, a spiritual quality, or a deity-like being. Thus, hiisi could refer to locations where spirits were to be found, but hiisi could also refer to the spirits themselves. In lore, hiisi were both worshiped and asked for favors, but at the same time, a hiisi is a dangerous place.

Lemminkainen is warned, "Thou wilt hunt in vain the wild-moose, Thou wilt catch but pain and torture, In the Hiisi fens and forests." Despite such warnings, Lemminkainen seeks out a famous maker of skis who builds him such magnificent skis that people brag that nothing will ever be able to outrun him. This, of course, is a violation of the sacred hunt and offends the hiisi, who tell the sacred animal to flee. Still certain that his skis and skill are enough to catch the hiisi animal by himself, Lemminkainen gives chase through the forests and fens. Over hills, snowfields, swamps and mountains he chases the animal, but in the end, his arrogance leads him to capture nothing.

Along with humility, generosity was an important part of the survival of many, if not all, hunting-gathering societies, and this need was often spelled out in fairy tales. I've already discussed generosity as one of the highest morals of the fairy realm, and it was so important to hunter-gatherers because success in the hunt was practically random. It was nearly impossible for anyone to go his or her whole life without bad luck leading to personal or family starvation. Thus, any family would need to depend on the kindness of another for survival at some point or another regardless of their survival strategy. Among the Yupik people, bragging about one's luck was taboo, and people who did it too often could be shunned. According to Cheng and Tracy (2014):

> Ecological and institutional forces help maintain the egalitarianism common to many hunter-gatherer societies. In the absence of sortable or predictable food packages, widespread resource sharing emerges to buffer risk in production and creates interdependence among families.=In some societies, such as the Ache of Paraguay and Hadza of Tanzania, it was often taboo for hunters to consume portions of their own kills.... Humility is not optional but is normative.

More than this, however, people in many societies couldn't even obtain food in the first place without help from others. Seal hunters in the north would often need at least fifteen different men standing over each air hole in the ice in order to successfully club a seal. This, as well as later need to share among agricultural societies, helps to explain why sharing was such an important part of fairy tales.

Getting back to the story of Lemminkainen, he fails over and over again, discovers his sin of pride and humbles himself:

Speaking words of ancient wisdom:
"Northland hunters, never, never,
Go defiant to thy forests,
In the Hisi vales and mountains,

There to hunt the moose of Juutas,
Like this senseless, reckless hero;
I have wrecked my magic snow-shoes,
Ruined too my useful snow-staff,
And my javelins I have broken,
While the wild-moose runs in safety
Through the Hisi fields and forests."

Thus, we see three important ideas in this story: first the need to maintain respect for the divine and sacred things and, second, the fear with which hunters needed to enter the woods. Finally, we see that, because hunting involves sacred spirits in an otherworld, it can be compared to a divine act, a spirit journey that gives the hunter the right to marry.

There are many stories in lore in which a hunter will chase a beautiful deer with unusual color, golden horns, or some other amazing quality. More than simply supernatural, this hunt is a foray into the otherworld, a spirit journey that brings the person closer to the divine—at least at times. In Evank lore, a man named Mani used his magical skis to chase an elk and her calf into the otherworld in the heavens. Here, he chased her across the sky— across the heavenly *taiga* (the entire breadth of the sky from east to west). The next morning, the calf had grown to full size, and the hunt began again, and so Mani continues to hunt. As a sky god, he hunts the sun, driving it on its course.

Stepping back from this, it becomes obvious that, if Mani ever succeeded in his hunt, the results would be tragic. The hunt itself, then, is a sacred act, even without success—one that can transform a person, a deity, or even the world.

Many hunts sound like imperial myths used to explain the divine right by which a chief rules over a land. In these hunts, when the hunter catches the deer, it will transform into a beautiful maiden and marry him and, in so doing, allow him to become the ruler of a nation. Hence, one gains the sacred right to rule through the hunt or through one's ancestors hunting. This right comes because of a marriage to a spirit with an animal form.

Hunts, too, are a means of proving one's worth and right to marry. Again, it was only through the hunt that Lemminkainen could marry into the divine. Having learned his lesson about his arrogance, Lemminkainen begins his next hunt with a prayer, which he continues as he journeys into the wilderness, greeting the keepers of each terrain in turn:

On the way to Tapiola,
Into Tapio's wild dwellings.
"Greeting bring I to the mountains,
Greeting to the vales and uplands,
Greet ye, heights with forests covered,
Greet ye, ever-verdant fir-trees,
Greet ye, groves of whitened aspen,
Greetings bring to those that greet you,
Fields, and streams, and woods of Lapland.
Bring me favor, mountain-woodlands,
Lapland-deserts, show me kindness,
Mighty Tapio, be gracious,
Let me wander through thy forests,
Let me glide along thy rivers,

He continues to pray as he journeys to the mistress of the forest, the spirits of the mountains, the children of Tapio (the forest King) and more. This is important because it shows that there is, in fact, an astounding array of spirits that the hunter must venerate as he journeys through the woods. In the end, however, this pays off, and Lemminkainen is, at last, successful (although Märkähattu, a cowherd whom Lemminkainen had offended, murdered him on his way home with serpents, but that's a different matter).

We see similar activities even into the modern day. Among many Altaic peoples, there is said to be a spirit being over every region.

> Passers-by usually stopped - and even today, they stop their cars - at these special trees, and place some money, tie a little piece of their clothes or handkerchiefs on it branches, put a comb or some other personal belongings. They attribute special powers to these trees, and they maintain that the trees bring good fortune in traveling, and that they protect people from accidents. This belief is a sign of unconditional trust in the power of nature, of a conviction which supposes the powers of nature to be so strong as to control human destiny as well. (Hoppal)

Such sacredness stems in large part from fear, but also from hope, dreams, and, of course, the fun one could have in hunting. Becoming a good hunter could, in fact, change a person's life. The best hunters were most likely to get the most desirable wives, after all, as hunting was what wealth was based upon. There is a Yupik fairy tale in which three sisters each get the opportunity to marry a man who brags about his skill as a hunter. The youngest sister rejects her suitor because he is ugly and old, but she is scolded by her sisters, because he is the best hunter, and that's what matters most.

In general, hunting was even more important to people's lives than our jobs are to us today. In a society that depends primarily on hunting and fishing, there were almost no other jobs to be sought out. The entire society was structured around hunting and fishing. People chose where to live based on where the hunting and fishing was good; they decided to marry based on the hunt. They told stories about it, and their gods were based on it. What's more, hunters could encounter a dizzying array of magical beings, both friendly and benign. Among the Komi, for example, there is a tall blue-eyed female spirit known as the Kalyan with the teeth of a horse and the feet of a cow. She tends to cause mischief; however, on cold days she might invite those out hunting to come and eat dumplings with her.

In one tale, a hunter discovers some giant footprints from a kurlaka (a man-eating monster so big that his head reaches into the otherworld in the sky. Realizing that the kurlaka, like an animal, will return along the same trail, the hunter sets up an ambush and shoots it. The kurlaka isn't so easily slain, however, and it manages to run off, forcing the hunter to track it a bit more to finish it off.

The spirits of the dead dwell within the wilderness, as well. For example, the laeter was said to have been a spirit of the dead that often appeared as a beautiful woman dressed in white. She travels through the taiga (northern forests) with a black dog with a gold ribbon around her neck. Interestingly enough, this spirit of the dead can still marry those men who encounter her, and they become wealthy from the number of squirrels she catches.

Such female forest spirits were common, as was the desire to marry them. Among the Ket existed spirits known as *kaigus,* which would meet hunters in the woods. Those who met these spirits, and who could build a relationship with them, would gain supernatural luck in hunting and so become wealthy. However, as with all forest beings, the kaigus were very sensitive, so many such stories end with the kaigus leaving their lovers because of some violation the other had committed. Most commonly, this violation involved a lack of cleanliness and purification as was required on the hunt. Such purification could involve jumping over fire, washing with water, and remaining clean as one hunted. Purity was of extreme importance to the spirits of nature.

As success in hunting was what gave people the right to marry, a number of tales exist about people marrying supernatural forest spirits. For example, in the Welsh story of "The Maiden in the Green Forest":

> *One day, he went out hunting in the Green Forest. While waiting for a wild boar to rush out, there rode past him a young woman whose beauty was dazzling. He instantly fell in love with her.*
>
> *The next day, while on horseback, at the same opening in the forest, the same maiden reappeared; but it was only for a moment, and then she vanished.*
>
> *Again, on the third day, the prince rode out to the appointed place, and again the vision of beauty was there. He rode up to her and begged her to come and live with him at his palace. (Griffis, 1921)*

Even after hunting became less important to people's livelihood, many of these ideas about the forest and hunting continued in people's tales and myths. Hercules, for example, was set to chasing the sacred hind. At the end of this successful hunt, he encounters the goddess Artemis.

Artemis and the Women

The sacred hunt's relationship to marriage and sex makes figures like Artemis confusing. On the one hand, she is sexually desirable, but on the other, she kills hunters who desire her. Further, she demands virginity from her companions. It may be, then, that Artemis' nature is a warning story that one shouldn't mess around with strange women in the woods. One shouldn't cheat on one's wife when traveling out into the wilderness.

This message is both opposite that of most sacred hunts, which hold that men gain the right to marry through hunting, and the same, in that it says that men should remain dedicated to their marriages. The need to keep men faithful on their hunts may be due to the...

> Unprecedented reproductive stress (that human women came under) owing to the high energetic cost of producing larger brained infants. Pregnant and nursing females would have needed regular supplies of high protein and fatty foods. (Mithen, 1988)

It was challenging for a woman to get the number of calories she needed to bear and nurse children in ancient times, and especially in hunter-gatherer societies. According to Knight, Power, and Mithen, this means that women needed to work together in order to prevent

87

philandering men from leaving their pregnant mates in order to try to impregnate others. One strategy for doing this was for women to act the role of animals, which might have led to things like bear dancers in some cultures. This could also have been used to try to prevent men from courting prepubescent girls before they were ready. This latter importance could be the reason why Artemis had young girls who would perform bear dancers in her temples. During this ritual, young girls and sometimes boys would dress as bears and dance in places holy to Artemis. In this way, they marked their willingness to be guided by the virgin goddess as they matured. Hughes (1990), however, believes that this ritual was meant more as a lesson to respect the environment than a means of guiding young girls through puberty.

Beyond that, women were known to use dancing to motivate men to perform better while hunting and or fighting for resources.

> According to this model, then, communal pretend play arises as a female driven strategy for motivating male hunting. Maximum male effort is secured by advertising the imminent fertility of cycling females while on the other hand signaling non-availability in the short term.

This, according to Knight, Power, and Mithen, also explains rituals such as pre-hunt celibacy, as well as why the hunting goddess Artemis is a virgin who punishes hunters that allow their eyes to wonder to her in the wilderness. This makes sense in another way as well; her virginity and punishing hunters could have arisen out of the need to create a morality preventing hunters from running away from their tribes and potential mates because of beautiful women they met from a different tribe while away from home. The Yupik people have a story in which a hunter gains the right to marry through the hunt and then is punished for cheating on this wife. I tell it now from my limited memory:

> There once was great hunter who lived alone. So great was his loneliness that he felt a strong connection with the natural world, and every time he went out onto the ocean to hunt for seals, he would leave gifts on a small island for the spirits that lived there.

> One day, when he went to leave his gift, he met a beautiful woman who told him that she was the spirit of the island. She had watched over him as he had gone hunting for many years and appreciated his gifts and admired him. The two of them soon got married and were happy for some time. The man would go hunting and bring back many game animals, and the women could make the most wonderful items.

> Soon, she was pregnant, and it seemed that her happiness was complete, but the man who went out hunting began to wander in his mind as well. Then, one day, the man went out hunting and didn't come back. The woman waited and waited for the man, but he did not return, and she could not go out and search for him for the baby was coming.

> The baby was born without the man, and for a few weeks, the woman lived and nursed the baby while waiting for the man, but he didn't come back. Tired of waiting, the woman finally went out and began her journey to search for her husband. She traveled for many nights and days until at last she came to a hut where an old man lived with his grandson. Seeing that she was tired from her journey, the old man offered to let her stay the night at his place.

88

That night, she told the old man and his grandson about her husband who she was looking for, and they told her there was a man who matched her husband's description in the village nearby. Wondering if this could be her husband, the woman traveled to the village that evening just as the people of the village were getting together for a celebration in a large house. The woman went into the house and soon spotted her husband with another woman. Angry, the woman got up and sang of her sorrow and her journey, and as she did so, the roof of the house caved in and crushed her unfaithful husband. The woman then ran back to the old man's house. She stayed there for some time and soon fell in love with the old man's grandson and married him.

The Importance of War

War, like farmiing or hunting, was important to the survival of many cultures. War was a way for many people to gain food, to find wives, and to protect themselves from others who waged war on them. War was a way for tribes of people to increase their access to the resources they needed to reproduce. Thus, one of the most common reasons for hunter-gathers to fight wars was to kidnap women or take revenge for women who had been kidnaped from their tribe (Azar Gat). This was also true among early farmers and pastorals; Genghis Khan's own mother was kidnaped and forced to marry the man who had essentially killed her previous husband. Even in the few hunter-gatherer societies without war, fights over women, blood feuds, and homicide related to jealousy were rampant. Some incidents were caused by suitors' competitions, some by women's abduction or rape and some by broken promises of marriage; most, perhaps, were caused by jealous husbands over suspicion of their wives' infidelity.

This shouldn't be too surprising, as those who didn't concern themselves as much with reproduction wouldn't reproduce. Young adult males' who are deprived of sex become restless and belligerent and engaged in risking-taking behavior (Gat, 2000), so fights for food and reproductive rights have been part of nearly every society at one time or another. It's important, to bear in mind, however, that this has little to nothing to do with Freud and his over-obsession with sexual symbols, both because he has largely been proven wrong and because fairy tales are rarely so subtle when discussing fights over women. In fairy tales, it is obvious that a man risks his life during a sacred hunt to get married. Similarly, the knight goes to battle monsters in order to get married. Fairy tales are filled with women being kidnapped by otherworldly beings and magical women being kidnapped by men.

The taking of wives or husbands is an important part of the relationship between humans and the magical world in fairy tales and is also closely tied to shaman's tales. Deusen found that spirits wishing to lure potential shamans into their role would sometimes purposefully appear as beautiful persons of the opposite gender. Thus, many shamans begin their path into the magical realm by being kidnaped by a spirit that has purposfully appeared sexually alluring. Similarly, other spirits would appear alluring in order to entice the shaman to kidnap them from the spirit world. Just as Hades carried of Persephone in Greek mythology, Theseus and Peirithoos decided to carry her off from the underworld (having already kidnapped the daughter of Zeus, Helen). Nilsson (1972) says of this act that Theseus...

> Was transferred to heroic mythology because the immigrated Greeks did not grasp the sacred nature of the myth.... It is highly improbable that this attempt was originally not considered a crime; success would have been the crowing end of a hero's career, just as the victory of Hades or the fetching of Cerberus crowned the career of Heracles. But the attempt of Theseus failed.

There is a flip side to this, however; such abductions can lead to war, and, indeed, there are tales from Northern Italy and Ireland in which wars between humans and fairies are started when a fairy snatches away a Queen to be his wife.

Tales from the sacred hunt and of abducting a spouse are closely related to those in which a hero gains the right to marry through his or her skill in arms. In other words, many heroes gain the right to marry through their war against dragons, enemies, giants, etc. Like the sacred hunt, war itself was often considered to be a sacred calling—although, interestling enough, in ancient Greece such legends, like that of Perseus and Heracles slaying sea monsters, the heroes were fighting to circumvent or overcome the divine will of offended deities. Once again, we see in these stories the complexity of human desire and thought.

The frequency with which potential brides were abducted in many early cultures led not only to stories of women being kidnapped but also to stories of women tricking their abductees. For men, gaining the right to marry was a heroic act; however, it seems that, for women in such tales, it was slaying one's abductor in order to be able to return home that was a heroic act.

In the Norwegian tale "The Old Dame and Her Hen," an old dame sends her daughters out looking for her hen one by one, and one by one, the eldest two are captured by an ugly fairy-like being, the Man o' the Hill, who seeks to marry them. They, however, mock the Man o' the Hill, so he locks them away forever. At last, the youngest sets out.

> *Yes! the youngest was ready enough to go; so she walked up and down, Waiting for her sisters and calling the hen, but she could neither see nor hear anything of them. So at last she too came up to the cleft in the rock, and heard how something said:*
>
> *Your hen trips inside the hill!*
> *Your hen trips inside the hill!*
>
> *She thought this strange, so she too went to see what it was, and fell through the trap-door too, deep, deep down, into a vault. When she reached the bottom she went from one room to another, each grander than the other; but she wasn't at all afraid, and took good time to look about her. So, as she was peeping into this and that, she cast her eye on the trap-door into the cellar, and looked down it, and what should she see there but her sisters, who lay dead. She had scarce time to slam to the trap-door before the Man o' the Hill came to her and asked:*
>
> *'Will you be my sweetheart?'*
>
> *'With all my heart', answered the girl, for she saw very well how it had gone with her sisters. So, when the Man o' the Hill heard that, he got her the finest clothes in the world; she had only to ask for them, or for anything else she had a*

mind to, and she got what she wanted, so glad was the Man o' the Hill that any one would be his sweetheart.

But when she had been there a little while, she was one day even more doleful and downcast than was her wont. So the Man o' the Hill asked her what was the matter, and why she was in such dumps.

'Ah!' said the girl, 'it's because I can't get home to my mother. She's hard pinched, I know, for meat and drink, and has no one with her.'

'Well!' said the Man o' the Hill, 'I can't let you go to see her; but just stuff some meat and drink into a sack, and I'll carry it to her.'

Yes! she would do so, she said, with many thanks; but at the bottom of the sack she stuffed a lot of gold and silver, and afterwards she laid a little food on the top of the gold and silver. Then she told the ogre the sack was ready, but he must be sure not to look into it. So he gave his word he wouldn't, and set off. Now, as the Man o' the Hill walked off, she peeped out after him through a chink in the trap-door; but when he had gone a bit on the way, he said:

'This sack is so heavy, I'll just see what there is inside it.'

And so he was about to untie the mouth of the sack, but the girl called out to him:

  I see what you're at!
  I see what you're at!
'The deuce you do!' said the Man o' the Hill; 'then you must have plaguy sharp eyes in your head, that's all!'

So he threw the sack over his shoulder, and dared not try to look into it again. When he reached the widow's cottage, he threw the sack in through the cottage door, and said:

'Here you have meat and drink from your daughter; she doesn't want for anything.'

So, when the girl had been in the hill a good bit longer, one day a billy-goat fell down the trap-door.

'Who sent for you, I should like to know? you long-bearded beast!' said the Man o' the Hill, who was in an awful rage, and with that he whipped up the goat, and wrung his head off, and threw him down into the cellar.

'Oh!' said the girl, 'why did you do that? I might have had the goat to play with down here.'

'Well!' said the Man o' the Hill, 'you needn't be so down in the mouth about it, I should think, for I can soon put life into the billy-goat again.'

So saying, he took a flask which hung up against the wall, put the billy-goat's head on his body again, and smeared it with some ointment out of the flask, and he was as well and as lively as ever again.

91

'Ho! ho!' said the girl to herself; 'that flask is worth something— that it is.'

So when she had been some time longer in the hill, she watched for a day when the Man o' the Hill was away, took her eldest sister, and putting her head on her shoulders, smeared her with some of the ointment out of the flask, just as she had seen the Man o' the Hill do with the billy-goat, and in a trice her sister came to life again. Then the girl stuffed her into a sack, laid a little food over her, and as soon as the Man o' the Hill came home, she said to him:

'Dear friend! Now do go home to my mother with a morsel of food again; poor thing! she's both hungry and thirsty, I'll be bound; and besides that, she's all alone in the world. But you must mind and not look into the sack.'

After rescuing the two eldest daughters, the youngest robs the Man o' the Hill and flees back home, securing her place as a trickster heroine. In another Russian tale, a princess agrees to marry a monster so that she can learn its secrets and tell the male protagonist how to kill him. In many other tales, a princess would put a monster to sleep by grooming it so that the male protagonist could slay it.

In the Welsh tale of "The Might Monster Afang," a beautiful girl dresses up and goes out towards the monsters den.

The maiden tickled his chin, and even put up his whiskers in curl papers. Then she stroked his neck so that his eyes closed. Soon she had gently lulled him to slumber, by singing a cradle song, which her mother had taught her. This she did so softly, and sweetly, that in a few minutes, with its head in her lap, the monster was sound asleep and even began to snore.

Then, quietly, from their hiding places in the bushes, Gadern and his men crawled out. When near the dreaded Afang, they stood up and sneaked forward, very softly on tip toe. They had wrapped the links of the chain in grass and leaves, so that no clanking was heard. They also held the oxen's yokes, so that nobody or anything could rattle, or make any noise. Slowly but surely they passed the chain over its body, in the middle, besides binding the brute securely between its fore and hind legs.

All this time, the monster slept on, for the girl kept on crooning her melody.

In one Oroqen tale, the need for a woman to trick her abductor is spelled out very clearly, with the kidnapped woman telling the man who kidnapped her that she loves him in order to distract him just as her husband is sneaking into the camp to murder him. In the tale of "The Giant Who Had No Heart in His Body," a prince speaks to the princess being held prisoner by the giant, and she eventually tricks the giant into revealing how he can be killed.

Other kidnaped women in these tales would sew up their captors' armor so that they couldn't put it on, didn't warn their abductors of hiding enemies, and more. What we see, then, is that many fairy tales of women being kidnaped by the spirit world or enemies aren't just about fears but are remnants of older lessons on how women should act should they be kidnapped.

Political Transformation

The transformation of the political system from small communities to large, centrally controlled nations has likely had the largest impact on shamanism and ideas about fairy land. This is because shamans generally lived as anyone else in their tribe would. The men would still hunt with the other men, herd animals, farm their fields, or whatever else might be appropriate in their context. The woman would still sew, make crafts and gather food. Indeed, one anthropologist said, "In everyday life the shaman is not distinguishable from other people except by an occasionally haughty manner. (Czaplicka, 2014)

Of course, they did, at times, become wealthier than most by earning trade goods or money from healing wealthy clients. However, since many of them existed on what amounted to tips in societies with very little, they could also become poorer than most other people in their tribe. After all, if, over the course of the year, a shaman must spend a large number of days on rituals to gain spirit helpers, foretell the future and heal people, he or she would have a lot less time to hunt, fish, or farm. This meant they would be poorer than many of the people they served. Regardless, however, a haughty attitude and a healthy amount of respect and fear from others also came with being a shaman.

This aspect of shamans—their living very much like the others in their society while being able to command respect and fear—leads to two of the most important reasons for their changing as society changes. The first is that, as society leadership became centralized, creative people had new opportunities to become wealthy. With the temptation of wealth before them, the most creative and intelligent people, who could have become shamans, would be less willing to live in poverty. It's therefore likely that this poverty was responsible for many people resisting becoming shamans in later societies. After all, the amount of work and stress involved in being a shaman is intense, and there is constant danger. Entering spirit worlds where people are devoured, demons fly through the skies, fields of bones and rivers of blood stretch before you is likely enough to cause some serious cases of posttraumatic stress disorder.

This, along with the shaman's sickness, might also make it hard for shamans to make friends, given how strangely they already act, which, in turn, could leave the shaman feeling even more alone and isolated. Even before they had other opportunities...

> In vain do many of the elect struggle against this innate tendency,
> knowing that the life of a shaman is not an enviable one, but this
> restraint brings greater suffering upon them; even the distant sounds
> of a tambourine make them shiver... (Mikhailovskii and Wardrop.
> 1895)

Many people, then, did not want to be shamans. Thus, they would have tried to resist the spirits. According to the beliefs about shamans, then, these spirits would have tortured and eventually killed them for resisting. Consider, for example, story of "Yallery Brown" from Lincolnshire, England.

In the story of "Yallery Brown," there is a young farm worker named Tom Tiver who hears a sad sobbing coming from under a large stone. Feeling bad for what he presumes is a child, he moves the stone to discover a strange, hairy little creature looking up at him. This opening seems benign enough. Tom is clearly a kind and good man, but, despite this, he's about to be severely punished in this story.

This contrasts with most other fairy tales in which the kind-hearted are rewarded. There are, of course, exceptions to the notion of kindness being rewarded, including the dark stories of Eastern Europe in which a person helps a wicked creature only to have it turn on him or her later, at which point the moral is told that 'good deeds are always repaid with bad deeds.' These tales also seem contrary to the primary thrust of fairy tales that tend to espouse generosity. This leads one to wonder what the moral of these stories is.

In the case of "Yallerey Brown," perhaps the simplest meaning is that one shouldn't meddle in the magical world. Indeed, the fairy tale of "Yallery Brown" prefaces Tom's sympathy by saying that he didn't like to meddle, but he made an exception for the sound of the crying thing under the stone. The story may be saying, then, that one should not be lured into meddling by the supernatural world.

Interestingly enough, this idea is shared by the Russians, who would avoid picking up strange looking rocks for fear that these might have a spirit under them, which would force anyone who touched the stone to become witch. In Lithuania, there is another similar tale in which a man helps a chicken that is caught out in a terrible storm. The chicken, as it turns out, is a spirit that helps the man become rich by stealing from his neighbors. Being a good man, he tries to stop the spirit but can't. At last, tormented by guilt for having unleashed the wicked spirit on his community, he burns down his house with the chicken spirit inside, but the spirit isn't harmed by fire.

These stories are important, because, as you'll recall, shamanistic experiences were often put into tales because they were too sacred to discuss directly. When people grew afraid of shamans and shamanism, it created the need for a warning tale against the experience of encountering a shaman's familiar.

Of course, it may be that, by the time of the telling of "Yallery Brown," few people (if any) would have been aware of the old connection of this story to shamanism. What the people of the 1900s likely got out of this story was a warning story about dangerous relationships with the fairy realm—although, at first, Yallery Brown doesn't seem like a bad fairy, and he even offers to get Tom anything he desires, from a wife to gold. Tom, being a simple man, asks for help with work. However, Yallery doesn't stop with just helping Tom. Like many similar spirits, he begins to attack the work of other people, upsetting their buckets, blunting their tools, covering their clean horses with muck, etc. When people...

> *saw that Tom's work was done for him, and theirs undone for them; and naturally they begun to look shy on him, and they wouldn't speak or come nigh him, and they carried tales to the master and so things went from bad to worse.*

> *For Tom could do nothing himself; the brooms wouldn't stay in his hand, the plough ran away from him, the hoe kept out of his grip. He thought that he'd do his own work after all, so that Yallery Brown would leave him and his neighbours alone. But he couldn't—true as death he couldn't. He could only sit by and look on, and have the cold shoulder turned on him, while the unnatural thing was meddling with*

the others, and working for him.

At last, rejected and friendless, Tom grows furious with Yallery Brown and tries to get rid of him. However, Yallery Brown isn't going to be easily driven off, for once a spirit attaches itself to a shaman, it was very hard to get rid of it. By trying to drive Yallery Brown away, all Tom manages to do is anger Yallery Brown that he would dare to try to dispose of their friendship. Because of this, Yallery attacks Tom for the rest of his life.

This ending leads to another possible meaning; that one shouldn't try to cast off the magical world once one has been chosen to be a part of it. Shamanism, after all, wasn't very often a choice; it was something the spirits forced onto a person, and if a person refused, he or she could grow sick and die. What we, in later eras, might see as a warning against getting involved in the magical world or as the cruelty of spirits those of earlier eras might have seen as a warning not to try to escape from the magical world of which they were destined to be a part. The change in meaning, from acceptance to avoidance, however, likely also led to people trying to banish and even demonize the spirits that possessed them.

In ancient Greece, we see something similar happen, with possession by nymphs originally being a sacred activity of those who became diviners, essentially shamanistic figures for their community. As time went on, however, people began to see such possessions as an affliction, an attack by dangerous beings. As a result, these nymphs went from being a bringer of power to something that needed to be exorcised—long before the coming of Christianity. Similarly, in Manchuria, a girl who would have been the last shaman of her tribe had the spirits that possessed her banished as well, thus ending shamanism forever among her people.

In addition to the problems created by poverty and the natural stress of dealing with the spirit world, the shamans' influence over society likely caused authorities in centralized governments to hate them. Shamans, after all, were potential rivals and even enemies of the leaders of their nation. A chieftain or king could try to convince people of his moral superiority and greater knowledge based on his position within the society, but shamans speak directly to deities and fairies and so can always claim greater knowledge then their king.

Shamans can even accuse a society's leader of being immoral or of having caused the wrath of the deities to fall upon a society. This, for example, is the primary reason shamanism was repeatedly outlawed in Japan. It's also why shamans and their decedents of previous eras led Russia to a number of localized revolutions. In Europe, those who had the ability to communicate directly with the divine continued to cause upheavals throughout the continent until just a few centuries ago. This is because shamans, with their ability to travel into the spirit world and talk directly to the gods themselves, had the ability to call into question any claims by the leaders of a nation.

In Germany in 1476, a man named Hans Bohm (a wandering drummer) had a vision of the Virgin Mary. After speaking with her for a time, he began to preach that the clergy and nobility were sinful and that all taxes, rents, and work for them should stop. He gathered tens of thousands of peasant followers from all over Germany. The peasants, however, were not well organized or trained, so their revolt was short lived, as most peasant revolts were. However, as with many peasant revolts, this one was started by someone who people believed had some form of religious authority separate from that of the leaders of the land (Leff. 1999).

95

Out of the turmoil of the Hundred Years War comes one of the most famous visionaries, Joan of Arc, who at the age of twelve had her first vision of Saint Michael, Saint Catherine, and Saint Margaret. Four years later she managed to convince the Lords of France that she was receiving visions from God and so was able to influence the French army in its war against England.

There was a long history of women in the medieval era gaining visions. Margery Kempe, for example, went through months during which she was possessed and tormented by demons until Christ came to her. She then became wholly devoted to him, but her public displays of wailing and writhing during her visions would scare the peasants and the clergy, eventually leading to her arrest. Another religious revolutionary named Anne Askew of England also refused to conform and so became the only woman recorded to have been tortured in the Tower of London. She was put on the rack and violently stretched out until her joints dislocated, but still she refused to change her Protestant beliefs and so was ultimately burned at the stake (Watt, 2001).

Over a thousand years before any of these women lived, another women named Veleda was practically worshiped as a living goddess and, in some ways, may be credited with the rebellion of the Germans against the Romans. Although she was left alone for a while by the Romans after the defeat of the German revolt, she may have eventually been captured, and she was certainly mocked by them (Goodman, 1992).

What's important to understand here is that those who had visions had the power to hurt a nation's leaders. These leaders saw those who claimed divine visions as competition. As a result, those who chose to be mystics risked not only poverty and a difficult life but also death and rejection. As time went on, fewer and fewer people would choose this life except for in times of great turmoil and or poverty.

Agricultural Societies and Shamanism

Many of the changes that fairy tales, shamans, and deities undertake during the transition from hunter-gatherer to agricultural societies involve a domestication and specialization process. Among larger agricultural societies, shamanistic and priestly classes grew more specialized, with magico-religious practitioners having very specific jobs. In larger societies, one shaman might be responsible for healing only certain illnesses, while another might become responsible for war and yet another for seeking advice from the deities. Further, group religious processes became more important (Kaplan, 1999). These changes may occur because of the typically larger community sizes and the ability of the community to support more religious practitioners.

In addition to these changes, it was common for animal spirits and fairies to begin to live in people's fields, bringing fertility to the land rather than game animals to hunters. Similarly, the spirits of locations, as previously discussed, often became the spirits of people's homes and their fields. We can see this in Celtic and English tales about fairies coming to help farmers with their work in the fields or other wilderness fairies coming to help people with their domestic chores. Mari-El farmers would enter into groves of trees, places where they once prayed for abundant game, and ask for a good harvest. It shouldn't be surprising that people would continue to ask the same beings to help them gather food as they always had.

Further, as specific jobs became more important, a certain sacredness was attached to working and cleverness just as had previously been attached to acts such as hunting and war. In other words, cleverness and work in fairy tales gave the protagonists of later fairy tales the right to marry or to become rich the way hunting once had. In Molly Whuppie, the heroine's ability to trick and steal from the ogre gives her and her sisters the right to marry princes. Similarly, in "The Brave Little Tailor," the tailor's cleverness in outwitting and ultimately defeating the giants gives him the right to marry a princess. In a fairy tale from the Amur River, a woman wins the right to marry by being skilled artist, for when the divine man atop the mountain of ice whom she was seeking to marry saw her beautiful cloak, he stopped the wind so that she could climb up to him.

The willingness to work hard became one of the means of surviving the otherworld where the beings all demanded that the protagonist work. In the Russian story of "The Girl in the Well," a girl enters the spirit world and gets a job as a herdswoman and because of this, is able to become extremely rich when she returns home. In the case of the Grimm Brothers' story of "The Four Skillful Brothers," four brothers gain their wealth by learning important trades such as how to be a thief, a tailor, etc. Rather than tales about the sacred hunt, these stories feature tales about the "sacred job," as it were.

With the switch to the sacred job, fairyland and fairies became the spirits who provided people with important skills, as the Greek muses did, or who provided them with work. As people had once dreamed of fairies protecting their cattle or helping them hunt, they then

97

dreamed of becoming nursemaids, carpenters, herdsmen, and more to the fairies, for the fairies pay very well, offering gold and eternal wealth to those who were willing to work hard for them.

The transformation of the folk religion with the shift to agricultural and other labor-based societies, however, isn't always clear cut. As I've asserted before, remnants remain from one belief system to another. More importantly for our discussion of fairy tales, however, is the fact that the peasants, the ones who kept fairy tales alive, have historically been slow to change and exhibit many of the ideas of previous eras in later folk religions.

Take the example of the benandanti (or vagabonds) of Northern Italy who, when summoned by an astral drummer, would send their souls from their bodies to go and fight against witches for a good harvest. On rabbits, cats, or other animals, their souls would ride over rivers and fields. At times, just as with the shamans of hunter-gatherers, the water would be too choppy for some of them to cross, and so the souls of the weaker Benandanti would stay behind. Indeed, it was said that they could retire at forty or some time thereafter if they chose. Until then, they didn't have a choice; they were bound to answer the call to battle witches. They believed that the witches, in service of the devil, had stolen the seeds of the earth, the fertility of the vineyards, and the fertility of the livestock. In order to get these back, the Benandanti had to fight against the witches with fennel stalks as weapons while the animal-riding witches carried sorghum stalks.
As the shamans before them, the Benandanti would travel outside their bodies in order to help their community obtain food. (Ginzburg, 1966)

There are a number of interesting ideas in the benandanti's soul flight that potentially made their way into a number of myths and fairy tales. The first, of course, is the witch's flight. Perhaps even more interesting was the idea that, if the soul didn't return to the body before the cock crowed in the morning, the person would die, tying them to ideas about witches and vampires. They were neither, however, but instead served God and Jesus, gaining instructions at times from a golden or white angel. Being agricultural shamans, however, their job wasn't to gain some metaphysical knowledge about the nature of sin or good but to help with the harvest.

As with many such sacred things, there was a lot of secrecy surrounding the benandanti. On the one hand, they would tell of their ability to fight witches, communicate with the spirits of the dead, and perform certain other magical services; on the other hand, they weren't supposed to discuss their work in detail. Indeed, they weren't even supposed to reveal who the witches they battled against were for fear of being attacked and beaten by them. If it weren't for the Inquisition forcing them to speak about what they did—without torture forcing them to admit to devil worship—we might never have heard a thing about them, for no one wrote a word about them outside of their trials. What's more, most Inquisitors tried to bend their words, to push them into giving a story that fit conventional thinking on witchcraft involving wild parties and dancing. The benandanti, however, only sent their souls from their bodies to fight against witches and so did none of those things (Ginzburg, 1966).

The benandanti weren't alone in traveling to hell to retrieve the fertility of the fields. In 1692, an eighty-year-old man in Livonia confessed to being a werewolf. Like the benandanti, he would travel to hell with an army of werewolves three nights before

Christmas. There, they would battle the devil and witches to retrieve not only the fertility of the land but also the catches of fish that fishermen depended on. Werewolves, it seems, weren't always considered bad. In Riga, a young man who was known to be a werewolf fell to the ground during a feast. When he got up the next day, he explained how a witch had flown into the banquet hall as a red hot butterfly, and he'd gone to fight it. It was the job of werewolves, after all, to keep witches away.

There is another interesting story out of Ireland:

> There was an old man named Fitzgerald, who lived in a neighbouring village. He was very fond of his garden and spent all his time in it. One summer he had a beautiful field of "white pink" potatoes. Once he had a fit of sickness, and was three days in bed. While the old man was keeping the bed the blight came on his potatoes and withered them.
>
> The saying was at that time that the fairies of Ulster were stronger than the fairies of Munster, and so they drove blight from Ulster to Munster.
>
> The fourth night the old man rose from his bed and crept out to take a look at his potato field, for his heart was in it. The night was very bright, the sky clear, and the moon full. He saw, sure enough, that the blight had come on his potatoes and destroyed them. He went into the house, took his blackthorn stick, and sat over the fire, and whittled it here and there. Then he went into the field with his bare head and feet, spat on his hand, took a firm grip on the slick, and, brandishing it, cried out time after time, as loud as he could, rushing the while from one end of the garden to the other: "Daniel O'Donohue, come and take me with you tonight to the fairies and show me the man among them who destroyed my potatoes. I'll go with you to-night and to-morrow night and every night, if you'll bring me back to this spot again."
> All the men and boys gathered around outside the ditch and listened to him, and he went on in this way a long while, calling on the chief fairy, Daniel O'Donohue, King of Lochlein, and challenging all the fairies of Ulster, and promising, if he couldn't do for them all himself, he had neighbours who would go with him and help him.
>
> "At that time," said the host, " there wasn't a man in ten who didn't believe in the fairies and think that it was they who caused the blight, so they listened to the old man as he went on challenging the fairies of the North, offering his help to Daniel O'Donohue." (Curtin, 1895)

It was believed in Ireland that there was only so much fertility within the land, and witches and others with knowledge of such things would sometimes seek to steal the fertility from their neighbors' land (Guidera, 2012). Similarly, on the opposite end of Europe, among the Votyak, thieves would sneak into their neighbors' fields, take a handful of earth, and say "Good luck, follow me give me a good harvest" with the intention of stealing the fertility of their neighbors' fields. In France:

> Many women believe and openly avow that in the hours of the night they ride on certain animals together with Diana, the goddess of the pagans with a numberless multitude of women. (Horsley, 1979)

In Milan in 1384 and 1390, two women were part of a society of both living and dead

99

people. They ate animals that were brought back to life by the goddess and traveled about villages in order to promote fertility, health and social welfare (Horsley, 1979).

In Votyak lore, when a field stopped producing, it was believed that the "Grain Soul" had vanished from it, often taking the form of a white butterfly. In order to get this "Grain Soul" back:

> The magician thereupon began searching for the vanished "Grain Soul." This ceremony was called "searching for the Grain Soul. Once the "Grain Soul" was discovered somewhere in the forest or in the field with the help of the magician it (I.e. the white butterfly) was wrapped carefully in a white cloth and was brought back to the field and freed there. After this, so it was believed, the field would thrive again and bear rich crops. (Paulson, 1965)

In all these cases, the people in the lower classes were aware of the shamanistic figures, while those in the upper classes—the people who wrote history—typically weren't. Indeed, the benandanti, for example, were such an important part of society that any children born with caul over their heads were told they would become benandanti. In some cases, it was stated that their mothers had even saved their cauls for them, which the person wore as a part of their calling. When a child or someone else grew ill, the benandanti were often called it to heal them, for they could fight against the witches that made people sick. The witches often did this by eating away the flesh and blood of children (while the witches' souls were out of their bodies). If the benandanti could use their power and the power of a scale to get the child to gain weight, the witches attacking them would begin to wither and eventually die. Sometimes, the Benandanti would also help people by providing them with good charms and removing cursed charms witches had put in their beds (such as finger nail clippings, pins, or other seemingly innocuous items that apparently carried a curse).

Despite these facts about the benandanti, priests only learned about their practices by happenstance and were greatly surprised by them. In other words, two societies existed simultaneously; to some extent I would argue that his occurred in even earlier agricultural societies as well. Because of this, shamanism remained even in societies where history books provide little or no mention of it. Aside from their role in helping people obtain food, there is another key difference between most agricultural- and hunter-gatherer-based shamans. Shamans among the hunter-gatherers tended to be very vocal; they jumped about, danced, sang, and worked themselves into a state of ecstasy. This makes me wonder if perhaps the depiction such activities by witches and fairies is a result of folk memories about the dancing shamans (Ginzburg, 1966).

In agricultural or pastoral societies, shamans or their dependents were often much quieter, falling into states of ecstasy through quite meditation and often requiring that no one else be around. For them, the state of ecstasy was private, and it was often dangerous for anyone else to be around when they went into their trance as, if they were moved, if their name was said, or if someone looked at them too long while in this state, that person might die.

Despite their importance, however, the Benandanti, like most shamanistic figures, were not religious leaders per se, nor were they wealthy. Some were servants, others cowherds and one was even reported to be an eight-year-old child. It could be argued, of course, that poverty was almost a requirement for agricultural shamans. Those who were wealthy

100

moved on into the priestly caste and changed their beliefs to conform to notions of polytheism or, later, monotheism.

Despite the fact that the benandanti were potential competitors to those in power, they survived for well over a thousand years after their practices were outlawed. They competed by focusing on healing those that the church could not, by blessing the fields when the church couldn't, and, most especially, by avoiding trouble. All this began to change during the 1600s, however, as they grew bolder and began to use their power to accuse witches for the first time (Ginzburg, 1966).

Accusing witches was nothing new. Inquisitions had been happening in Italy since the height of Rome. However, it is likely that these accusations led to anger for the same length of time. There was nothing people could do when the Catholic Church or a political leader accused someone of witchcraft. A benandanti's political power, like the political power of any shaman, was based on people's willingness to believe in them. Once they started accusing people's loved ones of witchcraft, their power vanished. One could argue, then, that the benandanti vanished because they overstepped their relationship with the people they were supposed to protect by going on the offensive against them.

Blacksmiths and Shamanism

Blacksmiths have a lot in common with shamans. They were transformative figures. With fire, they were able to change elements in inexplicable ways. They played with fire, subverting the most dangerous of elements to their will in order to bend and shape metal. Further, like the shaman, they had tot be creative and skilled members of their community while, at the same time, existing apart from ordinary people. Blacksmiths lived at the edges of villages, talked about things no one else understood, and weren't as concerned with seasonal changes as neighboring hunters and farmers.

Those who live on the margins were almost always thought of as magical, which is why beggars in Europe, mountain men in Japan, and the herders of Russia and the Alps were all considered to have their own magical powers.

In a tale from Scotland, a blacksmith's son was taken to the realm of the fairies in the hill where they taught him the art of blacksmithing—in much the same way as they would teach a shaman their craft. As with most people abducted by the fairies, the boy's body—or a replica of it—was left behind. Over time, this began to wither away with illness, causing the smith and his friends to worry that the boy would die. Eventually, his father, advised by a wise old man (who may have been a deity, cunning, or helping spirit of some sort) went on a journey into the fairy realm, where he managed to free his son. However, the boy still wasn't himself:

> For a year and a day the boy never did a turn of work, and hardly ever spoke a word; but at last one day, sitting by his father and watching him finishing a sword he was making for some chief, and which he was very particular about, he, suddenly exclaimed, "That is not the way to do it;" and, taking the tools from his father's hands, he set to work himself in his place, and soon fashioned a sword the like of which was never seen in the country before. (Douglas, 1901)

So, like the shaman, the boy was taken to the spirit world to learn his art, his body seeming

101

to die, allowing him to have a near-death experience. Then, on returning, he—like many shaman figures in tales—was perplexing, appearing to be lazy until at last revealing his brilliance.

In Irish lore, blacksmiths were protected against curses and the mischief of fairies and witches.

> Blacksmiths surely are safe from these things. And if a black-smith was to turn his anvil upside down and to say malicious words, he could do you great injury.

> There was a child that was changed (replaced by a fairy), and my mother brought it a nice bit of potato cake one time, for tradesmen often have nice things on the table. But the child wouldn't touch it) for they don't like the leavings of a smith.

> Blacksmiths have power, and if you could steal the water from the trough in the forge, it would cure all things. (Gregory, 1920)

Books, Necromancers, and Cunning

Some of the biggest changes to magico-religious traditions came from books and an overabundance of educated clergy with no real job prospects. These clerics created an underworld of people educated in religious rituals, Latin, and theology who studied necromancy and demonology as well as other forbidden rituals. Such rituals were different from previous shamanism for a number of reasons. The first is that such people, who were used to learning from books, began to write things down with greater frequency, and people think differently when reading and writing. Second, the fact that the Christian clergy, with their theological training, began to contemplate how magic worked as a structural system fundamentally altered the nature of how people thought of magic. Third, the necromancers didn't typically worship or even like the spirits they summoned, viewing them not as partners to be respected but as demons to be used. Finally, the primary concern for these marginalized clergy was opportunities to gain real power over others or to find their place in a society.

Instead of using their rituals to benefit a community or find food, these clergymen often used magic to satisfy their own sexual or greedy desires. Hence, there were spells to gain favor from a lord at court, to sexually manipulate men or women, to find hidden treasures, etc. Perhaps even more interesting than this, however, were the spells created to entertain oneself, for, as marginalized clerics with no real work, boredom was likely one of their greatest enemies. Further, there was a clear desire to satisfy their desire to understand forbidden secrets for intellectual curiosity as well as spells to help one connect with the divine (Kieckhefer, 1998).

All of this changed the nature of the magico-religious relationship with the spirit world. Instead of serving the powers they summoned, necromancers would use circles and runes, the names of God and his angels to entrap and essentially enslave demonic spirits. There were exceptions to this, with necromancers at times prostrating themselves and even praying to the demonic forces; however, even when doing this, the necromancers viewed themselves as controlling the dark forces through their will and often with the help of astrological magic and the power of the angels and God. This also further separated the

102

upper-class, educated society from that of the peasants, for a time, for even in places where the clergy and upper classes perceived the spirits as being demons, peasants, as already mentioned, still often believed that they were talking to fairies and the like.

It was not only educated members of the court and clergy who were influenced by books, however. As books dropped in price and literacy increased, many more people could be influenced by them. A cunning named Murrell had books on magic even though he lived in a village that was still culturally isolated. Nearly a century later, the Vicar of Little Wakering said that "deep in the hearts of country people is still a religion of secret paganism." As with the necromancers, the cunning believed himself to be a sacred person, knowing the Bible better than any local parson, and so he was able to consider himself superior to them in spiritual matters. As such, he battled against the evil forces. He would hunt the witches who used their magic for evil, exorcize demons, and go after ordinary criminals. His magical practices utilized a mixture of prayers, amulets, and sympathetic powers (Maple, 1960).

In one case, a young woman found an old gypsy hiding in a barn and ordered her out. She was a witch, and she cursed the girl, who began to scream like a cat and bark like a dog. Murrell was called in. He placed in the fire a bottle containing hair and nail clippings from the victim. He told everyone to keep absolutely silent while they awaited the arrival of the witch. Presently, there came a hammering on the door, and a woman's voice begged him to stop "the test" as the fire was causing her agony. The bottle burst. On the following morning, an old woman was found burned to death outside the Woodcutters' Arms, three miles away. It was the gypsy. The girl recovered.

Like many other cunning, Murrell existed outside the community. He seldom spoke, and when he did, he did so in a way that was difficult for others to understand. He tended to only come out at night, and those who went to see him might stand outside his home for hours trying to build up the courage to knock (Maple, 1960). In one story from Essex, a girl named Rosie went to see Murrell to get magical aid in winning back her love. As with many love spells, the one he gave her was fairly violent, requiring her to pierce red flannel with a thorn while calling out letters, after which there was an explosion.

There were still, however, some who had a shamanistic character, even if they were shunned by society as a whole. Again in Essex:

> The most sinister figure in Canewdon was old George. Old George Pickingill along with Cunning Murrell, boasted of being one of the 'cunning men' of Essex. Unlike Murrell, he was not liked. He was a farm laborer who it was said could clear a field at harvest time in half an hour with the help of his 'imps'. Local farmers were wary of him for he'd demand money or beer from them, threatening that if they not agree he would blight their crops or put a hex on their farm machinery. (Maple, 1960)

Like most shamans before him, George didn't make his living from his ability to communicate with the spirit world. Rather, he lived more or less like anyone else in the community, but he was able to call on the spirit world with his ordinary everyday tasks, and everyone feared him. This is reminiscent of the tale of "Yallery Brown" and the farm laborer who everyone came to fear. Just as Murrell was a real figure, it is possible that these now shunned cunning were also real, and, if so, it may be that they began to revel in the fear people had of them.

Lina Ivanits in "Russian Folk Belief" writes about one woman everyone feared was a witch who threatened those who made her angry. It is common in stories for old women, beggars, and so forth to threaten those who do not give them what they want and to take advantage of people's fear of them. Some of the rumors about witches might have come from those who claimed to be witches. Still, that is not the only reason that the nature of shamans had developed into that of witches. After all, shamans would threaten and cajole people as well. However, once people felt their services were no longer required, it was easy for the people to turn on them.

Agricultural Shamanism in Fairy Tales

Many of the elements of shamanism remained fairy tales, though there are often clear agricultural elements in them, such as in the following Cassock tale, "The Serpent Wife":

> *There was once a gentleman who had a laborer who never went about in company. His fellow-servants did all they could to make him come with them, and now and then enticed him into the tavern, but they could never get him to stay there long, and he always wandered away by himself through the woods. One day he went strolling about in the forest as usual, far from any village and the haunts of men, when he came upon a huge Serpent, which wriggled straight up to him and said, "I am going to eat thee on the spot!" But the laborer, who was used to the loneliness of the forest, replied, "Very well, eat me if thou hast a mind to!"--Then the Serpent said, "Nay! I will not eat thee; only do what I tell thee!" And the Serpent began to tell the man what he had to do. "Turn back home," it said, "and thou wilt find thy master angry because thou hast tarried so long, and there was none to work for him, so that his corn has to remain standing in the field. Then he will send thee to bring in his sheaves, and I'll help thee. Load the wagon well, but don't take quite all the sheaves from the field. Leave one little sheaf behind; more than that thou needs not leave, but that thou must leave. Then beg thy master to let thee have this little sheaf by way of wages. Take no money from him, but that one little sheaf only. Then, when thy master has given thee this sheaf, burn it, and a fair lady will leap out of it; take her to wife!"*

There is a lot going on in this short section of the story. As occurs in many shamans' stories, this tale begins with a farm laborer who doesn't fit in with society. In addition, just as many shamans in hunter-gatherer societies were isolated in the wilderness for some time before they found their first helping spirits, this person was also alone in the wilderness before he found his. At times, these helping spirits would threaten to kill the shaman, trying to scare him or her, and the shaman would need to avoid showing fear. If the shaman was successful in this, then he or she would be given power. For example, a tiger spirit in Southeast Asia or a jaguar spirit in South America would attempt to scare a potential shaman, eating any who showed fear and aiding any who did not.

The fact that the spirit, which appears to guide the shaman, takes the form of a serpent makes sense; serpents were one of the most important guardian and fertility spirits in

104

Eurasia's past. Finally, the last sheaf of grain in the field was commonly believed to hold the fertility spirit of the field within it (Frazer, James), so it makes sense that an agricultural shaman would seek this as a helping spirit.

"The Serpent Wife" Continued...

The laborer obeyed, and went and worked for his master as the Serpent had told him. He went out into the field to bring home his master's corn, and marvellously he managed it. He did all the carrying himself, and loaded the wagon so heavily that it creaked beneath its burden. Then when he had brought home all his master's corn, he begged that he might have the remaining little sheaf for himself. He refused to be rewarded for his smart labour, he would take no money; he wanted nothing for himself, he said, but the little sheaf he had left in the field. So his master let him have the sheaf. Then he went out by himself into the field, burnt the sheaf just as the Serpent had told him, and immediately a lovely lady leapt out of it. The laborer forthwith took and married her; and now he began to look out for a place to build him a hut upon. His master gave him a place where he might build his hut, and his wife helped him so much with the building of it that it seemed to him as if he himself never laid a hand to it. His hut grew up as quick as thought, and it contained everything that they wanted. The man could not understand it; he could only walk about and wonder at it. Wherever he looked there was everything quite spick and span and ready for use: none in the whole village had a better house than he.

Recall that we have already discussed two other cunning folk from England, Tom and George, who were able to do massive amounts of work with the help of the spirits. The notion of being able to perform a lot of work with the help of a spirit seems to be an important part of magico-religious belief in agricultural societies. We see a similar importance placed on supernatural workers in the tales of Paul Bunyan—though, in this case, Paul Bunyan is the supernatural being rather than a person receiving help from a supernatural being.

"The Serpent Wife" continued...

And so he might have lived in all peace and prosperity to the end of his days had not his desires outstripped his deserts. He had three fields of standing corn, and when he came home one day his laborers said to him, "Thy corn is not gathered in yet, though it is standing all ripe on its stalks." Now the season was getting on, and for all the care and labor of his wife, the corn was still standing in the field. "Why, what's the meaning of this?" thought he. Then in his anger he cried, "I see how it is. Once a serpent, always a serpent!" He was quite beside himself all the way home, and was very wrath with his wife because of the corn.

When he got home he went straight to his chamber to lie down on his pillow. There was no sign of his wife, but a huge serpent was just coiling itself round and round and settling down in the middle of the pillow. Then he called to mind how, once, his wife had said to him, "Beware, for Heaven's sake, of ever calling me a serpent. I will not suffer thee to call me by that name, and if thou dost thou shalt lose thy wife." He called this to mind now, but it was already too late; what he had said could not be unsaid. Then he reflected what a good wife he had had, and how she herself had sought him out, and how she had waited upon him continually and done him boundless good, and yet he had not been able to refrain his tongue, so that now, maybe, he would be without a wife for the rest of his days. His heart grew heavy within him as he thought of all this, and he wept bitterly at the harm he had done to himself. Then the Serpent said to him, "Weep no more. What is to be, must be. Is it thy standing corn thou art grieved about? Go up to thy barn, and there thou wilt find all thy corn lying, to the very last little grain. Have I not brought it all home and threshed it for thee, and set everything in order? And now I must depart to the place where thou didst first find me." Then she crept off, and the man followed her, weeping and mourning all the time as for one already dead. When they reached the forest she stopped and coiled herself round and round beneath a hazel-nut bush. Then she said to the man, "Now kiss me once, but see to it that I do not bite thee!"––Then he kissed her once, and she wound herself round a branch of a tree and asked him, "What dost thou feel within thee?"––He answered, "At the moment when I kissed thee it seemed to me as if I knew everything that was going on in the world!"––Then she said to him again, "Kiss me a second time!"––"And what dost thou feel now?" she asked when he had kissed her again.––"Now," said he, "I understand all languages which are spoken among men."––Then she said to him, "And now kiss me a third time, but this will be for the last time." Then he kissed the Serpent for the last time, and she said to him, "What dost thou feel now?"––"Now," said he, "I know all that is going on under the earth."––"Go now," said she, "to the Tsar, and he will give thee his daughter for the knowledge thou hast. But pray to God for poor me, for now I must be and remain a serpent forever." And with that the Serpent uncoiled herself and disappeared among the bushes, but the man went away and wedded the Tsar's daughter.

This tale, then, is the story of a shaman's family line—one that explains how a man or a family gained supernatural powers. At the end of many of these stories, the husband violates some taboo, and so his magical wife leaves. The reason for this might be the need for some explanation of why the supernatural being is no longer living among their descendants—why the supernatural mother or father isn't around to help them directly.

Deities and Fairies in Fairy Tales

It's often difficult to see the presence of former deities in fairy tales, for they have been replaced by wise old men, beautiful women, frogs, or sometimes nothing at all. A child born under a lucky star in "The Devil With the Three Golden Hairs" by the Brothers Grimm, is given his magical luck by three fairies who come down to him when he is born in a Slavic version of this story. Also in the Slavic version of this tale known as "The Three Golden Hairs of Grandfather Allknow" the Devil is called the Sun. In evening the Sun in this story is a cranky old man, but when morning comes he's reborn as "abeautiful golden-haired child, the divine Sun (Wratislaw, 1890)." In the Sleeping Beauty tales, the king and queen are given a child by a sacred fountain where a fairy lives or by a fairy in the form of a frog. In other tales, a wise old man appears to the protagonist, offering him or her information or magical gifts. Other times, the deity could be the villain of a story as many deities in mythology and lore did horrible things at times. Finally, sometimes fairy tale protagonists might be remnant of a deity themselves. Still, what all fairy tales with deity characters have in common is that they are about the connection between humanity and the deities. As a result, in order to understand many fairy tales, it is important to understand people's beliefs in the fairies and deities, a belief that very often centered on their relationship with these beings.

Our Relationship with the Fairies

Folk religions are, in essence, about trying to build and maintain a relationship with a spirit world, which, in turn, helps people be more productive, get along, and, essentially, survive.

Once, fairies were a projection of people's dreams, as well as their fears. People would call on fairies in forbidden love spells or dream of the day when fairies would offer them gold and wealth. They would dream of escaping the mundane, getting enough food to eat, or successfully rebelling against social norms. In this latter case, rebels would invoke their right to rebel because the Queen of the Fairies or the Virgin Mary had appeared to them.

At the same time, fairies were also important to societies. Fairies and folk religion helped to enforce social and cultural norms and ensured that both these things survived. Fairies would punish servants who stole from their masters, reward hard work, punish laziness, and even concern themselves with such mundane matters as whether or not someone was dressed in a culturally acceptable way. This was important because any society that didn't have some form of constructs to support its existence will collapse, and for a long time, many of these constructs were based on supernatural ideas.

In other words, fairies have a multitude of functions, both personal and social, which leads to a lot of confusion about their nature. Further, since so many aspects of their nature are based on society and individual needs, fairies morph and change from society to society and era to era. This means that, while people thought of fairies as having individual personalities, any fairy being is made up of many different ideas and stories that often do not seem to fit together.

This led to another important point about many ancient and folk religions. There wasn't a single text or group of people determining what was cannon. Because of this, there were likely as many ideas about fairies as there were individual people to have them. Yet, at the same time, many aspects of a fairy's nature could be passed on very diligently, because people believed that their relationship with the otherworld was of the utmost importance— that their fates were controlled by the spirits of the otherworld. Given that deities controlled people's fates, it became clear that they weren't always kind. People suffered and dreams failed to come true more often than not, so deities were perceived as having a dual nature, being both cruel and kind, helpful and harmful. We could see this dual nature very clearly by the fact that Kore, the deity who makes the grain ripen, and Persephone, the queen of the dead, were the same being with different functions.

These earth mothers—perhaps of which there was the most speculation of all the deity motifs—also composed the group of deities that best personified the duality between dark and light. Persephone and her mother were the goddesses of fertility in ancient Greece; they were earth mother figures that caused the crops to grow, but who also caused them to fail. Persephone—and sometimes her mother, as well—was a chthonic deity; that is, she was a deity of the earth where plants grew and the dead dwelt.

> The Chthonic gods of the realm of the dead "were invested with a mysterious dread just by reason of their connection with the souls of the departed. In the fact that they were terrible gods whose anger was easily roused and difficult to allay, we saw the reason why these divinities were chosen to protect the sanctity of the oath. Not because they were such ancient gods, but because of their dreaded nature, they were invoked in this connection. Perhaps the practice went back to the period when the souls of the dead were thought to pursue with vengeance the oath breaker, as well as other evil-doers. (Fairbanks, 1900)

In Russia, people would swear oaths to the Damp Mother Earth; however, it's unlikely that they originally did so because she was a kindly figure. As Fairbanks pointed out, people wanted others to swear oaths to a vengeful deity who would punish them for breaking their promise. There were exceptions, of course, but there was also a propensity in Europe for Earth Mothers, in general, to be fairly vindictive and dangerous.

Persephone's closest companion, Hecate—the one who made certain that she returned to the world, that fertility returned to the earth, and who was also able to grant people their heart's desires—also had for her servants...

> The filthy demons called Empusae, children of Hecate, are asshaunched and wear brazen slippers - unless, as some declare, each has one ass's leg and one brazen leg. Their habit is to frighten travelers.... Empusae disguise themselves in the forms of bitches, cows, or beautiful maidens and, the later shape, will lie with men by night, or at the time of midday sleep, sucking their vital forces until they die. (Graves, 1992)

A portion of the odd behavior of these deities may have come from the fact that ancient Greece, and nearly every other nation of the past, didn't have a singular religion. Rather, they had many. Therefore, Persephone had different personalities and roles from one city to another, which could explain some of the confusion surrounding her as a multi-natured being, a characteristic that could be difficult to try to interpret today. Nevertheless, there seemed to be something in the thinking of many cultures that made them give the supernatural beings both positive and negative traits, which made the same being both good and evil.

This duality was often perplexing to people in the modern day. The notion that Zeus was both kind and a wild monster disturbed us. His nature reflectd and expanded the nature of people. At one time, parents beating children, husbands beating wives, and so forth, were the norm. Indeed, it was encouraged. Yet, children still loved their abusive parents, and, in Russia, anthropologists said that they would even sing and dance when parents came home. Because of this, many people thought very differently about the nature of love compared today. They often believed and accepted that good and bad events were caused by the same being.

The Japanese formally codified the idea of multiple personalities into their religion by giving each kami (deity) multiple souls and multiple natures. Europe seemed to do something similar by giving each deity multiple titles and incarnations. Zeus, for example, was also Telios (of marriage rites), Basileus (King), Konios (of dust), Obrios (of Rain), and, literally, dozens upon dozens more.

One important consequence of the multiple nature of spirits was the extreme importance for a person to constantly work to avoid breaking with what the deities considered acceptable behavior. This could include anything from avoiding whistling in the house to being generous to beggars. To anger the deities was to cause them to turn destructive. In other words, the multiple natures of deities forced people to do specific things while avoiding others. More than this, however, it pushed people to have a social relationship with the spirits. This went beyond just fearing them, however, as what mattered most, at times, was building an emotional connection with the fairies.

Take, for example, the Aka Pygmies of Congo, who had two rituals specifically designed to call out the good forest spirits. In the ritual performed by children, "singing and dancing were used to call and enchant the mokondi (forest spirit)." This, in turn, led to the mokondi blessing of everyone in the camp with good luck. The song began with the young boys going a short distance into the jungle where they bundled together and clothed some sticks. Then, singing and dancing, they led the Bolu spirit, the forest deity, back into the camp where they were joined by dancing girls. "The girls' singing and dancing must lure Bolu into camp by the beauty and enthusiasm of their performance. They will dance provocatively forward"(Lewis, 2002).

Singing and dancing were the delight of fairies, and particularly deities, the world over. Indeed, one was likely hard pressed to find more than a few religions in which the people did not sing and dance to their deities. Music was likely a common part of the religious experience and beliefs of many people, not just for cultural reasons, but for deeply seated psychological reasons, as well. Music had many of the same roles that fairies did; songs reflected our dreams and fears and help to cement our cultures together.

> Music has the power to exert enormous influence on the human mind, especially when people are gathered in large groups, and the euphoric power of group dynamics is brought to play. (Till, 2010)

Music has the power to enhance social bonding and induces the brain wave patterns that are involved in altered states of consciousness, increasing the chances of religious experiences or shamanistic journeys.

Rituals, in general, are an important part of human belief. Indeed, rituals are often the defining characteristic of religion. Neuroscientists have seen a decrease in activity in the partial lobe when people are taking part in religious activities. This indicates that, during religious experiences, people lose a sense of self and their own surroundings. At the same time, both focus and concentration increase. Further, rituals can result in a state of pleasure (Gross, 2012).

In other words, any religious ritual involves both the outward acts that we as observers can see and inward mental experiences. These internal experiences include a release of opioids, which "stimulate the immune system; produce a sense of euphoria, certainty, and belongingness; and enhance coping skills, maintenance of bodily homeostasis, pain reduction, stress tolerance, environmental adaptation, and group psychobiological synchronization" (Winkelman, 2002).

Returning to the Aka of Congo, the adult's dance is similar to that of the children's, in that it involves singing and dancing with masked figures dancing among the participants. These dances can last for hours—at times, days—and over such extended periods; the trance-like states of *okondi massana* are easy to slip into. These are a sort of dreamy, heightened experiences and appreciation of sound and movement, as well as an irresistible desire to sing and dance combined with tremendous energy and control.

> As the singing builds up to ever more intense and beautiful crescendos, the sounds of the okondi drift into camp. The mokondi begin coming in from the forest, and their hoots and cries can be heard echoing under the canopy as they approach. Suddenly, as if from nowhere, small luminous dots and shapes begin swirling around the camp, moving rhythmically to the singing and drumming while whistling beautiful, short melodies. Perfumes drift up as the rustling luminous mokondi pass by (Lewis, 2002).

Those not participating in the Aka's ritual would only see people dancing and singing for long periods of time—people acting strangely. They wouldn't experience the emotions or the connection that the Aka do, nor would they have any hope of seeing the mokondi emerging from the forest to dance with people.

The fact that people had both rituals and songs and performed other acts to celebrate certain spiritual beings, and that such rituals made them feel a connection with these beings, meant that many people likely believed that the spirits themselves were participating, or were at least present. Certainly, the spirits of Europe seemed to love festivities and participating in the activities of humanity.

> In Lithuania, the name for the last sheaf is Boba (Old Woman), answering to the Polish name Baba. The Boba is said to sit in the corn which is left standing last. The person who binds the last sheaf or digs the last potato is the subject of much banter, and receives and long retains the name of the Old Rye-woman or the Old Potato-woman. The last sheaf—the Boba—is made into the form of a woman, carried solemnly through the village on the last harvest-wagon, and drenched with water at the farmer's house; then everyone dances with it. (Frazer, 1922)

This festival from Lithuania wasn't unique—though it wasn't exactly common, either—for there were nearly as many harvest festivals in Europe as there were villages to hold them. Some were violent, some were fun, and many were confusing to our modern comprehension. The most important thing to understand, however, was that, in all cases, people were trying to form and maintain a relationship with the fairies and spirits around them. This was what folk religion was about.

In Europe, long festivals and dances, held at specific times, were scheduled when it was believed that the spirits would be out and about or in places where they were believed to dwell (such as sacred groves of trees). People specifically held these festivals in such a way that spirits could participate. They would set food at the tables in their houses or go out and eat in places where the fairies were thought to exist.

In his book "The Neuroscience of Religious Experience," Patrick McNamara developed a list of 17 common religious experiences of rituals. Though not every experience would include all of these features, and the intensity of them would vary from ritual to ritual and person to person, they were fairly enlightening:

1. Unity or sense of integration within oneself and with others
2. Transcendence of time and space
3. Deeply felt positive mood
4. Sense of sacredness
5. A prophetic quality or feeling of insight
6. Paradox or the ability to respectfully hold opposing points of view
7. Alleged ineffability (the experience is felt to be beyond words)
8. Transiency of the euphoria
9. Persisting positive changes in attitudes and behavior
10. An enhanced sense of personal power or even that one has been specially blessed by God
11. Enhanced theory of the mind
12. Changes in sexual behaviors (these can be enhanced or dramatically diminished)
13. Changes in reading/writing behaviors; most often these manifest as an enhanced interest in writing
14. Enhanced awareness and appreciation of music
15. Complex visual and metaphoric imagery (These complex visual metaphors are usually related to the sense of noetic insight that accompanies intense religious experiences. The religious ideas are felt to be so meaningful that only complex symbolic visual imagery could capture them.)
16. Ritualization (the propensity to perform ritual actions when religious experiences are heightened.)
17. Encounter with God or spirit beings

Upon examination of this list, it is easy to see many of the aspects that people tended to associate with fairies from ideas about prophetic insights, alterations in how time works, love of music, and so forth. Number 13, changes in reading and writing habits, is particularly interesting because it clearly depends on the availability of reading and writing to a person. What if reading and writing aren't available? Would this, instead, lead people to speculate on the nature of the spirit world without writing? Would it lead them to want to share these ideas through stories? It is impossible to definitively answer this question without some specific research into people who perform religious rituals absent a written language. However, it does lead to some interesting questions about how an enhanced interest in discussing the spirit world might change people's stories.

The last of these points, however, is perhaps the most interesting: the idea that the spirit beings are encountered, and that the ritual calls to them. Through festivals and other rituals, that bond iss formed with the fairies that, while frightening, are also benevolent.

Of course, not all rituals were part of a wider festivalnor were they even performed by all people. Fairy doctors and cunning folk were a common feature in many communities across Europe, and they were often the only ones to perform certain rituals to connect with the fairies. At the same time, however, they were also considered to be authorities on such beings, so their beliefs would have affected the community as a whole.

In general, such rituals could lead to the belief that fairies were at times benevolent, such as the predecessors of Santa Claus, fairies who would leave coins for good people, help the poor, or provide for the sick. Some specific examples of these kindly spirits included a magical woman who lived on Teckberg Mountain; she would ride a golden chariot pulled by two winged cats. Before leaving the land behind, because of her shame over the wickedness of her sons, she left places where grain and trees would grow more lushly than elsewhere. Another example of kind spirits included the elves in the Italian version of "The Elves and the Shoemaker," in which the fairies sneaked into a shoemaker's house at Christmas time in order to make him wealthy.

There is, however, a competing point to this generally positive notion. As already mentioned, many of these same spirits had negative aspects to their nature that were enhanced by stories. As you'll recall from the list of common neurological religious experiences, the ability to hold opposing views is one of the most common aspects of religious experience; people can love the beings for whom they are performing a ritual and fear and, or, hate them at the same time.

Festivals vs. Stories

It's early spring. The ground is still touched by spots of melting snow with little rivulets of clear, cold water running down between the budding flowers and through fields that will soon be ready for planting. In the distance, a Christian church bell can be heard ringing, as it has in this village for over a thousand years. Even so, a small group of young girls still follows these rivulets of water towards the river to sing and perform ceremonies in a beautiful cluster of trees which cling to the side of a river, as they have done since long before the coming of the Christian church. The girls tie scarves to trees beside the river. They perform circle dances, sing, and pray to the spirits of the water, imploring them to dampen the earth and keep it damp until harvest time. The nature spirits, known to the Russians as Rusalka, comply as they come out of the water, dancing through fields while dampening the ground for the year, and bringing their lifegiving water to what would otherwise be a lifeless earth. Meanwhile, the girls cast divinations or swear oaths of eternal sisterhood as they dance once more, free as the nature spirits they worship for just that moment.

Based upon these rituals, one would think of the Rusalka as positive, benevolent beings. Yet, in stories, the Rusalka would rip people apart, drown them, steal their souls, kidnap children, and more. One would see two competing ideas - one of horror, and the other of positive emotions. This, in turn, can also help to explain people's dual beliefs regarding the nature of fairies, and which likely contributes to the topsy-turvy nature of fairyland. This has, perhaps, always perplexed and confused people.

The differences between story and ritual are interesting, in part, because, as Bulbulia and Slingerland (2012) contend, "Myths are open to variation, whereas ritual is more bound to

112

tradition." In other words, rituals are far slower to change than are stories. This isn't to say that rituals don't change; they do with some frequency. Typically, though, they are only likely to do so because of some social upheaval, something that forces people to readapt to a new way of life.

Yet, at the same time, rituals and stories do often sync together—that is, they both begin to draw on the positive and negative elements from the other. To understand this, let's begin with an examination of the festival of Perchta in Tyrol.

Perchta is both exactly what you would expect from an Alpine Goddess whose name means "the splendid and magnificent one" and exactly the opposite. She is one of the many fairy beings that come out around Christmas time, giving small silver coins to good children and slitting open the bellies of bad ones. Furthermore, she leads a troop of followers on a wild hunt to eliminate the dark spirits from the earth. In a legend from Styria, a man goes out to fetch a midwife when he encounters a beautiful woman with a cricket on her long nose. She needs him to carve a wooden nail for her wagon, and the shavings from this turn into gold. In another tale, she kidnaps a man and returns him dead in the morning with flowers from distant countries between his toes, indicating that he has traveled far (Johns, 2004).

> Perchta has her troops of followers, strange beings half-way between mortals and immortals. These do not live among the children of men but appear amongst them at such times as Advent and the Feast of the Three Kings. Like Perchta herself, they are divided into disposition. Some are good, kindly creatures, such as the "beautiful" Perchten; while others, like the Schiachen Perchten, are wild, irresponsible, malicious things. They are more felt and heard than seen. In swarms, they come down on men's dwellings and are recognized by their weird screams and laughter. They love to draw men into danger by alluring sounds and spells and to punish undiscovered crimes. The Perchten dances originated among the peasants of the mountains, who desire to imitate these mythological beings, (Vivian, 1908)

Around Christmas time, a number of Alpine communities held festivals, dances, parades, and other rituals in her honor. Sometimes, the participants went from house to house and receive food in return for blessing the occupants. In other cases, the dance was more of a parade-like affair, with troops of people dressed in various costumes dancing through the city streets. As one would expect, these dances were wild affairs, performed only by men, many of whom imitated the female Perchta, dressed up and wearing massive headdresses so expensive that only the wealthiest farmers could play this role. "In their right hands, the 'beautiful' Perchten clasped a naked sword, and with the other Hand they led their partners — young men dressed as women." Other men dresed as Schiachen Perchta, a terrifying monstrous figure that looked exactly as modern-day people would depict the devil, for she had a goat-like face, horns, and teeth and was generally terrifying to look at.

The fact that men dressed as women for this festival was fairly typical, as many festivals tended to turn conventions on their heads. In some festivals, slaves and servants acted as the masters and could actually speak their minds without being punished. In others, children would tie up their teachers, lock them out of the schoolhouse, and battle them with pop guns ().

The topsy-turvy nature of fairies and, in particular, the opportunity to act in a way that was contrary to cultural norms, was something that humans often desired. In Japan, during the planting season, women teased and harassed men, pulling them into the mud even though they usually had specific norms frowning upon such behavior. In addition to these, there was often a lot of sexual innuendo and humor involved in planting festivals. In ancient Greece, indecent jokes, talk, and games were a part of the women's celebrations at Holoa. During the spring in the Ukraine, it was expected that a man and woman would roll in the fields as if they were coupling. Beyond the obvious symbolism of fertility being transferred to the fields through such activities, there was likely another important reason for this frolicking

.

Recall what was stated about shamans and creativity; about how, by acting contrary to social norms, they were able to create diverse thinking about what would otherwise be a homogeneous community. Creative people, in general, often seemed to be slightly crazy; they didn't fit with social norms. Since such people were often considered to be under the influence of the spirit world, one could only conclude that the spirits themselves were a bit topsy-turvy. More than this, however, the topsy-turvy nature of festivals gave people in the lower castes of society a chance to speak their minds, and it has been found that giving everyone a chance to speak freely will ultimately lead to innovations and better outcomes (Jana, 2009). (Although he is a literary character, Puck perhaps simply exemplified the world of fairies. By turning everything on its head, he made it possible for everyone to have a moment of actual self-reflection on their lives—to realize what they should be doing.)

These festivals served two other important social functions; the first was to give people a chance to have a vacation and cut loose. It was common for fairies to have specific days when people weren't allowed to work and for fairies to grow angry at those who didn't celebrate. They hated teetotalers in parts of Britain, demanded that people feast, and grew angry at those who worked on holidays. What one saw reflected in them was the human need to unwind, to escape the drudgery of daily life, and to be someone else for a moment. This demand cut two ways, for it not only forced the peasants to take a day off, but it also forced the people in charge to give a day off. Much as many of those in charge might have hated vacation days, there were numerous studies which showed that vacations and breaks from work increased productivity (Thompsongaug, 2012). Thus, by enforcing certain days off, fairies ensured that humans would be more productive, and that they and society would be more likely to survive.

Second, festivals created a social glue. People must work together to prepare for them, and they take part in them together. This social glue—this creation of a community—is something that spirits have always seemed to do.

Shamans' Helping Spirits and Totems

"You must call on the raven," said the Wolf.

So the Prince called on the raven, and in a trice the raven came, and flew up and fetched the keys, and so the Prince got into the church. But when he came to the well, there lay the duck, and swam about backwards and forwards, just as the Giant had said. So the Prince stood and coaxed it and coaxed it, till it came to him, and he grasped it in his hand; but just as he lifted it up from the water, the duck dropped the egg into the well, and then Boots was beside himself to know how to get it out again.

"Well, now you must call on the salmon to be sure," said the Wolf; and the king's son called on the salmon, and the salmon came and fetched up the egg from the bottom of the well.

Then the Wolf told him to squeeze the egg, and as soon as ever, he squeezed it. The Giant screamed out.

"Squeeze it again," said the Wolf; and when the Prince did so, the Giant screamed still more piteously, and begged and prayed so prettily to be spared, saying he would do all that the Prince wished if he would only not squeeze his heart in two.

"Tell him, if he will restore to life again your six brothers and their brides, whom he has turned to stone, you will spare his life," said the Wolf. Yes, the Giant was ready to do that, and he turned the six brothers into king's sons again, and their brides into king's daughters.

"Now, squeeze the egg in two," said the Wolf. So Boots squeezed the egg to pieces, and the Giant burst at once. (Dasent, 1904)

As illustrated by this tale about a shamanistic figure who must slay a giant, shamans and their kin couldn't succeed without help from specific helping spirits. It came as no surprise, then, that many of these helping spirits found their ways into fairy tales as helpers, not only of heroes on journeys, but also as protagonists in Cinderella stories, such as the tale of "Biancabella."

"Biancabella" was very different from what people accustomed to the sterilized expectation of Grimm Brothers' fairy tales. In this tale, a marquis named Lamberico wished for a child, after which his wife fell asleep in the garden. While she was sleeping, a small snake climbed up her dress, making its way into her womb. A short time later, it was discovered that she was pregnant. When their daughter was born, the snake was wrapped around her neck and crawled off.

This snake later became the girl's helping spirit, appearing to her when she grew older, professing to be her sister. The snake told her to bring two buckets—one of milk and one of rosewater—in which to bathe at the garden. The girl did this, and jewels began to fall from her hair whenever it was combed, and flowers sprung from her hands when they were washed. The story became reminiscent of Cinderella when Biancabella married a man she didn't know, and, additionally, was forced to live with a psychotic, wicked stepmother who blinded her and cut off her hands. Ultimately, the snake came along and saved her, using its magic to restore her eyes and hands (Giovanni, 1901).

Given the importance of helper spirits to shamans, it comes as no surprise that, of all the rituals, the most personal are those in which shamanistic figures call to their helping spirits. Helping spirits take the form of nature spirits, the ghosts of their parents or uncles, and more. These helping spirits are also one of the most common fairy types within fairy tales. From "Puss in Boots" to the animals saved by a hero that later returns the favor, fairy tales are filled with familiar spirits. On top of this, they are one of the most prominent features of witches, who are very often depicted with black cats. Despite their prominence, however, it is common for people to misunderstand the relationship between a witch and his or her familiar spirit, for most people view the witch as owning the familiar. More often, however, it is the other way around. As Mikhailovskii and Wardrop stated:

> Shamans are the property of the spirits, who though subject to his summons, have yet full power over him.

Certainly, a shaman's helper spirit quite often seeks to help befriending the shaman. However, shamans/witches, as a general rule, work for the spirits of the otherworld with the familiar spirit serving as a representative. For example, the Celts' cunning and witches tend to work for the king or queen of the fairies within their region. This fairy king or queen seeks to either help or harm humanity and use the witches to this end, having their familiar spirits act as go-betweens in order to relay their orders.

In Buryat lore, the Tengri were good spirits who were upset because the evil spirits were killing mankind. To protect humanity from their eternal enemies, the Tengri turned an eagle into a shaman. The people, not understanding what had happened, shot at the Eagle, so it returned to the Tengri and asked to be given the power of speech and/or for a human to be made into a shaman. The Tengri agreed and gave the Eagle the power of speech, and as the bird returned to humanity, he saw a beautiful woman and fell in love with her. Through their union, the first shaman was born.

This story highlighted two important points. The first was that certain human lines were often believed to have been established through marriage to various spirits. The Bulgarians, who invaded Europe, had many clans based on animals that were likely thought to be their ancestors, and so stories of people marrying animals in the folklore of the Steppes were stories of the beginnings of shamanistic lines. Another shaman of Siberia's family gained its power from an ancestral marriage with a wolf, while many others seemed to have gained their power through marriage with a swan.

There were similar tales of divine ancestry in Europe—certainly many of the "Beauty and the Beast" tales seemed to point to this. It was common in lore to claim descent from an important spiritual being, and among hunter-gatherers, many animal, such as bears, were the spirit owners of the land that one must ask for permission to hunt. It came as no surprise that some groups in Asia and Northern Europe claimed to be decendants of the bear. Such a descent gave people not only permission, but the moral right, to utilize the land exclusively while driving out intruders.

Consider the story of "The Bear Prince" from Switzerland. In this tale, a father, before setting out on a journey, asked his daughters what they wanted, and one of them asked for grapes. As he was returning home, the father started to wonder where he might find some grapes. At that point, a dwarf appeared and told him about some grapes owned by a bear. As he was harvesting the grapes, the bear appeared and demanded that he give him the first thing to greet him, upon his arrival home, in return for the grapes. Unfortunately, this turned out to be his daughter. This outcome was similar to the tale of "East of the Sun and West of the Moon," in which a white bear promised to make a poor man rich if he gave him his youngest daughter to be his wife.

European fairy tales are filled with traces of totemism, the idea that people are descended from the combination of a human with some divine being (Alinei, 1985). It is interesting to note that, when these stories are about women marrying magical men, they tend to follow the "Beauty and the Beast" motif in which the woman must transform her husband. However, when a man marries a magical woman, the stories tend to follow a Swan Maiden motif in which the woman ultimately leaves her husband.

In one story, a young man from Wales married a fairy who told him that, if he ever touched her with clay, she would leave him—which, of course, he eventually did. In another story, a king promised his magical wife that he wouldl never be surprised by what their son did, but he did show surprise when their son was able to jump into a tiny bottle, and so she, too, left him. There were exceptions to these stories, such as those in which a deity like Zeus appeared in animal form and impregnated a woman. In these cases, the fact that the divine ancestor left his or her mortal children was likely necessary to explain how a family could claim divine descent without the abiliity to communicate directly with their divine ancestor.

Many of these divine descent tales could grow very twisted. In Japan, people would often kill the kappa (water spirits) that had impregnated a woman. Similarly, there was a Sami tale that was fairly similar to the Beauty and the Beast story in which a Sami man was starving in the cold and was taken in by a *stállu* (an ambiguous monster of Sami lore). In return for shelter and food, he was forced to promise his daughter in marriage to the stállu's son. In this story, the man's daughter threw hot oil on the stállu's son, killing him. The people filled themonster's mother's pipe with hot coals so that she sucked these into her lungs and died, and they beat the stállu to death. In another story, a girl laid with a stállu, but her father tricked him and killed him. The story ended with the statement that...

> The stálut are now almost all gone, but some Sámi are still related to them. And that came about when stálut married with Sámi girls, and people were born who were half stállu and half human. And they are different from other people both in appearance and nature. (Dubois, 2011)

In addition to the "Beauty and the Beast" motif, there was also a group of tales in which the animal husband takes on a role similar to that of a helping spirit, such as in the "Frog Prince." It was fairly common in lore for shamanistic figures to have children with some supernatural helper, and, given that most helping spirits were animals, this made them common candidates.

Shamanistic lines were an important part of mythology such that children might be left a magical cat by their parents, as happened in "Puss in Boots." Because the spirits tended to pick shamans who were related to another shaman, at times it was even a person's own ancestral spirit who taught him or her how to be a shaman. For example:

> At the age of nineteen Anga saw several dreams. In them her (deceased) father taught her to be a shaman. In her childhood, she had dreamed several times that she was living with the tiger. She gave birth to three baby tigers, but wouldn't agree to raise them, and instead gave them to the tiger-father. (Deusen, 2011)

Eventually, Anga flew off to seven burning mountains where a tiger came and held her spirit in the otherworld, an event that manifested itself in the physical world as sickness. Eventually, her grandmother rescued her soul and brought it back to her body. Now, the winged tiger acted as her "helping spirit" but also forced her to act as a shaman. In many tales, early shamans would have their souls taken to the otherworld, leaving their bodies behind to grow sickly or lie in a catatonic state.

The spirits that took over the lives of shamans were believed to be either good or bad, and the nature of the shaman themselves often depended more on the types of spirits that approached them than on the personalities of the shamans themselves. A person might resist the pull of evil spirits for a while but, eventually, through abuse and attacks, would bend to their will. In fairy tales, however, the helping spirits that were most often encountered were good and not after anything in particular. In "One Eye, Two Eyes, and Three Eyes," a young girl named Two Eyes was crying because she was abused and given

117

nothing to eat by her mother and sisters. That was when a woman appeared and gave her a magical goat, telling her:

> *Just say to your goat - `Bleat, my little goat, bleat, Cover the table with something to eat,' and then a clean well-spread little table will stand before you with the most delicious food upon it of which you may eat as much as you are inclined for, and when you have had enough, and have no more need of the little table, just say, `Bleat, bleat, my little goat, I pray, and take the table quite away,' and then it will vanish again from your sight.*

From the perspective of those left behind on earth, a shaman figure would often collapse, become sickly, or be on the verge of death, but, as with a near-death experience, what they thought was happening would be very different. In one Greek fairy tale, for example, a young girl named Tasoula collapsed and so must carried into her house by her neighbors:

> *Tasoula's mother still knelt at the bedside, moaning, while the women who stood about wailed in despair. Tasoula was lying just as she had been since she was carried in, when all at once she gave a little sigh and opened her eyes.*
> *She seemed startled as she looked about. Then she realized where she was and after she had been given a little food and wine, she was able to tell what had happened.*
>
> *Six beautiful fairy maidens had appeared before her while she was drinking from the spring at the foot of the tallest pine. It was the very Kreovreshe where the fairies had appeared to Grandmother Adamis. The maidens begged Tasoula to dance with them and, when she refused, they grew very angry and, by joining hands, they formed a ring around her so that she could not escape. They took her up, up, dancing all the time and never touching the ground, until they reached the highest peak of all the mountains. There was snow, deep snow, everywhere, and it was bitterly cold, but they danced in the snow and made Tasoula dance with them.*
> *Then their anger seemed to have left them. They whispered together a little while, looking at her. Then the tallest, the most beautiful, waved her handkerchief above the ground. The snow melted and a great, black hole opened beneath their feet. They dropped into the mountain and went whirling down, down, down. It was dark and terrible. Tasoula could not see, but she felt the fairies holding to her, and their voices echoing through the passage rang in her ears. All at once, they were out again in the hot sunshine on the side of the Sotera.*
>
> *"The fairies laughed and flew away," Tasoula said, "and then I don't know how it was, but when I started to the spring to drink again, I was here!"*
>
> *"She doesn't know it was only her soul they took with them," whispered a neighbor.*

Another girl in England collapsed into an epileptic fit when the fairies came to her but, from her perspective, she went on a journey to the fairy court where the fairy men would flirt with her, and she was wined and dined by the Fairy Queen. In both of these cases, the journey to the spirit world was not predicted. Most often, shamans took their first journey after extreme physical and/or emotional suffering or, at the very least, at a time of transition. Very often, shamans were sickly for some time before the spirits called them and often died during their first spirit journey—what could now be called a near-death

118

experience. Spirits and fairies were frequently the dreams of the desperate, appearing most often to those in emotional turmoil.

It wasn't atypical for the shamans to be afraid during their first encounters with the spirit world. In the Italian story of Tlipana, for example, a woman had fourteen daughters, and the youngest, named Tlipana, was not well behaved (as was typical of shamans as children). When her mother (who was an herbalist) sent her and her sisters into the mountains every morning to collect herbs, the youngest spent her time chasing butterflies and doing other unproductive activities.

Upset that Tlipanawasn't helping them and tired of her shenanigans, her sisters left her in the forest. Scared and alone, Tlipana called out, "Oh wolves of the woodland, come to me. All ye animals of the forest come to me. Come, you dogs, and cats of the forest." Then, a large cat with fiery eyes and two humps appeared. As was common in these tales, Tlipana was afraid during her first real encounter with the otherworld, but the kindly cat comforted her and helped her to gather herbs before showing her a shortcut so that she was able to beat her sisters home.

Once home, the cat continually took Tlipana's food, leaving her to starve (helping spirits often demanded the shamans go through a period of fasting). At last, Tlipana began catching mice, making them a blood sacrifice to the cat. The mice pleaded with her and begged her to let them go, but she ignored them. Each time she fed the cat, it lost a hump and finally turned from red to a beautiful white.

Eventually, the cat left for the castle of red coral, so the girl told her mother she was going there, as well. She set out and, after a long time, came to a house with no windows or door to get in. From out of the house came a butterfly; she caught it and took one of its wings. She put this in a hankerchief on which she fell asleep (perhaps symbolizing her own soul's upcoming spirit journey).

When she woke up, the house was gone, and in its place was a massive lake filled with swans. One of the swans told her to climb on its back, and it carried her to the other side of the lake. It told her how to get to the Castle of Red Coral.

When she made it to the castle, a wolf appeared at the gate, but she needed only to touch him on the head with a pen; he let her in. The same was true with a lion and a snake inside the castle. At last, she found her helping spirit, the white cat, who turned into a handsome young man, and the two of them were able to marry.

The story of Tlipana illustrated a number of common aspects of the shaman's relationship with a helping spirit, including the notion that they would eventually marry. There were exceptions to this generally positive relationship, however. While most of these spirits were good, demanding that the shaman help humanity and act kindly, there were evil spirits as well, which forced people to become evil witches. Indeed, rival shamans would often accuse each other of being evil witches. When, for example, a Tlingit shaman failed to heal someone, he or she would accuse someone of being a witch. The village would then torture this individual for a confession and execute him or her.

Among the Aborigines, murder done by magic was one of the major reasons for cross-social warfare. Other tribes and rival shamans were often used as scapegoats in these accusations. The shamans from different Haida and Crow clans would use their mystical powers to try to kill each other, while the Klamath would blame sickness and bad weather on a spirit that had been placed on Mount Shasta by a shaman of the Modoc people. In South America, the accusation of one shaman against another could lead to military raids against another tribe while, in the agricultural societies of later Europe, one of the cunning folks' primary jobs was to discover and accuse other witches, a job that was eventually passed on to the newest religious leaders. What this meant, however, was that there was a clear belief that the neighbors helping spirits were as harmful as one's own spirits were helpful. Thus, stories could be told about both kind and wicked helping spirits of the same type, depending on with whom they were working.

When Fairies and Deities Are Born

Frigid winds buffet the small shelter in which people have gathered to share stories with the coming of darkness where a primal wilderness stretches out for thousands of miles . . . a wilderness in which humans are not always the dominant the species. Bears and lions stalk this wilderness, and wolves can be heard to howl around them. The sounds grow ever closer, causing children to huddle against their mother, and men to look to their weapons
.

Quite often, the tales these people shared were much more than just stories; around the world, many people attached a certain religious importance to the sharing of tales. Perhaps even more common, however, was a fear of darkness – the night. The darkness contained earthly beasts but, perhaps most horrifying of all, were the others. Bogymen, dark spirits that snatched children away and stole souls, leaving behind empty sickly husks were common in European tales, and they, too, haunted the night. Giants and trolls who opposed the gods, as they did in Germanic, Kalasha, and Greek lore, were also thought to be outside.

This scene of people huddled in the darkness probably wasn't the origin of people's belief in fairies and deities. Believing in powers greater than oneself was likely altogether natural, hardwired into our brains (Linden, 2007). It was, however, where people likely had the time and inclination to share stories of the otherworld, along with their ideas about the nature of the deities that inhabited it. This was one of the two most important places where deities and fairies took form; the other was the one in which people searched for food, struggled to survive and, in general, were most likely to call upon unknown powers.

One of the first places people were likely to call on help from the divine was on the hunt for food. This was perhaps why so many fairies and their kin were closely tied to the animals of the forest and hunters, in general. In the Highlands of Scotland, for example, deer were believed to be the cattle of the fairies; fairy women would take the form of deer and take revenge on those who killed them. Therefore, the hunter must win his game through the use of iron and so forth. The Kalasha had fairies that also owned the ibex (mountain goats), and these, too, would either help or hinder hunters. At the same time, Japan had mountain kami, which were most often (though not always) conceived of as female and were closely tied to the hunters. In turn, each of these spirits also became agricultural and/or pastoral spirits, though many continued to help and hinder hunters in tales.

120

The Glaistig of Scotland, for example, was a fairy being who dwelt in the forests, rocks, and lakes. She appeared quite frequently to hunters out in the lonely woods and would appear in some cases to be a spirit of hunting. Yet, she now took an interest in cattle and the herding of animals. She would help herd the cattle, and an offering of milk was poured into a hole for her in gratitude.

> When the family was at dinner, or the herdsman had fallen asleep and neglected his charge, she kept the cattle out of mischief; and, though not seen, was heard shouting after them and driving them to their proper pastures. In this respect, she behaved like an old and careful herdsman. If the cows were not clean milked, she punished the dairy-maid by some unchancy prank. At night, she kept the calves from the cows (a needful and useful occupation before the days of enclosures and plentiful farm accommodation), and its substance in the milk. In summer, she accompanied the cattle to the hill pastures, and there had her portion of milk duly poured out for her in the evening in a stone near the fold. Unless this was done, the calves were found next morning with the cows, the cream not risen from the milk, a cow was found dead, or some other mischance occurred. She was not supposed ever to enter a house, but to stay in some ravine near a Fairy residence. (Campbell)

Despite her typical occupation of herding cattle in the Highlands, however, in some places she became a household spirit attached to a specific home. She would not follow the family to a new home, even if it was rebuilt on the same property. As a house spirit, she would do all the things typically expected of these spirits (sweeping, arranging the furniture, etc.).

In addition to these two occupations, the Glaistig became an industrial fairy who would bestow skills on craftsmen. In one tale, a Glaistig worked a smith's forge every night and left things in a different order. Annoyed that someone appeared to be interfering, the smith hid to attack whoever entered. Soon after night rose, the Glaistig entered with a pet chicken. Though the chicken warned her that someone was watching, she ignored it, saying, "It's only mice."

> *At this point, the smith struck the old one on the head with his hammer and caught hold of the little one... Before the smith let his captive go, the Glaistig left a parting gift— that the son should succeed the father as smith in the place till the third generation. This proved to be the case, and the last was smith in Strontian, some forty years ago (Campbell, 1900).*

Just as previous people had won the right to farm, others had to win the right to be skilled at their craft. Other stories about the Glaistig, granting people their craft, were less dramatic, however, with the Glaistig allowing them to choose either to become masters of their craft, but always poor, or clumsy, but always rich. Thus, from her, a person could gain skills as a tailor, a carpenter, a poet, and so on. This perhaps tied, in part, into another feature of the Glaistig - her nature as a protector of those whom people would consider fools. She despised people who looked down on fools and punished them. It may be that she only gave the rest of humanity limited gifts, so they would always know that they weren't perfect and would be kinder to those in need. Her limited gifts may also have been related to the fact that so many skilled people remained poor, while those who seemed terrible at their jobs could inexplicably become successful.

With her four separate roles—in hunting, herding, housework, and providing skill in crafts—one could see a fairy's ability to transform with society. At the same time, she retained many of her old traits because there were still hunters while there were tailors. Perhaps more interesting than the transformation in her role, however, was the notion that she sometimes had to be dominated. She was chased by the hunter's dogs as if she was a wild animal, and she was threatened by blacksmiths. While she was involved with hunters, it was the herdsmen with whom she had a good relationship.

As already discussed, people got along with the nature spirits better, in many places, right into the modern day. So why did the people of Britain seem more willing to threaten and cajole fairies than many others? They were by no means the only ones who did so, of course, yet it still seemed interesting that this should be so pervasive in their stories. One might presume that this was because of Britain's history of new people coming in to conquer a land's previous inhabitants, but nearly every place in Europe and Asia had a similar history of conquest. Rather, it would seem that this idea of needing to dominate the spirits of nature came from something within the way the people of Britain lived and thought, though exactly what this was could be difficult to ascertain. Again, it was this difficulty in coming up with satisfactory theories about fairy tales and deities that made understanding folklore so frustrating and fascinating at the same time.

Part of the challenge to finding this understanding was that the nature of fairies came to vary, not only from era to era, but also from place to place and person to person. This situation was made all the more complex by the fact that Europe was once awash with stories of fairies told in thousands of languages as migration after migration of people found their way into the continent. These stories mixed together changed with social upheaval and then were overwhelmed by the next migratory wave. While it's true that deities altered form to fit the needs of the people who believed in them, it was also true that they altered form as new people added to their stories. As they were passed down generation to generation through stories, the beliefs of many people mixed together to form the roots of the fairy tales known today.

Given that fairy tales were tied to the people who told them, it was interesting to note that there were only three primary language families remaining in Europe. These included the Basque, tucked away in the mountains between France and Spain, the Uralic Language Family in the North, which included the Sami, Finns, Estonians, Hungarians, Mari-El, along with few others, and the Indo-European language families, which dominated nearly everything else from Ireland to India.

When people learned how thoroughly the Indo-European language dominated Europe, they often wondered two things about folklore. The first was simple: Can we discover root ideas that were likely held by the original proto-Indo-European speakers? The answer to this was likely "yes." By looking at the religious ideas contained in the language itself, as well as the common elements among most all Indo-European speakers, we came to understand what they may have believed before they split into so many different peoples.

The other question people often asked was, what did the people believe before the Indo-Europeans came to dominate Europe's languages? This question was much harder to answer, for it was not as simple as searching for ideas different from those of the Indo-Europeans. There were also people who migrated to Europe after the Indo-Europeans. What's more, we could not be certain when the Indo-Europeans migrated into Europe. We could trace the genetic changes that occurred in Europe due to migrations of new people, but as of yet, scholars still questioned whether the Indo-Europeans entered Europe during the beginning of the Neolithic Era, bringing farming with them, or thousands of years later as a migratory people from the Steppes who were likely very much like the later Huns and

Mongols.

The question is not small, because it speaks to the origins of figures such as Zeus, Jupiter, and Thor, the culture in which these deities were developed for thousands of years before entering Europe, and the one in which they survived in Europe afterwards. Many, for example, look at the art of the Neolithic era and imagine a different world, a different religion than the one of the Ancient Greeks, Germans, and Romans. However, if the Indo-Europeans entered Europe during the Neolithic Era, then nearly every interpretation of Neolithic Art and religion in Europe is likely wrong, and many of the beings people claim to be pre-Indo-European deities likely are not.

Either way, I would argue that the pre-Indo-Europeans and the Indo-Europeans likely had enough in common that many of their beliefs merged together fairly easily. Take the example of the Etruscans who spoke an extinct non-Indo-European language. Despite their different language family, the Etruscans have enough in common with the Greek beliefs that they easily adopted many of these. It might be, then, that many of a pre-Indo-Europeans' beliefs and deities were similar to those of the Indo-Europeans—similar enough, in any case, that separating the two could be difficult. As an example, the Etruscans seemed to have added many tales to that of Hercle, making him the slayer of the Minotaur in place of Theseus amd. in one work of art, a protector of Hera against a band of satyrs, a job the Greek hero would never have undertaken (Grummond, Nanc). An even more pertinent example could perhaps be found in the case of the Sky Father. The Thunder God figure wasn't the king of the deities only among most Indo-European people; he was also important among many other peoples.

Waller and Kolar (2014) argued that part of the purpose of Stonehenge and similar monuments was to create acoustics similar to thunder when clapping one's hands. He found that caverns, which had the best acoustics, were most likely to have cave paintings in them, indicating that these acoustics had some impact on the selection of sacred sites.

Among the Pygmies of the Rainforests in Congo, Khonvoum, a sky god, was the supreme god, and he sent messages to humans through his elephant, Gor (The Thunderer). He also was responsible for hunting (Bartlett, 2009).

Among the Babylonians, Marduk was a thunder deity who defeated Timat. Like the Roman sky and thunder god, he was associated with the planet Jupiter. In addition, China's head deity, Shangdi was another heavenly/sky deity of weather, victory in battle, and so on. Anu was a sky god who was the supreme god of the Sumerians. In Northern Asia, the head deity was often a sky god, as well. The Selkup believed that this sky deity gave them their souls and took them away at the time of their death. He caused the wind and the thunder, the snow, and the rain. Like Zeus, he was the bringer and controller of weather. Like God in Russian folklore, he contended with the evil spirits that dwelt on the earth, throwing lighting at them, even when they tried to hide inside trees, rocks, or people.

In other words, nearly all people groups had a sky god associated with lighting, and whether he was their king deity or not, one could easily see how the legends of such a deity could be absorbed into those of Zeus, Jupiter, Thor, and others likewise. Further, in both places in which the Proto-Indo-European language was presumed to form (Turkey or the north end of the Black Sea), it could easily have influenced and been influenced by the existing Eastern European belief system, long before becoming the dominant language.

Perhaps the question wasn't what came before the Indo-European people, but what was different from their primary belief systems. One clear difference between the Germanic,

Irish, and Greek myths came in the form of the magical creatures that worked as craftsmen for the magical realm. Among the Greeks, the being that forged magnificent and magical things was the Cyclops. Among the Germanic peoples, the dwarfs were the ones who forged magical items for the gods, such as Thor's Hammer. Yet among the Irish, it was the leprechauns who acted as craftsmen for the fairy race, the faded deities. What was interesting about these three beings was that, while they all had the same job as craftsmen within the realm of fairies and gods, they were wildly different from the others, especially with regard to their role in human tales.

The best-known tales of Cyclops involved them acting as giants and kidnapping humans, while the best-known stories about leprechauns had them being captured and robbed by peasants. This would seem to indicate that, despite their similar roles in the pantheons of their respective peoples, these beings were completely different—that is, one didn't come from the other. It seemed unlikely that these differences were due to the Cyclops shrinking in size to become leprechauns or dwarfs in places like Germany, where giants were so famous. The opposite idea—that the Cyclops grew in stature to match that of the deities—while possible, still seemed unlikely.

These differences may be due to the fact that, unlike the coming of agriculture, in which the spirits of a location, plants, the earth, water, and weather could all easily be adopted to become the spirits of the field, or the coming of pastoralism, in which the spirits of the animals and hunting could be adopting to help care for domesticated animals, there was no obvious spirit to take on the role of metal working. Without one, people were left to either develop a completely new one or adopt a less obvious one, resulting in the differences between these fairies.

The spread of bronze in Europe occurred after the spread of agriculture, but before the spread of wagons. In other words, these fairy smiths either survived the coming of the Indo-European language, or they were adopted after it. Once again, one could see that trying to determine pre- vs. post-Indo-European ideas was nearly impossible without some information regarding the exact date of this event.

Regardless, however, the difference between these three beings was interesting, because it pointed to another aspect of each of these cultures that cropped up repeatedly. Among the Celts, with their belief in capturing Leprechauns, threatening Glaistigs, and tricking Bogles out of their land, there was a frequent theme of winning treasure by capturing and overpowering weaker magical beings. Among the Greeks, while one could trick a Cyclops or capture a satyr by getting it drunk, the bulk of their beings often loomed large over humans. The Germanic dwarfs potentially were powerful and weak. They had magnificent halls, great weapons, and belts that made them ten times stronger than a person, but, at the same time, they could live in poverty and be assaulted by peasants just like Leprechauns. I would argue that, in this sense, each of these creatures helped reflect many of the fairy tales of their respective peoples, showing that, despite any similarities from language or otherwise, there were also clear differences between them.

Another outlier from the typical goddess of the Indo-European people was the aforementioned Glaistig. For one thing, threatening a goddess figure in order to gain magical gifts seemed to go against the general thrust of Indo-European lore (though it fits in nicely with Celtic lore). Perhaps more interesting, however, was the Glaistig's unusual fear of dogs, for, as Davidson pointed out, goddesses are continually depicted as having dogs at their side. This was true in Celtic and German lands, in Greece where Artemis and Hecate both had hunting dogs, and in Germany with Pertche and Holle. So the Glaistig was clearly different from the typical Indo-European Goddess figure.

Perhaps the difference cave from the fact that the Glaistig was often considered to be a spirit of a person who had died, making it separate in some ways from the general wilderness court. This would mean she could be a potential target of the dogs that sought to bring ghosts to the realm of the dead. It was also possible that her fear of dogs was related to the Germanic notion that the wild hunt would chase down spirits of nature, though there was very little evidence for this aspect of the Wild Hunt in Scotland otherwise. It seemed more likely that this aspect of her nature was one of the things that made Scotland unique. Whether this uniqueness was new or very ancient, however, I can't say.

Turning to the gods of Europe, perhaps the most unique of all is Odin.

The Evolution of Odin

Odin was the king of the deities in Germanic lore, making him unique among the Indo-European peoples, and even among the neighboring Ugric peoples, for whom the thunder god was usually the king. Such thunder deities included Zeus in Greece, Jupiter in Rome, Perun in Russia, Indra in the Veda of India, Ukko of Finland, and more. According to Davidson, this role in Germanic lore was initially filled by Tiwaz (Tyr), who once shared power with Wodan before his role was taken over by Odin and Thor.

While Odin was a sky god, he was also psychopomp (a Grimm Reaper figure that leads souls to the land of the dead), a lord of the dead, and a shamanistic figure who lacked the power of lighting, which, instead, belonged to his son, Thor. As stated before, this was an extremely unusual situation, leading to the question of where Odin came from. This wasn't a minor question when it came to folk religion and fairy tales. Odin, after all, was a very hands-on god at times; most of the founding dynasties in Europe claimed linage from him at one time. Odin also had a tendency to wander the world in disguise, so he could very well have inspired many of the tales in which the hero encountered a funny old man who helped them; he certainly showed up in this role in Estonian tales. What's more, his servants, the swan maidens (Valkyrie), appeared in many tales as well, so understanding his origins could tell us much about many of the different elements of European lore.

Unfortunately, the questions of Odin's origin and the reason he became King of the Norse pantheon don't have an easy answer. There is a lot of debate and a lot of evidence for different opinions. It is likely that no one alive today can know for certain why Odin became the head deity of the Norse. However, this is also certainly one of those cases in which merely trying to answer the question can teach much about the past and, perhaps, our own present.

The Roman historian Tacitus stated that, among the Germanic people, "Mercury is the principal object of their adoration; whom, on certain days, they think it lawful to propitiate even with human victims." With this statement, Tacitus was trying to explain the nature of Odin in terms that the Romans could understand, so his statement should not be taken at face value. However, this does point to the notion that Odin seemed to have a lot in common with Mercury, as well as Hermes. To begin with, they were all psychopomps, leading the souls of the dead to the afterlife. They were all lords of poetry, and they were all masters of deceit. Odin, like Hermes, was even represented at times by a phallus. Given that these three deities were shamanistic characters, and that they were all deities of the European branch of people with the same root language, it was tempting to presume that they might all stem from the same deity. However, this still begs the question: Why would the Romans start worshiping Hermes, a shamanistic deity of the liminal realm between the living and the dead?

One place to begin searching for the answer to these questions was among the Etruscans, who were genetically related to the Neolithic tribes that entered Europe 7,500 years ago (Ghirotto, Silvia; et al, 2013). What's more, they didn't speak an Indo-European language. However, like the Indo-Europeans, they had a lighting god at the head of their pantheon named Tinia. Unlike Zeus, he didn't have a beard, and he led a more prophetic religion than that of the Greeks or Romans, - one similar to that of the Hebrews in the sense that prophets would read and interpret the word of god. (This made sense, given that the Etruscans had origins in the same region as the Hebrews and had been farmers for a long time.)

Odin, too, was a very prophetic god, having sacrificed to gain the power of divination. However, Tinia was a lord of lighting, so why would one think that a deity similar to him could have influenced Odin? There were two reasons: first, he, like Odin, was associated with the afterlife. Second, and perhaps most interesting, he ruled over a divine tribe known as the Aiser, just like Odin. Given that they were both weather gods, it is very tempting to connect them (Grummond, 2006). One could, for example, see a scenario in which two peoples, one related to the Etruscans, and the other to the Indo-Europeans, encountering each other and mixing their gods in a way that kept Zeus/Thor intact by allowing him to keep lighting while Tinia/Odin took over as king of the deities. This isn't necessarily likely to be the case, however. As previously stated, this is, in many ways, a question without an answer; it has only possibilities and relationships. There is no serious evidence, beyond the single word similarity, that the Norse were influenced by a people similar to the Etruscans at all.

Perhaps the best place to look for an answer was with the Lithuanian neighbors of the Scandinavians, where we found that the deity Velinas was very important. Velinas, like Odin, was a one-eyed seer, a trickster figure, whose name conjugated to veles, meaning the phantoms of the dead, which he led on a wild hunt across the earth and sky. He was important enough that nearly 400 place names had one of his many epitaphs within them. Forty percent of these were swamps, for his home lay beneath the water in the underworld. He was a lord of the water and the hanged. In lore, he would change his shape in order to bring this death to others, becoming a pretty boy in order to lure girls to dance with him and then caused them to hang themselves. He would also use his power of persuasion to lure men into an illusory castle to dance in what turned out to be a bog, where they sank to their deaths. He could turn into a black horse and drown people in swamps or pull them into the water directly, often leaving behind the sound of fiddle music to mark the person's passing. Like almost all deities, then, he was both harmful and helpful (Gimbutas, 1974).

He brought gifts to the poor, stole from the wealthy, swindled the swindlers, and gave supernatural aid to those who needed it. Sometimes, he appeared to be a small shepherd boy and, in this form, he played with the others; however, when he threwa disk, it traveled for miles, giving him away.

In the Estonian tale of "Slyboots," a hero was trying to find his way into the underworld realm, and an old man appeared to give him a magical shellfish that allowed him to do this. This old man may have been the consort to the Queen of the Meadows, a role filled by an Odin-like figure with one eye. In another tale with this one-eyed Estonian deity:

126

A girl who was out in a wood all night saw a fire on a hill and finds an old man standing by it. He had a long gray beard, and only one eye, and wore an iron helmet. He threw it on the ground, when two girls appeared, and the village child stayed with them till morning, when a young woman gave her a brooch which would enable her to return to the Misty Hill whenever she pleased. On reaching home, she found she had been absent seven years. On the first opportunity she returned to the hill by night, and her friend, who had given her the brooch, told her that the old man was the King of the Misty Hill, and the consort of the Meadow Queen. She was their daughter. The girl continued her nightly visits to the Misty Hill; but after her marriage, her husband discovered her disappearanced and, taking her for a werewolf, tried to burn her; but the King of the Misty Hill carried her away to his dwelling uninjured (Kirby).

In many ways, this darker aspect of Odin is similar to Varuna, lord of the dead in the Veda (another source of knowledge of Indo-European Lore), which has many aspects of the chief deity. Each of the stars is one of his eyes, spying on the world. He can catch lies in snares and is essentially the omnipotent creator. He is also the lord of the drowned and the underworld beneath the waves and swamps, and horses were born from his waters (Heestermman, Hoek, and Oort, 1992).

One couldn't help but see similarities between Varuna and Odin. People would offer Odin the treasures won at the end of a battle by sinking these in the water of a swamp. This method of sacrifice seemed to indicate that, perhaps, at one time, people viewed Odin as living beneath the waves before he took over the role of sky deity as well. Further, Odin's role as the god of the hanged was clear, not only due to the fact that he hung himself in order to gain secret knowledge, but also from the fact that those sacrificed to him were hung as well:

> And they (Scandinavians) incessantly offer up all kinds of sacrifices, and make oblations to the dead, but the noblest of sacrifices, in their eyes, is the first human being whom they have taken captive in war; for they sacrifice him to Ares, whom they regard as the greatest god. And the manner in which they offer up the captive is not by sacrificing him on an altar only, but also by hanging him to a tree, or throwing him among thorns, or killing him by some of the other most cruel forms of death. Thus, then, do the inhabitants of Thule (Norway) live. (Heinemann, 1919)

The brutal picture that this paints of human sacrifice, and especially the hanging, certainly points to Odin as a deity of death. Presuming, then, that Odin is a god of the underworld and a lord of the dead who took on many of the aspects of the head deity, this still begs the question, why would people start worshipping a deity of the dead as the king of the gods?

A man from the Ottoman Empire observed the Rus merchants going to one of the figures of their gods, asking it to help him make a good trade in return for some offering. If this failed, he would go to the next statue, then the next until, at last, he made a good trade. The Norse, it seemed, were very willing to go from one god to another until they got what they wanted. Imagine a situation in which it seemed that their head deity had stopped listening, and fear became endemic.

During the Iron Age, death from violence began to increase, as shown by an increased number of bodies uncovered that had been assaulted from behind. Women, men, children—it didn't matter; they were shot and hit from behind in substantial enough numbers that the evidence remains strong for these types of attacks even today. Looking at

Tacitus's description of this time period, we saw that a chieftain's ability to rule was based on his ability to act valiantly and win battles. War was so craved, according to him, that if a people's...

> native country be long sunk in peace and inaction; many of the young nobles repair to some other state then engaged in war. For, besides that repose iss unwelcome to their race, and toils and perils afford them a better opportunity of distinguishing themselves; they are unable, without war and violence, to maintain a large train of followers.

This situation sounds similar to the Grecian Dark Ages. However, we might also think of it as similar to gangs fighting for money, prestige, and territory. Currently, the uncertainty created by such violence is causing the people of Mexico to turn, in ever-greater numbers, to Santa Muerte, the saint of death.

Although there are massive differences between the Ancient Germanic and Modern Mexican cultures, it is still possible to see in this example a series of situations by which a deity like Odin could become the most important of all. This is especially true given that Odin was a shaman figure with the powers of both male and female shamans—an enticing figure for a time of crises, given that we know that the Germanic peoples did turn to a powerful female shaman during times of crises.

In Germanic lore, female shamanistic figures, known as Volva, had a lot of political influence, for they seemed to have had a near monopoly on predicting the future. They would often be invited by kings and lords to feasts where they were honored above everyone else. That the Volva were shamans was made very clear in a number of sagas and records of their doing. In one incidence, for example, the fish grew scarce, and people began to starve, so a Volva was called forth:

> She had had nine sisters, and they were all spae-queens, and she was the only one now living. It was a custom of Thorbjorg, in the winter time, to make a circuit, and people invited her to their houses, especially those who had any curiosity about the season, or desired to know their fate; inasmuch as Thorkell was chief franklin thereabouts, he considered that it concerned him to know when the scarcity, which overhung the settlement, should cease. He invited, therefore, the spae-queen to his house, and prepared for her a hearty welcome, as was the custom wherever a reception was accorded a woman of this kind. (Sephton, 1880)

Though records of them are not frequent, it does seem likely that Volva typically traveled in groups of nine or three, and there seems to be a number of tales about them—or perhaps the goddesses they are meant to reflect—in which one of these "fates" grows angry and curses a newly born child. The most famous group of these stories, of course, is the "Sleeping Beauty" tale.

There is, however, another role for the Volva and their kin in fairy tales, and that is as the magical woman who advises the hero. In one story, a girl, trying to journey to the Well at the End of the World, was lost and could find no one to help her. That was until, at last, "a queer little old woman, all bent double, told her where it was, and how she could get to it." This little old woman could be one of many things; she could be a goddess, a helping spirit, or a seer akin to a Volva. It is often difficult to know the difference in such stories because, in many ways, the Volva reflects goddesses.

A high seat was prepared for her, and a cushion lay thereon in which were poultry-feathers. Now, when she came in the evening, accompanied by the man who had been sent to meet her, she was dressed in such wise that she had a blue mantle over her, with strings for the neck, and it was inlaid with gems quite down to the skirt. On her neck she had glass beads. On her head she had a black hood of lambskin, lined with ermine. A staff she had in her hand, with a knob thereon; it was ornamented with brass, and inlaid with gems round about the knob. Around her she wore a girdle of soft hair, and therein was a large skin-bag, in which she kept the talismans needful to her in her wisdom. She wore hairy calf-skin shoes on her feet, with long and strong-looking thongs to them, and great knobs of latten at the ends. On her hands she had gloves of ermine-skin, and they were white and hairy within. Now, when she entered, all men thought it their bounden duty to offer her becoming greetings, and these she received according as the men were agreeable to her.

The franklin Thorkell took the wise-woman by the hand, and led her to the seat prepared for her. He requested her to cast her eyes over his herd, his household, and his homestead. She remained silent altogether. During the evening the tables were set; and now I must tell you what food was made ready for the spae-queen. There was prepared for her porridge of kid's milk, and hearts of all kinds of living creatures there found were cooked for her....

The preparations were made for her which she required for the exercise of her enchantments. She begged them to bring to her those women who were acquainted with the lore needed for the exercise of the enchantments, and which is known by the name of Weird-songs, but no such women came forward. Then was search made throughout the homestead if any woman were so learned. Then answered Gudrid, "I am not skilled in deep learning, nor am I a wise-woman, although Halldis, my foster-mother, taught me, in Iceland, the lore which she called Weird-songs."
"Then art thou wise in good season," answered Thorbjorg; but Gudrid replied, "That lore and the ceremony are of such a kind, that I purpose to be of no assistance therein, because I am a Christian woman."
Then answered Thorbjorg, "Thou mightest perchance afford thy help to the men in this company, and yet be none the worse woman than thou wast before; but to Thorkell give I charge to provide here the things that are needful." Thorkell thereupon urged Gudrid to consent and she yielded to his wishes. The women formed a ring round about, and Thorbjorg ascended the scaffold and the seat prepared for her enchantments. Then sang Gudrid the weird-song in so beautiful and excellent a manner, that to no one there did it seem that he had ever before heard the song in voice so beautiful as now. The spae-queen thanked her for the song. "Many spirits," said she, "have been present under its charm, and were pleased to listen to the song, who before would turn away from us, and grant us no such homage. And now are many things clear to me which before were hidden both from me and others. And I am able this to say that the dearth will last no longer—the season improving as spring advances. The epidemic of fever which has long oppressed us will disappear quicker than we could have hoped.

It is interesting that only one person could be found who could sing the necessary songs, and that more people hadn't memorized them. This points not only the sacred nature of these songs but, also, possibly to the fact that singing them involved more than following a script. Often, a shaman's assistant must react to and change his or her song according to what is happening with the shaman.

In the "Tale of the Nisan Shamaness" from Manchuria, there is a similar difficulty in finding a singer for the shamaness.

> *She struck her tambourine and drum, praying in a murmur to the spirit; however, the three or four village shamans who struck their tambourines and accompanied her were so out of harmony that the Nisan shaman said, "If it is as discordant as this, how will I travel to the underworld?"*

In Nisan's tale, someone must be fetched from a distant village who could sing in harmony with Nisan In both and, indeed, nearly all shaman ceremonies, the music was meant to summon spirits who could help the shaman/Volva gain knowledge or perform some other task.

The story of Erik the Red illustrated two important points. The first was that the Volva were very clearly related to shamanistic traditions. Second, the Volva were of the utmost importance to the society of the Germanic peoples. They forced peace settlements between warring parties by causing amnesia. They also cast spells to dull the weapons and hardened the bodies of those trying to kill each other. Through stories like these, one could see that the Volva were often figures who worked to maintain peace.

Finally, the Volva also were figures of justice and would refuse to take money from tyrants who overcharged their people for rent. The importance of these female shaman figures in people's lives meant that they likely had a lot of influence, and Odin used their powers, or, as Loki accused him:

> *They say that with spells | in Samsey once*
> *Like witches with charms didst thou work;*
> *And in witch's guise | among men didst thou go;*
> *Unmanly thy soul must seem.*

In other words, Odin once traveled the world as a Volva, even dressing and possibly appearing as a female. This wasn't atypical of male shamans (nor was it atypical for female shamans to dress as men). Perhaps the most interesting idea contained in this statement was that Odin would likely have been more important to the Volva than a deity, like Tyr, in many regards. Like Odin, they were often associated with death cults and may have been the females so often mentioned as preparing sacrifices, as well as funeral rights, to him. They were also often symbolized, like Odin, by the horse, the symbol of the underworld. It was likely, then, that Odin was one of their most important deities, which, considering their influence, could have elevated Odin in the eyes of the people.

David Miller had another interesting theory about Odin's rise to prominence, believing that the Roman frontier created a...

> violent, dangerous, and treacherous world. Roman military supremacy deprived men of any expectation but that of eventual destruction. Therefore, religion reoriented itself to represent the condition in which the frontier world then existed as the normal condition of the world....

Further, according to Miller, the cult of Odin was a pessimistic cult. Odin was a dour, violent, and deceitful god. Prisoners of war were sacrificed to him; "He was the lord of the carrion eaters that haunted the battlefield. He was a god who would deliberately cause war where none existed, in order to claim for himself the souls of the slain." He did this to prepare, for Ragnorok, a hopeless battle that would spell the doom of the world and all life. His Hall was a mirror of the beer hall society of the warlords that sprang into prominence during the chaos of this time.

According to this hypothesis, Odin worship began to take shape in Germany, sometime between 2050 and 1800 years ago, as a reaction to the Roman invasion of Germany.

This is an intriguing idea, and it would seem to answer a lot of questions about Odin's nature. However, it has one flaw. How did the cult of Odin push north into Scandinavia, well beyond the Roman frontier? It seems more likely that Odin's origin is in the North, in Scandinavia, among the Proto-Germanic peoples, hundreds of years before they traveled south to the Roman Empire. In this case, the Roman frontier would have altered Odin's character, creating new stories that would have spread throughout his cult, but he wouldn't have originated there.

If we presume that Odin's origin lies with the Proto-Germanic people in Scandinavia, it may be that he emerged from the constant cultural clashes that must have occurred between the Neolithic peoples and the hunter-gatherers in this region. Scandinavia has one of the highest percentages of DNA from the first hunter-gatherers of Europe, a percentage that is likely much higher in the past before intermarriage with the rest of Europe diluted it. This means that Odin himself may have been, in part, a pre-Neolithic deity mixed with an Indo-European deity.

The mingling of large numbers of Neolithic and pre-Neolithic peoples in the same place possibly also led to much of the conflict early on, leading Odin to be a deity, not only of the Roman frontier, but, also, of the Neolithic frontier. Regardless, it does seem likely that much of Odin's character is due to a traumatic event, one that reshaped the pantheon that people worshipped.

Despite Miller's assertion that Odin's is a pessimistic cult, there is a much hope in his nature. It is often true that to those standing on the outside—figures like Santa Muerte and Odin—seem dark and depressing. This, however, is a misunderstanding of their nature and human emotion. Santa Muerte is believed by many to protect them from violence and death. Odin, too,is called on for protection. He gives hope as well as knowledge. In the Skaldskaparmal, he flies over the earth in the shape of a bird, dribbling wisdom and life from his beak. He is the bringer of knowledge to humanity. This gives him a different role than Zeus, who also turns into an eagle, but is often associated with trying to withhold knowledge, such as the knowledge of fire.

This bringing of knowledge to humanity, along with his use of Valkyries, led to another possible source for much of Odin's character. Mongolia, North Eastern Europe, had genetics from Mongolia/Siberia which showed us that there was a large migration of people from this region, even if we couldn't be certain when this migration occurred. Further, Odin had much in common with the deities of the peoples of Mongolia and Eastern Siberia. Among the Beryut, for example, the Eagle was the one who brought the knowledge of shamanism to humanity, just as Odin did to the Germanic people. European deities had this form. Rather, it was in the form of an eagle. This wasn't to say that Odin got his eagle from the east, as many Indo-Europeans had a deity that could turn into an eagle. Rather, it was to point out that the two people had similar deities that took the form of an eagle, so their ideas could easily have been adopted. Further, Odin, like Erlik, the lord of the dead in parts of Siberia, had Swan Maidens under his command. Finally, Odin's eight-legged horse was similar to the eight-legged reindeer that an Eastern shaman rode, or an eight-legged horse ridden by a Buryat shaman.

Odin also had much in common with Finnish and Sami shamanism, including his ravens and his wolves. As will be discussed, further in the section on "Neighboring Peoples," it was common for those Scandinavians, wishing to learn magic, to travel to Finland to learn from a shaman. We shouldn't be too surprised that this practice could influence the religion of the Scandinavian people and, quite possibly, the nature of Odin.

There was another possible source for Odin's Eastern Shamanistic behavior, however, regarding Attila the Hun and his armies. The invasion of Europe by Attila, the Hun was one of the most shocking and transformative events on record in Europe. Hedeager (2011) pointed to a number of similarities between Odin and Attila's historical stories. They both came from Asia during a time of Rome; they were both great warriors who won all but one battle, which they fought to a draw with a people who eventually became their most important allies, and they both had three sons. Perhaps more important, however, was that Odin came from a land of shamanistic peoples. This didn't mean that Odin came from Attila, however, as the Germanic peoples worshiped an Odin-like figure hundreds of years before the Huns. It was possible, however, that Attila altered Odin's character.

There are just three more points I would like to make. First, we have no way of knowing what the pre-Indo-European deity of the Norse people was like, so it's also very possible that Odin's character is related to him, or even to her. Second, the father of the Thunder Gods in Greek and Roman lore (Cronus and Saturn, respectively) are not the monsters in movies in which they are now depicted. Instead, they are benevolent gods that ruled over a golden age for humanity. In many ways, Zeus/Jupiter's overthrow of them makes the world a worse place. Further, in India, the thunder deity Indra is such a letch that he, too, is toppled from his position as the head deity. He is portrayed as in the Rigveda. So perhaps the real question we need to ask is, "Why did people continue to worship Zeus and Jupiter as the king of the gods?" Perhaps the reason for this is that they saw kings as lecherous tyrants, so they simply accept that this is the nature of Zeus in stories. Perhaps, too, Odin is related to the father of the gods, in Indo-European lore, to Cronus or Saturn.

Finally, John Carey points to the notion that the idea of Odin sacrificing his own eye may have come from Irish lore, in which such stories are more common than in Scandinavian or Germanic lore. Here, figures such as Saint Brigit would pluck an eye from their faces in order to be able to serve supernatural powers, and a fountain would burst forth; Odin sacrificed his eye before a sacred fountain. Thus, in both cases, there was a deity who sacrificed of an eye and a magical fountain. Thomas Africa points out that Hannibal, the man who nearly defeated Rome and who lead an army of Celts through the Alpine mountains, had a single eye.

Hannibal's crossing of the Alps, with strange troops and monstrous beasts (elephants from Africa), must have left an impression on the Alpine tribes and the Celts of Northern Italy.

> Long after the great captain had returned to the mysterious land from whence he came, the barbarians of Spain and Italy who served him recounted the exploits of the guileful, one-eyed, war chief, who could change shape, had supernatural contacts, and had once led them against the hated Romans. (Verlag, 1975)

To the Germanic people whose world was being overwhelmed by the Romans, these tales of a hero who could fight the might of Rome, told by Celtic refugees, must have been very

132

appealing.

Returning to the original question of the exact reason that the Germanic people worship Odin as the king of the deities, it is something we'll never fully know. However, one thing likely is certain. Odin is the result of multiple deities and ideas mixing together, as well as a continuous evolution of religion over thousands of years. It is likely that all deities and all fairies are very much like Odin, the result of many events and many people. If such transformations weren't common, then all deities, and certainly all Indo-European deities, would be the same.

This transformation leads to the next chapter.

Influence from Neighbors and Migrations

As already mentioned in the discussion on fear, aspects of people's tales are often borrowed from, or inspired by, their neighbors. More than this, however, people sometimes use humans from other cultures as supernatural beings. In recent times, stories have used gypsies as a sort of mysterious mythological being, knowledgeable of the magical world. When someone needed to defeat a vampire or werewolf in the movies of the past century, they were likely to go to a gypsy for information. This was in spite of the fact that England had cunning, Ireland had fairy doctors, and Romania had magical practitioners that also existed into the modern era. In Hawaii, the Menehune were also a previous people who existed alongside the later Hawaiians and were treated in lore as essentially magical, fairy-like beings. The desire to turn outsiders into magical beings might have come from a tendency to tie magical knowledge to the unknown, which, in turn, meant neighboring peoples and outside elements could have a large impact on a people's folk beliefs. Another current example of this came from the Congo, where agricultural groups valued the Mbendjele (hunter-gatherers who lived in the forests) as healers; they admired them for their musical and dancing skills, often hiring them to perform at festivals. Indeed, one of the first mentions of these hunter-gatherers was in relation to their performing in Egypt. In essence, the agricultural peoples saw them as magical beings. For their part, the Mbendjele believed that the Bilo (their term for agricultural peoples) had the magical ability to curse them, so the Mbendjele avoided doing anything to openly offend the Bilo. Thus, both people saw each other as magical (Lewis, 2002).

In Scandinavian sagas, the Sami were considered to be highly skilled wizards and sorcerers, earning them both fear and admiration. Further, in early Norway, the law put witches and Finns in the same category by making it illegal to believe in Finns or witchcraft. Despite being few in number, it is arguable that the Sami had a huge impact on the Scandinavian folk religions. Sami women in lore were treated as seductive, often supernatural beings who would take revenge on Norse men who had wronged them or would gain power over kings through their supernatural powers. Further, in sagas, many Scandinavian heroes were trained by Sami wizards in the art of magic. If there was any truth to this idea that Scandinavian magico-religious practitioners would go to Sami shamans to learn, then many of the religious beliefs of the Sami would have been passed on in their folk religion from teacher to student. These students then became the most important influencers of Scandinavian folk religion and lore (Palsson, 1999).

It is fairly common in general for people to view what seems unique and rare to them as magical, or to place their focus upon it. Thus, things like voodoo have a much larger impact on our own ideas of magic than the percentage of the population would indicate. Indeed, despite the fact that so-called "voodoo dolls" exist in Europe, Japan, and many other places, we still think of these in association with voodoo, specifically, having forgotten our own roots in this regard. The problem is that most of the ideas of the other people are misunderstood and misinterpreted. Take Britain prior to and during 19th century, for example, where...

> It commonly happens that a neighbor folk speaking an unknown tongue gain the character of having something uncanny about them. Mr. Baring-Gould amusingly tells us how, in his childhood, a Devonshire nurse impressed him with the belief that all Cornishmen had tails. He actually asked a Cornish bookseller of his acquaintance if this were the case, and finally 'satisfied' his 'own mind that the good man had sat his off.' Professor Rhys observes that the children of Englishmen and Scotchmen settled in Wales are reported to be descended from the fairies, and it cannot surprise us to find a Welshman playing the part of an elfin serf (in an English fairy tale).
>
> In Germany and Holland, England is regarded as the native country of witches and night-hags. In Brittany, .it is the land of the dead. A North German legend, in Thorpe's Title Tide Stories, shows a Russian princess as a being of superior powers. All over the north of Europe, Russians, Finns, and Lapps are accounted wizards by other nations. In Napier's Folk-Lore of the West of Scotland, a Highland herd-boy is accused by his Lowland fellow servants of practicing the Black Art. (Jackson, 1883)

On top of all of this, the places where other people lived were often thought of as magical, an otherworld. In one Irish tale, for example, a man travels to Scandinavia, the land of the Vikings, in the same way people travel to the spirit world in other tales. Here, he encounters many magical beings, including a mouse who gives him the power to see the "treasure that the Danes had left hidden in Ireland." So the Vikings are made to be very much like the fairies of lore in this story, and they were even depicted as inhuman.

> Vikings are depicted as small, stocky, fierce old men with long red hair and sometimes having hairy skins and short tails, they have foxes for dogs, weasels for cats and crows for hens, and make bear out of a wild plant, heather, instead of from a domesticated plant.... Some Vikings are depicted as giants... they are also the originators of many skills such as burning stones for fertilizer, irrigating land, harvesting turf, making wheels for carts. (O'Giollain, 1994)

134

This means that the stories outsiders told about the supernatural and the taboos of which they warned carried quite a weight of importance. As discussed in the section on "Migrations," the people of Europe constantly came in contact with outsiders.

Vikings may not have been the only ones to be depicted as giants, however. One must think of the meaning behind the most famous quote by the giant from the story of "Jack and the Beanstalk:"

> Fee-fi-fo-fum,
> I smell the blood of an Englishman,
> Be he alive, or be he dead,
> I'll have his bones to grind my bread."

Here, the giant specifically mentions smelling an "Englishman," not just a human. Perhaps the reason he's so specific about this is that he's conceived of as a foreign entity, a foreign monster, or even a foreign person.

The strange relationship that exists between hunter-gatherers and agriculturalists, such as Sami and Scandinavian people, can perhaps help to explain the odd nature of Loki. In early lore, Loki is called a friend of Aesir, a friend of the deities of the Scandinavian people. In other words, he was an outsider to the regular deity system of the Scandinavian people and was best known in the far north among the people who were closest to the Sami.

There are also some interesting Sami tales about their encountering Russian migrants in their territory:

> The Sámi's best safety is to flee and hide from others. And that is why the Sámi of old built their goađit underground and hid there. The Sámi have had many enemies, such as the ruoššačuđit, who roamed across the Sámi homeland and killed everyone they found and took all their property. And, for this reason, the Sámi also hid their silver and money in the earth. And there is still a lot hidden in the ground in these parts even today. And the Russians also hid money in the ground here in the Sámi homeland. And at length the Sámi began to think of how they might kill those Russians. And they finally came upon a method with which to kill many ruoššačuđit. (DuBois, 2011)

These stories of killing the Russians often involved a lot of trickery, causing the Russians in the wilderness to become lost, to freeze to death, and so forth. Many times, the one doing this would be a brave noaidi (shaman). In one story, an old woman used the promise of food to lead some Russians into the dark forest, and some fires to lure them over a cliff.

Many Sami tales tend to be about tricking monsters in order to kill them. We see something similar in the behavior of the Selkup, in which deceit in war was not only heroic but also highly moral. This was necessary, given that both these peoples were surrounded by enemies that greatly outnumbered them. The impact on their tales is interesting. It also seems likely that these shamans tricking people had a huge impact on the people who encountered the native hunter-gatherers and their stories. In other words, our own fairy tales were likely influenced by encounters between hunter-gatherers and agriculturalists. Keep in mind that nearly everyone is related to both these peoples, and so our stories would have both perspectives, to a point—that is, we trick the giant and are tricked by the fairies.

Claire Porter and Frank Marlowe (2007) argued that hunter-gatherers in modern societies live in marginal regions, having been pushed into worse areas by agricultural and pastoral

135

societies. These marginal and more difficult to survive areas result in lower population density and resulting in more egaltarian societies. When people are struggling to survive, it's difficult to spend too much time on war, and people are dependent upon each other. This could also explain why it is so difficult for many of them to survive without trade with agricultural people.

> For example, pre-Holocene foragers, living in more productive habitats, may have had a considerably higher population density, resulting in different social organization. Larger groups in smaller areas could have favored greater territorial defense and perhaps resulted in more warfare. Bigelow suggested that domination by agriculturalists might account for the relatively peaceful nature of so many ethnographic foragers, and may explain their egalitarianism as well. It is, therefore, an important question whether foragers live in more marginal habitats. But the impression that they do may derive from the prominence in the more recent literature of certain foragers like the !Kung and Central Australians in very arid deserts, or the Inuit in icy tundra.

Those who refused or were unable to join the larger agricultural societies would likely have been pushed to the margins, just as fairies often were believed to have been. In the lore of the Celtic British and Irish, for example, the fairies were often believed to have been defeated people. In addition, there were many stories about fairies who lived in rags, in poverty, and so on. These fairies would often steal from the people, often nothing more than food, or they would demand food and punish those who didn't provide it in the same way that beggars would. This wasn't to say that the stories of fairies came from these refugees - just that it was likely that refugees influenced them.

When trying to understand the nature of stories about the Sami from an outside perspective, it is important to keep in mind that there isn't a single Norse belief system. Instead, there is a series of fluid folk religions, which vary from place to place. Much of this divide between ideas exists between the north and south. Indeed, there are clear genetic differences between the two peoples, just as there are clear differences between north and south with regard to the Huldra and Odin as the leader of the Wild Hunt.

The Huldra are incredibly beautiful nature spirits that, in the northern part of Scandinavia, tend to have tales of foxes, cows or lynx, while in the southern part, they have hollow backs.

Similarly, there is a story of Odin hunting down fairy women like game animals that exists in Denmark, the Netherlands and Oslo in Norway—in other words, the southern regions of Norse/Germanic lore.

> A man was once walking from Ersted to Årestrup, when he saw two elf-women come running towards him as fast as they could. They sat down there on the south side of the village, saying to each other, "He won't catch us yet, for he's not clean."
> The man continued on his way, until he was met by one on horseback, who was no other than Jons, the hunter.
>
> "Did no one meet you?" he asked of the man.
>
> "Yes," said he, "there came two little things running as hard as they could."

"What did they say to each other?" asked the horseman.

"They said, 'He won't catch us yet, for he's not clean.'"

He took water in his hand and washed himself, and then said to the man, "If you will lie down now and put your fingers in your ears, I shall pay you well for it when I come back again in a little while."

The man did so, but began to think the time long, and wanted to take his fingers out of his ears. First, he took one finger out and heard someone fire a shot, though at a considerable distance; he thought it might be as far as Hobro. At this, he lay down again for a little, but once more he grew tired of lying like this, and so raised himself from the ground and took the other finger from his ear. Again he heard a shot, but this time as far away as the neighborhood of Horsens. At this, he made haste to put his fingers into his ears again, and lay down in his old place.

Soon after that, the horseman rode up with the two women, tied together by the hair and hung over the horse's back, one on each side, and said to the man, " You shall have good payment, but it should have been better You have taken your fingers out of your ears, and that did me so much damage that I had to ride from Hobro to Horsens to catch the last of them. My horse has lost a shoe on the road there, which you can go and pick up, and that will be payment enough for you."

When the man reached the spot and found it, it proved to be of gold. (Craigie, 1986)

Here, then, we see Odin taking on a darker edge in the south, likely in later eras, than he did in the north, which Loki seemed to have done, as well. According to Laidoner, Loki developed his devilish character as Christianity and modernization changed people's attitudes towards the Sami and their shamanistic magic. Still, given his foreign nature, Loki was already likely an ambiguous character, just like the Jotnar, from whom he might have been descended. People tended to feel afraid and fascinated by foreign people, just as people were fascinated by and afraid of the Sami. Perhaps most interesting, however, was the fact that the Jotnar, like the Sami, were found to the north and east regions of the Norse people. This meant that, in addition to inspiring their magico-religious thinking, the Sami might also have been the mythological characters within the Norse sagas. What's more, Loki possibly was inspired by Sami shamanism and their helping spirits.

In one tale, Loki became a female horse and mated with another horse, giving birth to an eight-legged horse that became one of Odin's helping spirits, carrying him between worlds. One could a similar idea among the Nganasan in which a shaman was given an eight-legged reindeer to carry him to the land of the dead. This gave Loki at least one aspect in common with a deity from a hunting-gathering people in another, albeit, fairly distant northern land. It was possible, of course, that the eight-legged steed was a Scandinavian invention, and that the Nganasan got it from them, or that they both developed it independently. However, Loki was clearly an outsider in Scandinavian mythology, so it seemed more likely that aspects of his character were borrowed. Regardless, one could imagine that Loki was built up of tales about Norse encounters with shamans from other lands, or those shamans, whom, for whatever reason, ended up living among the Norse.

There was an interesting exception to the pattern of neighboring people becoming the monsters of lore: vampires. Gregoricka, Betsinger, Scot, and Polcyn (2014) conducted a study in which they examined the remains of people who had been treated as vampires in Poland. Their initial thought was that people were most likely to have accused foreigners, those who hadn't grown up in the village. As it turned out, however, such people were less likely to be accused of being vampires than local people were. This might have had to do with the fact that those accused of being vampires were thought to have started a plague. Loners and those who lived more isolated lives from the village were less likely to do this.

Still, despite a very few exceptions, it was true that neighboring peoples were often thought of as particularly magical, and the fact that neighboring people could have such a large impact on a culture's belief system and thinking about the magico-religious world was significant, because no people ever lived in an isolated bubble. Rather, the people of Europe were made up of a series of migratory waves.

Migratory Waves

The Great Migration of Huns/German Tribes

People and wagons slipped over a thick, seemingly endless sheet of spring ice as they herded their animals to their traditional grazing lands. Their horses and sheep stopped to paw the icy ground to get at the grass beneath, but they couldn't crack a large enough section of the ice's shell to get enough food to eat. The wagon train stopped for a moment; axes and hammers hit the ice over and over again. It was exhausting work to chip away enough ice for even a few animals to graze, and long-term survival required dozens of animals per person. There was no way for anyone to break enough ice to feed all the animals they needed to survive. Late spring snow would be followed by a short cold summer and an early winter. Thousands of animals would be lost, and the people who would later form the core of the Huns would starve. They would then do what the Steppes tribes had done for generations; they would move. They would expand, pushing west into Europe, collecting other cultures and warriors on the way.

The Huns weren't a single people but a mishmash of many groups that lay between the Altai region and Europe. They would conquer most of Northern Europe, possibly including parts of Scandinavia for two generations—though, as with most things, whether the Huns entered Scandinavia and the amount of impact they had is debated by scholars. Regardless, within Central Europe, the people shared a common experience: the Huns. "The importance of this painful historical event that accompanied the end of the Roman Period and recast the European political landscape needs to be emphasized." (Hedeager, 2007)

Archaeological finds from the period between 150 and 600 A.D. show that the Germanic people began to adopt many forms of Hunnish art, including metal mirrors, earrings made of round thread, Eastern-style cauldrons, long two-edged swords, short one-edged swords, and various forms of horse equipment. Perhaps most interesting is the purposeful deformation of skulls; a number of Germanic tribes from the Ostrogoth to the Lombards imitated the Huns' method for extending the skull during infancy (Marianne, 1993). Although this practice fell out of favor once the Huns fell, it does indicate that they likely had an influence on people's stories and ideas.

138

It was conceivable that the invasion of Europe by the Huns was a portion of the catalyst that drove German tribes to invade Rome repeatedly over the course of the next century. At the very least, their attack caused this to happen earlier. It also changed the scale of the migration. While Germanic tribes and Romans needed only small areas to farm, the Huns needed massive pastures for their flocks and herds (Maenchen-Helfen, 1973). This meant that the Huns would drive far more peasants off their land than a conquering Germanic tribe possibly would. Further, the Huns, a nomadic people, likely moved much faster than did the Germanic tribes..

What was certain was that, during this time period, many Germanic tribes were set to wandering, almost like bandits, looting and conquering. During this period, kings created stories about their ancestry, and perhaps of themselves, that were larger than life. Further, these kings were often strangers in the lands they ruled. They were essentially supernatural outsiders in the lands they came to conquer, although sometimes only briefly.

This is perhaps one reason Europe has so many stories about ogres, giants, ettins, and so forth, ruling a kingdom nearby. The giants and similar monsters throughout the medieval era often do seem like neighboring or rival nobility. This shouldn't be too surprising; such nobility were often monstrous, having gotten their start as warlords and bandits during the Great Migration or later eras of conquest. Some knights outside one town chopped off the hands of a craftsman, simply because they thought it was funny to take away his ability to feed himself and his family. In other cases, they roasted people alive, broke into homes and killed everyone inside to loot the place, and otherwise acted the role of ogre. This isn't to say that the idea of ogres and giants came from the knights and conquering lords. Rather, it is to point out that, because we often draw our idea of villains from the world around us, these people may have helped alter the character of people's beliefs about giants and ogres.

Consider, for example, the story of "The Red Ettin."

> So the young man went to seek his fortune. And he went all that day, and all the next day; and on the third day, in the afternoon, he came up to where a shepherd was sitting with a flock of sheep. And he went up to the shepherd and asked him who the sheep belonged to, and he answered:
>
> "The Red Ettin of Ireland
>   Once lived in Ballygan,
> And stole King Malcolm's daughter
>   The king of fair Scotland.
>
> He beats her, he binds her,
>   He lays her on a band;
> And every day he strikes her,
>   With a bright silver wand.
> Like Julian the Roman,
> He's one that fears no man.
>
> It's said there's one predestinate
>   To be his mortal foe;
> But that man is yet unborn,
>   And long may it be so."

This shepherd also told him to beware of the beasts he should next meet for they were of a very different kind from any he had yet seen.

So the young man went on, and by-and-by he saw a multitude of very dreadful beasts, with two heads, and on every head four horns. And he was sore frightened, and ran away from them as fast as he could; and glad was he when he came to a castle that stood on a hillock, with the door standing wide open to the wall. And he went into the castle for shelter, and there he saw an old wife sitting beside the kitchen fire. He asked the wife if he might stay for the night, as he was tired with a long journey; and the wife said he might, but it was not a good place for him to be in, as it belonged to the Red Ettin, who was a very terrible beast, with three heads, that spared no living man it could get hold of.

Here, the Red Ettin lived in a castle, had workers who care for his sheep, and, in every way, seemed to live just like a king. The same was true of "Puss in Boots" and similar tales from further east, though the Red Ettin, within this story, was clearly of foreign character.

This transformation of the early warlords and nobility into giants, if that's indeed what occurred, likely happened over time, both because the monsters who committed horrible deeds were made more monstrous over time, as a political farce, and because this was how people expected tyrants to live and act. In other words, people simply applied the template of the evil tyrants that they knew to the evil tyrants of the supernatural world.

A thousand years earlier, the Greeks had seen the monstrousness of the Cyclops in the Celtic pastorals who were big, uncouth, and violent (Green). One could easily see how, as these people came into conflict; the Greeks would have compared not only them to Cyclops, but the Cyclops to them. In this way, they would have shaped the Greek's thoughts on the monster of mythology to some extent. Similarly, hundreds of years later:

> Christopher Kininmonth had a temporary Nanny in the mid-1920s who was about sixty. If they were naughty, she would say: "Boney will get you." A tribute to the immense fear Napoleon had inspired. (Gathorne-Hardy, 1993)

The migration period brought many people into contact with each other for the first time, often under the worst of circumstances, as refugees and raiders moved about the countryside. It also brought Northern fairy tales and folk religious ideas south, as the Germanic tribes conquered Italy, France, Spain, and so on, while, in all probability, bringing ideas from the Steppes into Europe.

> A new ethnogenesis of Germanic Tribes took place; the social structure, settlement pattern, and economic bases changed. A significant part of the shaping and development of Germanic kingdoms began. A totally new development and change in Central European settlement areas took place on which the later Medieval and Christian societal order was built. It is tempting to state that without the Hunnic impact, this development would not have happened until much later. (Ulf, 2008)

In many ways, one can think of the migratory period and the eras that followed it as a blender that sliced up and violently mixed around previously separate cultures, never fully combining them but very definitely changing them all. For example, the Franks, a series of Germanic tribes, suddenly settled and passed laws in Southern France and parts of Italy, and they believed they were descended from Trojan refugees. Further, the Migratory period also brought numerous Danish ideas and stories into England, such as Beowulf, as well as tales of dwarfs south into Northern Italy.

What's interesting is that, despite the significance of this migration in restructuring the culture and history of Europe, it had very little genetic impact on Northern Italy, France, and a number of other regions. What this means is that even migrations that are so small they are almost genetically undetectable can have a substantial impact on a region's folklore. Europe is made up of multiple migrations, some of which now make up a majority of the population in certain countries.

A Continuous Movement of People

Genetic studies have shown that even individuals on opposite ends of Europe still share millions of common genealogical ancestors over the last thousand years (Ralph and Coop, 2013). This is important for fairy tales and folk religion as these are passed down from parent to child, generation to generation. If you go back just one thousand years, anyone from any European country will have had relatives from any other country in Europe. Presuming that a story can survive just a thousand years, and many have, then the bits and pieces of any story can end up in any other region in Europe. Consider, for example, the Irish story of the Salmon of Knowledge. In this story, a man named Finn Eces catches a salmon that contains all the worlds' knowledge and gives it to his servant Fionn with instructions not to eat it. However, Fionn ignores this, cooks it and then burns his finger on hot oil from the salmon and sucks it to ease the pain. The wisdom of the salmon was concentrated in that one drop of fish fat, and so he gains all the wisdom. In an Eastern European tale, a girl gains this secret knowledge when she puts a little fat her father has rendered out of a magical snake onto a cracker. Similarly, in the Grimm Brothers' tale "The White Snake," a servant brings a king a secret dish every day:

> This had gone on for a long time, when one day the servant, who took away the dish, was overcome with such curiosity that he could not help carrying the dish into his room. When he had carefully locked the door, he lifted up the cover and saw a white snake lying on the dish. But when he saw it he could not deny himself the pleasure of tasting it, so he cut off a little bit and put it into his mouth. No sooner had it touched his tongue than he heard a strange whispering of little voices outside his window. He went and listened, and then noticed that it was the sparrows who were chattering together, and telling one another of all kinds of things which they had seen in the fields and woods. Eating the snake had given him power of understanding the language.

It seems likely that, although these stories are different, the motif of the fat from a magical animal of knowledge being accidentally eaten by a servant or daughter comes from a single source. So, on the one hand, there are often striking similarities between the stories of one land and another due in part to the relationship between those lands. Yet, at the same time, there are still important differences between these stories from one region to another. The same is true of genetics in Europe:

> Southeastern Europeans, for example, share large numbers of common ancestors that date roughly to the era of the Slavic and Hunnic expansions around 1,500 years ago, while most common ancestors that Italians share with other populations lived longer than 2,500 years ago. (Ralph, Coop, Tyler-Smith, 2013)

While people were always moving, there are regions where certain ideas are more common, and big movements of people shifted cultures. At times, these migrations can be understood through linguistic and genetic studies, which can tell us a lot about the history of folk tales in a region. The challenge to utilizing major migratory events to understand Europe's history is that there is still a lot of debate with regard to the genetic and linguistic history of Europe. Still, it is possible, to some extent, to figure out what migrations took place. The meaning, origins, and impact of these migrations is largely debated. A general timeline of some of the largest genetic movements into Europe can be reconstructed to a point, but Europe is a complex hodgepodge of multiple migratory events that make it difficult to get a clear picture of anything.

Before continuing, it would perhaps be useful to give you some idea of what haplogroups are, as they will be discussed extensively in this section. Haplogroups, in simple terms, are genetic markers used to identify related populations on the male (Y-DNA) and female (mtDNA) lines, which can be used, at times, to help track the origins of different people groups. As we'll see, however, they are not a magic key for figuring out history, but they are useful for figuring out some of the relations we would not have otherwise seen.

Hunter-Gatherers
Mesolithic and Paleolithic Europe

The first humans to enter Europe did so before the last massive Ice Age. When this Ice Age struck, people were driven south to a few separate colonies scattered along the southern part of the continent. Here, in isolation, they developed their cultures for generations. As the weather warmed, they again spread out, each recolonizing Europe. Yet, interestingly, despite the centuries of isolation from each other, the remains that have been tested from the Mesolithic/Paleolithic era tend to be fairly genetically homogeneous across Europe, primarily containing mtDNA Haplogroup U on the female line. In the modern day, this haplogroup is all but gone in most of Europe except for among the Sami, the Baltic nations such as Estonia, and, interestingly, in the Berbers of North Africa; which seems to indicate a connection between them and the Sami in the North (Achilli, 2005). These two groups of people have two interesting sets of folklore in common. One is the worship of spirits in large rocks, and the other is an idea of ancestral spirits that dwell in the natural world rather than a separate spirit world (much like the fairies are reputed to do).

While these early hunter-gatherers obtained their food from a variety of places, they seem invariably to have gotten a large percentage, if not most of their food, from the water. As with many people who survived on ocean fish, people in places like Brittany were able to develop large sedentary communities; the dumping grounds for their refuse were filled primarily with shells from marine invertebrates, bones from a large variety of fish and seals, and some bones of deer and boar. Communities of people who were further inland in places like Northern Germany ate a large amount of freshwater fish, waterfowl, beaver, and moose that lived in marshy areas. Thus, their survival was largely dependent on the water as well. Given that any people's folk religion and fairy tales are largely based on what they eat, this surely had an impact on their beliefs. On top of this, these villages were small and mobile, very much like those of the people of Siberia many years later. This might explain why water spirits are among the most important beings in early Europe and were believed to be the founders of cities and civilization; though water is generally important to many people all over the world.

Water Goddess and Fishing

Given that the early hunter-gatherers lived largely on fish, one can presume that the spirits of water would have been important to the early people of Europe. This is interesting because Briggs held that water fairies were the most common of all the fairy types the Celtic people believed in. Danu, the mother of the Tuatha De Dannan, which became the Daoine Sidhe or fairies of Ireland (Briggs), was associated with rivers in the Indo-European languages and mythologies. Among the Gaulic people, Dea Matrona was a mother goddess associated with the river Marne. In later years, sacred wells would retain so much importance for the Celts that the Catholic Church would be forced to rededicate them to Saints because they could not stop people from worshiping them. Similarly, Larson indicates that water nymphs were often thought of as being related to the deities of the indigenous people of Greece. Many of these well spirits appear to have existed before the Indo-European invasion and so were so important the belief in them survived from Neolithic Europe until well after the post-Christian era. There can be...

> "No doubt the Indo-Europeans had no monopoly in religious feeling and observance of this (the worship of water) type; it may go back tens of thousands of years. But it must have been part of their religion, and its prevalence among their linguistic and cultural heirs must be due at least in some degree to the power of Indo-European tradition." (West, 2008)

It would make sense that water spirits would be the most likely to survive from one generation to the next, because they were still important right into the modern day. The names of rivers are among the features of the land most likely to continue to have the names of the indigenous people long after their language is no longer used. Further, both fishermen and farmers need clean water. Water is, in general, among the most valuable resources for any people.

> Water is scarce in Greece, and so the benefits received from rivers are especially appreciated. In ancient times the rivers were holy. An army did not cross a river without making a sacrifice to it, and Hesiod prescribes that one should not cross a river without saying a prayer and washing one's hands in its water. The aid of the rivers was sought for the fertility not only of the land but also of mankind... When a young man cut his long hair, he dedicated the locks to the neighboring river.

> The rivers each had their god. These gods are represented in the shape of a bull or a bull with a human head. River spirits in the shape of a bull are well known from European folklore of the present day, and they are certainly an ancient heritage. The river spirit appears just as often, however, in the shape of a horse. This is true, for example, in Sweden and Scotland. (Nilsson, 1972)

First Neolithic Migration

The Neolithic Age began with the entrance of farming from Anatolia about 9,000 years ago. This migratory event spread slowly across Europe, making the incoming farmers and the hunter-gatherers neighbors for thousands of years before they started seriously mixing together. As I've already discussed, when two people live side by side for a long time, they begin to affect each other's thinking. This was likely especially true with the small mobile communities, which could easily have seemed supernatural to the farmers as they came and went with the seasons. Sometimes, the two peoples lived in such close proximity that, in places like Hagen, Germany, it was found that the hunter-gatherers and the farmers even buried their dead in the same cave. Also of interest is the fact that women from the hunter-gathering culture would marry into the agricultural culture.

Second Neolithic Migration

Around 6,500 years ago, another group of farmers entered Europe carrying Haplogroup H, which is now one of the most common mtDNA haplogroups in Europe. This indicates that these newcomers replaced a large percentage of the previous farming peoples and the hunter-gatherers. This second wave of farmers might also have carried R1b, which is the most common haplogroup in Western Europe by far. (There is a geat deal of debate on the exact origins of R1b, and I'll discuss this in greater detail later.)

Before its push into Central Europe, Haplogroup H was found in Mesolithic remains from Karelia Russia and in Northern Spain. This may indicate that the people carrying this Haplogroup pushed into Europe from either or possibly both of these locations. It might also indicate that this Haplogroup was present in Mesolithic Europe only in small amounts.

Regardless of the origins of this Haplogroup, however, what its appearance in Europe means is that there were then three people groups living side by side for a long time— people who likely would have seen each other as outsiders, "others," and possibly magical but also "unclean." Nevertheless, in many similar situations hunter-gatherer women would, on occasion, marry into the agricultural community, though the men almost never did, and agricultural women almost never married into the hunter-gather community. Given this state of affairs, consider the following Alpine fairy tale, for example:

> On the plateau between Brugg and Wldshut, seven Zwerg (dwarfs) lived together in the black forest. One night a lost peasant girl asked for shelter for the night. The Zwerg argued with each other, as each wanted to give up their bed to the girl. Finally the eldest took the girl to his bed.
>
> Before they could go to sleep, however, a woman came to their house. The girl began trying to explain herself to the woman, saying that she had no choice. The woman wouldn't listen, however, and became angry, accusing the girl of being a slut, for she thought that the girl was sleeping with all seven men. Vowing to end such wickness she stormed off.
>
> She returned a while later with two men. They broke into the Zwergs home, killed all seven and buried their bodies in the garden outside, then burnt the house to the ground. No one knows what happened to the young girl. (Druck und Verlag von H.R. Sauelander)

Despite stories of such harsh punishments for women who would sleep with the fairies, however, there is evidence that women from farming communities did join those of hunter-gatherers in Northern Europe. It's difficult to know in ancient Europe if such marriages occurred of people's own free will or if this was the result of kidnapping between

144

the two groups. After all, there are a number of stories from Europe of forcefully taking supernatural wives, and history is filled with such incidences. There are, however, some few happier tales of fairy and human unions. For example:

> A poor girl went out one day, and as she was passing by a hill she heard a Dwarf hammering away inside of it, for they are handy smiths, and singing at his work. She was so pleased with the song that she could not refrain from wishing aloud that she could sing like him, and live like him under the ground. Scarcely had she expressed the wish when the singing ceased, and a voice came out of the hill, saying, "Should you like to live with us?" "To be sure I should," replied the girl, who probably had no very happy life of it above ground. Instantly the Dwarf came out of the hill and made a declaration of love, and a proffer of his hand and a share in his subterranean wealth. She accepted the offer and lived very comfortably with him, as he proved an excellent little husband. (Keightley, 1870)

It's likely that, since these three peoples lived side by side for so long in so many places, the relationship between the different peoples manifested in many ways. Further, this would also seem to lend credence to the idea that fairies were stories about a conquered and subsumed people, and motifs from this are certainly present. However, there's likely a lot more to this.

Imagine for a moment that you live in a region with another people, a people whose beliefs are clearly different from yours. If we presume that the hunter-gatherers had something resembling the Sami belief system, and the Neolithic people had something resembling the Celtic or Germanic belief system, then we must also presume that they both believed in sacred places. To them, there were certain groves of trees, rocks, rivers, hills, and other places that needed to be respected. What's more, the hunter-gathers likely would have believed that many of the spirits of their dead would wonder about the hills, live within large rocks, etc. The same is true of the farmers, who likely believed that the spirits of their dead ancestors traveled the world on specific days.

It was important for these people groups to explain their beliefs to each other in order to get the others to respect their sacred spaces and days. How would they have done this? Imagine trying to explain to another culture, one that doesn't necessarily respect your beliefs, the importance of staying away from taboo places. Imagine, for example, the farmers trying to explain that it was forbidden to hunt animals or fish for food in certain sacred groves or the hunters trying to explain to the farmers that they couldn't plow up certain hills or move large rocks—especially given that they had limited understanding of each other's language. The best way to do this would have been to warn the other group of the scary, unlucky things that could happen if one group entered the other's sacred spaces or to try to impress on the other people the importance of the spirits living in the sacred spaces.

From such warnings and a limited understanding of the spirits that the other worshiped, a number of fairy tales would have arisen. In other words, the fairies weren't necessarily just the previous people; they could also be the spirits of the previous people's dead. This would explain why many of the original burials mounds in Europe are now considered to be homes to otherworld beings such as the *huldra* and fairies that would curse anyone who damaged their sacred places.

This doesn't mean that the Neolithic peoples didn't have ideas resembling *huldra* and fairies before moving into a region. After all, people often simply incorporate multiple

145

ideas into preexisting notions, and the idea of magical others is common among nearly all peoples. What it means is that the notions about different magical beings likely have many sources, some of which came from contact and difficulty communicating with neighboring peoples.

R1a – Migratory Event

Adding to this already confusing picture came another wave of people from Southern Siberia around 4,800 years ago carrying the R1a Haplogroup. It is often presumed that this Haplogroup is related to the Indo-European language family that includes the Celtic, Germanic, Greek, Romantic, and Iranian languages as well as the languages of India—though, as already stated, there is a lot of debate on this point.

What we can say for certain, however, is that this migratory event left a substantial genetic mark on Eastern and Central Europe. Considering how dramatically the later migration of the Huns would impact Europe, this event may have also thrown Europe into complete chaos for a time. However, archeological records don't show many major indications of genocide or other large-scale wars at this time, so the exact nature of this event isn't entirely clear. This migration from what was originally a Siberian people might explain the many similarities between the spirits of Siberia and those of Europe.

The British, the Celts, the Basques and the Debate Over R1b

Perhaps the biggest challenge in assessing the beliefs of any Pre-Indo-European people group comes from the debate on the origin of Haplogroup R1b, which is the most common haplogroup in Western Europe. In fact, R1b is present in 80% of all men in places like Ireland, so the origins of this genome can tell us a lot about the origins of Western European beliefs in general. There are, however, two primary arguments about R1b and, hence, about the very origins of the Celtic, British, and Germanic peoples.

On the one hand, some argue that, since R1b hasn't been found in any remains before the Neolithic era, it wasn't present in Europe until then. As a reasult, it is argued that the Neolithic people carrying it replaced the hunter-gatherers in Western Europe more extensively than had happened in Eastern or Central Europe.

However, other genetic studies indicate that R1b comes from a group of Paleolithic Europeans who were pushed into an ice age refuge on the Iberian Peninsula. With the end of the Ice age, they were able to recolonize Europe, and so they represent an indigenous population. This means that the British and Celtic belief systems may or may not be based primarily on pre-Indo-European elements.

Two Sides of Britain

Regardless of the origins of R1b, there are a few things we can likely discern about Pre-Roman Britain.

146

Britain at its simplest can be sub-divided into two groups of people. In the North and West are speakers of Celtic languages, in places such as Scotland, Wales, and Cornwall. The Celtic language family also includes languages from Ireland and Brittany and the ancient Gauls of the Iberian Peninsula. In the East are the originators of the English language, which is part of the larger Germanic language family.

Thanks to Gilda, a writer from the early medieval era, many people believe that this split is due to a Saxon invasion at the End of the Roman era. However, it seems more probable that, while there was a Saxon invasion, the division between Celtic and Germanic language families in Britain occurred long before this, with the seafaring Celtic-speaking peoples arriving from Spain into Cornwall, Wales, Ireland and eventually Scotland around the same time as a Germanic-speaking people arrived in Britain from across the English Channel. There are both genetic and linguistic reasons for thinking that this is the case. For example, Britain has a number of rivers with names from a preexisting people, but none of these rivers have Celtic names. Even with massive replacement events, such as happened along the Delaware River when the Europeans arrived in North America, many rivers still retain names from a previous people. It bears repeating that, while we do indeed see pre-English names for rivers in England, none of these names are Celtic; they are from an unknown pre-Indo-European language.

If it's true that the split in Britain occurred long before the Roman era, this would mean that many of the myths in England that we associate with Celtic remnants were instead Germanic. Of course, it is also true that the Celts and Germans have mythologies that are very similar to each other. Further, regardless of when the split occurred, all the people of Britain and Ireland are, in fact, fairly closely related, which means that some of their myths and fairy tales would have similar origins. The only question is: are they closely related to the original inhabitants of Britain and Ireland (i.e., the people who built Stonehenge)? Or were these people wiped out along with their language?

There is no real answer to this, so there is no way to know for certain if the differences between their tales and typical Indo-European tales are a result of some pre-Indo-European influence.

Additional Migrations

European history is filled with migrations both large and small from Asia. From the Gypsies to the Hungarians, people have been bringing ideas and stories into Europe from the East since the very beginning of humanity in Europe. Indeed, there have been so many migrations that they are too numerous to cover. Further, there are likely many more that we do not know about. However, there are two more worth mentioning briefly. At some uncertain point, likely a few thousand years ago, a group traveled into Finland and the Scandinavian countries from Central/North Asia. These people were most closely genetically related to the Bayrut and Yakut peoples, which, as I've already mentioned, likely had a substantial influence on Norse and Germanic tales.

Second, the Scythian raiders from the Steppes became an important part of Greek history. However, it was Eastern Europe that they conquered, so they likely had a much larger impact to Northern Greece than we have been able to record; there is very little writing about the people of the North during this time.

Dreams of Philosophers

The Germany of the Brothers Grimm was a land that, for so long, had clung to two pasts. The first was that of the ancient shamanistic Germanic peoples, the tribes from the north that had crushed Rome under their heel. The second was that of Rome, for even as they defeated them, the Germanic people wished to be Roman. Thus, their later Emperor took on the mantle of the "Holy Roman Emperor." Two pasts, neither of which fit together, pushed into a future neither brother was prepared to handle. The world around the Grimm brothers was changing faster than ever before. This was an unstable world in which the wealthy Grimm family became impoverished in the blink of an eye, leaving the brothers as young men to find a way to support their younger brothers and sister. As with the Brothers Grimm, many highly educated upper-class people found themselves marginalized or hurt by the new push to industrialization. They saw the austere system of utilitarianism and the reason of industrialism as crushing happiness, so they began to seek more romantic images. According to Jack Zipes, they began to rebel against their own class's utilitarian tales:

> Beset by a changing world, the Victorian could find stability in the ordered, formulary structure of fairy tales. He could be called from his time and place to a soothing other world by the faintly blowing horns of Elfland. He could be taken from the corruptions of adulthood back to the innocence of childhood; from the ugly, competitive city to beautiful, sympathetic nature; from complex morality to the simple issue of good versus evil; from a different reality to a comforting world of imagination.

For the Romantics, fairy tales were a way to push forward philosophical agendas. It was at this time that the countryside, the folk, and children began to be romanticized. Children especially came to be viewed as existing in a state of innocence.

> Transforming earlier religious myths and ideologies, the Romantics created a new myth of original innocence in contrast to the myth of original sin. The child became the sacrosanct image of innocence opposed to the fallen adult. It is this myth the modern world has inherited, a myth as complex as it is fascinating.

(Sky, 2005)

This idealism often manifested itself as a sugary counterweight to the austere writing that was popular at the time. This is clearly seen in the story of "Red Rose and Snow White."

There was once a poor widow who lived in a lonely cottage. In front of the cottage was a garden wherein stood two rose-trees, one of which bore white and the other red roses. She had two children who were like the two rose-trees, and one was called snow-white, and the other rose-red. They were as good and happy, as busy and cheerful as ever two children in the world were, only snow-white was more quiet and gentle than rose-red. Rose-red liked better to run about in the meadows and fields seeking flowers and catching butterflies, but snow-white sat at home with her mother, and helped her with her house-work, or read to her when there was nothing to do. The two children were so fond of one another that they always held each other by the hand when they went out together, and when snow-white said, we will not leave each other, rose-red answered, never so long as we live, and their mother would add, what one has she must share with the other. They often ran about the forest alone and gathered red berries, and no beasts did them any harm, but came close to them trustfully. The little hare would eat a cabbage-leaf out of their hands, the roe grazed by their side, the stag leapt merrily by them, and the birds sat still upon the boughs, and sang whatever they knew.

No mishap overtook them, if they had stayed too late in the forest, and night came on, they laid themselves down near one another upon the moss, and slept until morning came, and their mother knew this and did not worry on their account. Once when they had spent the night in the wood and the dawn had roused them, they saw a beautiful child in a shining white dress sitting near their bed. He got up and looked quite kindly at them, but said nothing and went away into the forest. And when they looked round they found that they had been sleeping quite close to a precipice, and would certainly have fallen into it in the darkness if they had gone only a few paces further. And their mother told them that it must have been the angel who watches over good children.

Snow-white and rose-red kept their mother's little cottage so neat that it was a pleasure to look inside it. In the summer rose-red took care of the house, and every morning laid a wreath of flowers by her mother's bed before she awoke, in which was a rose from each tree. In the winter snow-white lit the fire and hung the kettle on the hob. The kettle was of brass and shone like gold, so brightly was it polished. In the evening, when the snowflakes fell, the mother said, go, snow-white, and bolt the door, and then they sat round the hearth, and the mother took her spectacles and read aloud out of a large book, and the two girls listened as they sat and spun. And close by them lay a lamb upon the floor, and behind them upon a perch sat a white dove with its head hidden beneath its wings.

This is one of the longest openings of any fairy tale, most of which provide very little actual description and almost never any unnecessary flowery prose. Romantics, however, loved flowery, long descriptions like this. The purpose of such descriptions was to paint a picture of innocent children and the perfect idyllic country life. This, of course, is far from the reality of the heavy labor that peasants suffered through, but for those in the city, the country has always held a certain romanticism.

Charles Dickens believed greatly in the idea of "fancy." He fell in love with the story character of Little Red Riding Hood. He used his writing to shine a light into the darkest corners of the Industrial Age (Ostry, 2013).

In addition to seeking after whimsy and an imaginary country life, these primarily male authors "sought to recover a lost 'femininity.'" Both of these desires—for childhood and for femininity—led to the more childish image of fairies and, ultimately, to today's view that fairies are for little girls.

Painting idyllic pictures was not the only purpose that Romantics had. They also wished to use fairy tales to consolidate national and cultural identities according to their own wishes.

> These writers did not write their fairy tales for children, but for each other. They came from the haute bourgeoisie or the aristocracy. They took stories from the lower classes, and they also made up stories as part of their word games in the salons of famous women. (Ostry, 2013)

Yeats sought to use fairies as a way of creating an Irish identity, and fairies in general came to be associated specifically with the Celtic world, even though most peoples in Western Europe had tales them. Even the Grimm Brothers hoped to use fairy tales as a means of inspiring cultural unification among the many divided Germanic states during a time when they were occupied by Napoleon's armies.

What the Romantics sought to do in creating an imaginary and romantic country life was nothing new. As the Ancient Greeks lived in larger and larger city-states, they, too, began to idealize country life—as did the later Romans. This is made clear by the popularity of the deity of the countryside Silvanus among city dwellers. As Peter F. Dorcey states:

> Most female, as well as male adherents mentioned on Silvanus inscriptions, lived in cities and did not practice farming. For them, Silvanus' appeal lay in the distance or inaccessibility of the countryside. Lurking behind many of these urban offerings is a sentimental nostalgia for the rural world and a longing for a simpler, quitter way of life. By the imperial period, Silvanus was rarely invoked as protector of fields and flocks, but served as an outlet for the stress of urban life and a constant reminder of real or imagined country roots. (Dorcey, 1989)

Fairies play an active role in urbanized societies by acting as a symbol for something beautiful and distant. The things that the romantics, such as the Brothers Grimm, idolized included childhood, rural life, peasants, and nationalism. Like the Romantacists, in general, the Brothers Grimm had an interest in folktales and mythology as well as an enthusiasm for human rights and nature. They tended to be very sentimental about the world around them and about traditions. More specifically, the Grimm Brothers believed that a peoples' character, that which made Germany special, could be found in the tales of peasants.

Yet despite this belief, they did not collect many of their tales from peasants. Rather, they collected them from women who were members of literary circles, women who likely changed the nature of these stories based on their own desires, which came from living sedentary, largely upper-class lives. Further, many of the Grimm Brothers' tales were collected from a woman who had heard these stories in France, where, for instance, "Little Red Riding Hood" was written down as a warning story for noble girls. This has led to a great deal of debate about the nature and origins of this story. So perhaps the best place to begin examining the mixture of old traditions and the philosophical and literary agenda of a pre-Romantic is in "Little Red Riding Hood."

Little Red Riding Hood

Few stories have intrigued people more than "Little Red Riding Hood." Indeed, if literary success is measured in longevity and universality, then "Little Red Riding Hood" is one of the most successful stories of all time (Sugiyama, 2004).

With so much interest, there has been a lot of debate about the meaning and origin of this story. This debate centers on the fact that the story collected by the Grimm Brothers came from a French woman, so it is not clear whether or not all the versions of the tale are, in fact, French in origin. Perrault's involvement in the story has also led to discussion of whether or not the red cape Little Red Riding Hood wears is a literary invention, and whether it has any actual meaning to the original fairy tale, for he clearly uses this tale to teach his era's sexual morality.

To answer the question of the origin of the story, Tehrani examines a number of stories using phylogenetics. According to his research, the original "Little Red Riding Hood" comes from Germany, after which the story spread to France, then made it back into Germany. Therefore, while the original story is German, the version that the Grimm Brothers collected is French.

Italian version of "Little Red Hat" analyzed
(Schneller, 1867)

> Once there was an old woman who had a granddaughter who was called Red Hat. One day when they were out in the field together the old woman told Red Hat, "I'm going home now; when you come, bring me some soup.

This opening is pretty straightforward, quickly establishing the character of Red Hat and her grandmother. There is no discussion on the nature of childhood and no romanticization of the family relationship.

Now consider, for example, the version told by Perrault:

> Once upon a time there lived in a certain village a little country girl, the prettiest creature who was ever seen. Her mother was excessively fond of her, and her grandmother doted on her still more. This good woman had a little red riding hood made for her. It suited the girl so extremely well that everybody called her Little Red Riding Hood.

One day her mother, having made some cakes, said to her, "Go, my dear, and see how your grandmother is doing, for I hear she has been very ill. Take her a cake, and this little pot of butter."

Little Red Riding Hood set out immediately to go to her grandmother, who lived in another village.

In writing, the story becomes not only more detailed but also more sentimental—enough for people to romanticize Little Red.

Perhaps the most interesting aspect in both these openings is the red hat, because colors like this are so rarely used in fairy tales. According to Tehrani (2013), this red hood was likely worn by the protagonist in the oldest version of the story, though this is often controversial and still leaves the question of what the color red really means.

There are a number of possibilities. First, and perhaps what scholars have focused on most often, is the possibility that red is a sign of Little Red's sexuality. It is certainly true that red has been a symbol of sex among many human cultures and even among many non-human primates for thousands of years (Elliot and Pazda, 2012). The common association with red and sexuality makes it seem possible that the color red in this tale is sexually based, especially given that the ending involves Little Red and the wolf getting in bed together, naked.

There is a possible hitch in this idea, however: in 17th century France, red was also considered a color of power. Red was associated with King Louis XIV and with palaces and nobility (Stamberg, 2007). If Perrault's tale was meant for people of the court, people who knew girls who were meant to wear red because of their station, would red have been a sign of sexuality or of nobility?

However, if the use of the color red predates Perrault's tale, we have to consider that it was used in the way red was typically used in fairy tales. In fairy tales, red was most commonly a symbol for the fairies. When Prince Pwyll sees dogs with red ears, he knows that the fairies are near. So this begs the question, could Little Red have come from the idea of the little wood wives, the fairies of the forest, being hunted and attacked by evil forest spirits? Perhaps this is one of the fragmented ideas contained in this story; indeed...

In Cox's "Comparative Mythology," Little Redcap, or Little Red Riding Hood, is interpreted as 'the evening with her scarlet robe of twilight,' who is swallowed up by the wolf of darkness, the Fenris of the Edda. It appears to me that this explanation may suit the colour of her cap or hood, but is at variance with the other incidents of the story. I am inclined to look upon the tale as a lunar legend, although the moon is only actually red during one portion of the year, at the harvest moon in the autumn. Red Hood is represented as wandering, like Io, who is undoubtedly the moon, through trees, the clouds, and flowers, the stars, before she reaches the place where she is intercepted by the wolf. An eclipse to untutored minds would naturally suggest the notion that some evil beast was endeavoring to devour the moon, who is afterwards rescued by the sun, the archer of the heavens, whose bow and arrow are by a common anachronism represented in the story by a gun. Though the moon is masculine in Slavonic, as in German, yet she is a lady, 'my lady Luna,' in the Croatian legend. (Wratislaw, 1890)

While this interpretation of "the moon" seems unlikely, it is possible that the meaning of the color red is magical, as red was often considered to be a magical color. The case of Little Red's tale is perhaps best exemplified in the first written story of a girl in red being attacked by a wolf.

> *A certain man took up a girl from the sacred font, and gave her a tunic woven of red wool; sacred Pentecost was (the day) of her baptism.*
>
> *The girl, now five years old, goes out at sunrise, footloose and headless of her peril.*
> *A wolf attacked her, went to its woodland lair, took her as booty to its cubs, and left her to be eaten.*
>
> *They approached her at once, and since they were unable to harm her, began, free from all their ferocity, to caress her head, "Do not damage this tunic, mice," the lisping little girl said, "which my godfather gave me when he took me from the font!"*
>
> *"God, their creator, soothes untame souls."* (Ziolkowski, 1992)

In this version, the color red is used to protect against evil spirits—against the wolf—so, in later versions, the wolf may have Little Red strip off her clothes because he can't eat her as long as she is wearing red. This would also explain why he bothers with the whole deception of pretending to be her grandmother in the first place.

This magical explanation of the color red is reinforced by another story in which Little Red's grandmother is very clearly a witch. In this version of the story, a girl named Maria is sent to visit her grandmother who wishes to give her a red hat. On the way, she encounters the wolf, which beats her there. In this story, the wolf pretends to be the sleeping grandmother, but the grandmother wakes up before the wolf can eat the girl. The grandmother then enchants the wolf and sets it on fire. She then scolds Maria for having been tricked and gives her the red cap. (Vaz, 2000)

The fact that the color red originally had magical meanings that were misinterpreted and misunderstood by modern thinkers and philosophers makes it this the perfect example of how ideas in fairy tales were subverted by literary agendas.

"Little Red" Continued...

> *After a time Red Hat returned home as well, and on the way she met an Orco (ogre), who greeted her, "Hello Red Hat, Where are you going?"*
> *"I'm bringing some soup to my grandmother."*
> *"Good, I'll come along too," The wolf told her. "Are you going to go over the stones or through the thorns?"*
> *"I'm going over the Stones," Red Hat told him.*
> *"Okay, then I'll go through the throne bushes," the Orco said.*

In this version, the wolf has been replaced by Orco, who is likely a remnant of the idea of Orcus, the ruler of the underworld in Roman mythology. Orco are maneating monsters that very often specifically target children; in the modern era, the term has been used to as slang for people whose crimes target children, such as pedophiles.

The Perrault version of the tale adds a bit more detail, describing "the poor child, who did not know that it was dangerous to stay and talk to a wolf." This ignorance is the reason Perrault has Little Red punished by the wolf. He was trying to teach a lesson, which he elaborates on at the end of the book. This lesson is that men are wolves, and young ladies need to watch out for them.

In general, Perrault is "unforgiving in his depiction of father figures" He uses fairy tales not only to teach morals but also to specifically attack societal patriarchs. In addition to warning young girls about male suitors, then, this story may also have been a way to demonize men who take advantage of women. One could say that it was meant to reflect the negative reality of rape; rather than just an attack on Little Red's ignorance, it was an attack on society for letting "wolves" get away with their villainy. (Patricia Hannon).

"Little Red Hat" Continued...

> So they each went their way, but as she traveled she came to a meadow filled with every color of beautiful flower. She began to pick these to her hearts content.
> Meanwhile the Orco hurried through the Thorns to Red Hat's Grandmother's home. When he got there, he went inside and killed Red Hat's Grandmother and ate her up, and climbed into her bed. Before he'd climbed into bed, however, he tied her intestine on the door in place of the latch rope, and put her blood and teeth in the kitchen cabinet.
> The moment he got into bed, Red Hat knocked on the door.
> "Come In," Orco answered, doing his best to soften his voice.

In some ways, it seems as if Little Red's picking of the flowers is a way of saying that children, especially girls, shouldn't dally at their tasks. Feminist folklorists have taken great offense at this part of the story, saying that the girl has the right to dally and to be happy.

Still, I'm not certain how important this is to the story other than that it gives the wolf time to attack Little Red's grandmother. It is never explicitly mentioned that Little Red's delay is a bad thing; even Perrault, who chose to turn this into a moral tale warning girls against early sexuality, merely states that the moral is a warning against talking to wolves. Red Hat's delay, at worst, seems like the typical romantic line about the fancy of childhood.

Much more than the delay, what I find most striking about Little Red's dallying in the woods is that she is so at ease in the wilderness despite having just spoken with a wolf or an Orco. The exact reason for this isn't certain. Perhaps it is merely a way of moving the story along. Still, it does make me wonder if there is something supernatural about Little Red, in general, that she isn't afraid of normally dangerous beings—especially given that she seems to be a magical figure in many of the stories.

If there is a moral to this section of the story, it's that Little Red "violates the interdiction against dallying in the forest and is punished by being eaten (or nearly eaten) by the wolf." This isn't a punishment for idleness; rather, it's a punishment for spending too much time in a dangerous place" (Sugiyama, 2004). In this case, this story is still a supernatural tale about the danger of associating with and staying in the spirit world, the place outside of the community.

> There's something innately terrifying about a wolf. First there is their sheer power. I've experienced the fangs of an angry she-wolf hovering above my neck. I've had my head held vice-like in a wolf's jaws. These are animals which can crush a human skull and snap thigh bones, with a bite twice as strong as a German shepherd dog...
>
> They listen to their prey's heartbeat from several meters away with their uncannily powerful hearing and can judge when it is petrified — the moment they decide to go in for the kill. (Ellis, 2011)

The natural fear inspired by wolves was heightened during the medieval era when their territories and humans' began to jut up against each other with sometimes terrifying results.

It wasn't Little Red's failure that put her in the forest and in harm's way in the first place. It was her mother who sent her out into the woods alone. This, then, may not originally have been a warning tale for children at all; rather, it could be a warning tale for parents about sending their children into dangerous places.

> The majority of predatory attacks (pre 20th century Europe and present-day India) have occurred in very artificial environments where a number of circumstances have occurred. These include; little or no natural prey, heavy use of garbage and livestock as food by wolves, children often unattended or used as shepherds, poverty among the human population, and limited availability of weapons among people so wolves might not be very shy. (Linnell, Andersen, et al, 2002)

Notice that one important element in wolf attacks is unattended children. Indeed, Red Hat is sent into the woods alone—or, in this case, left unattended. The moral of this story may be about parents leaving their children in the woods. Just because a writer later tried to give it a moral relevant to the aristocracy doesn't mean that his moral was the original one.

"Little Red" Continued...

> "Oh, your rope is really squishy Grandma," Red Hat called (Remember she had to grab the intestines to open the door as they had replaced the latch rope)
> "Be quite, and just pull the door open," Orco told her. "Those are your grandmothers guts."
> "What did you say?" Red Hat asked uncertainly.
> "Just open the door and be quiet," Orco told her.
> Red Hat pulled the door open and on entering the house said, "Grandmother, I'm hungry."
> "Go to the kitche cabinet, there's some rice in there."
> Red Hat went to the cabinet and found the teeth, "The rice is hard grandmother."

155

> *"Eat it and be quiet, they are your grandmother's teeth"* Orco told her.
> *"What, did you say?"* Red Hat asked.
> *"Just eat it and be quiet,"*
> A little while later, Red Hat said; *"Grandmother, "I'm still hungry."*
> *"There's some chopped meat in the cabinet ,"* Orco told her.
> *"This meat is very red Grandmother,"* Red Hat said on finding her mothers jaws in there.
> *"Eat it and be quiet, those are your grandmothers jaws,"* Orco told her.
> *"What did you say?"*
> *"Just eat it and be quiet."*
> A few moments later Red Hat said, *"Grandmother, "I'm thirsty."*
> *"There's some wine in the cabinet,"*
> Red Hat found her Grandmother's blood and commented on how red the wine was.
> *"Be quiet and drink it, it's your Grandmothers blood"*
> *"What did you say?"*
> *"Just be quiet and drink it."*

This is a fairly macabre scene, one that, like the later scene in which Little Red begins to slowly realize that the wolf/orco isn't her grandmother, seems designed to build anticipation, to act as a horror story, introducing us to unusual ideas.

There are other incidences of evil beings getting people to eat someone they loved in fairy tales. In one tale, a vampire tries to get a girl to eat her sister, and when she refuses, he kills her. In France, there was a group of bandits that roasted a knight and tried to force his own family to eat him, and in "The Juniper Tree," a wicked step-mother secretly feeds a man his own son. As previously mentioned in the discussion on fear, many fairy tales act as horror stories and so are likely purposefully gruesome for gruesomeness's sake.

"Red Hat" Continued...

> *"I'm getting tired Grandmother"* Red Hat said.
> *"Take off your clothes and come to bed with me,"* the Orco replied.
> So Red Hat got into bed and felt something hairy. *"Oh, your so hairy Grandmother."*
> *"That comes with getting older,"* said the Orco
> *"Wow you have such long legs, Grandmother."*
> *"Yes, that comes from walking"*
> *"Oh my, you have such long hands Grandmother"*
> *"Yes, that comes from working."*
> *"Wow, you have such long ears Grandmother."*
> *"That comes form listening."*
> *"You have such a big mouth Grandmother."*
> *"That comes from eating children!"* said Orco and she wolfed Red Hat down in one big bite.

This ending varies greatly from place to place. In some cases, Little Red is eaten, as she is here. In others, she manages to trick the wolf and escape. Still other times, Little Red is saved by a woodsmen and cut out of the wolf. This likely means that the ending of this story has many different sources, some of which may be remnants of older ideas. In Perrault's version of the story, Little Red couldn't escape, because the moral was that those who had sex were socially doomed; there was no coming back from this.

Perhaps more interesting, however, are the stories in which Little Red is eaten and comes back out of the wolf's stomach as if being reborn. Shamanistic figures were often devoured in lore, then reborn as more powerful beings. In Yupik lore, a man might be eaten by a bear spirit while, in Southeast Malaan lore, a person would be eaten by a tiger spirit. In both cases, the animal spirit would regurgitate them. Others could be eaten by worms, by giants, or by twisted weird monsters. If they managed to avoid screaming or showing any pain at this time, they would be reborn as shamans.

Little Red is a story with a number of sources, many of which are very old. However, the later people who wrote this story down didn't understand it and so were able to use it to enhance their own agendas, turning it into a tale about sexuality, a warning against men and strangers.

Perrault did something similar with his tale of "Cinderella." While the initial story likely involved some evidence of the Cinderella character's own personal skill in using folk religious ideas to get what she wanted, Perrault's version is substantially different from this. Gone is any mention of Cinderella's power, her ability to grow magical trees, or any other connection she might have had with the supernatural—other than the appearance of a godmother. In his version of the story, she had so little involvement in the magic of the story that she might as well have won the lottery. His focus is instead on her behavior in court and at home. He wrote these tales for court, so within his world, a person's behavior at court and being the center of attention was what both men and women aspired to. Thus, his Cinderella is led to the most honorable seat by the prince:

> *And afterwards took her out to dance with him. She danced so very gracefully that they all more and more admired her. A fine meal was served up, but the young prince ate not a morsel, so intently was he busied in gazing on her.*
>
> *She went and sat down by her sisters, showing them a thousand civilities, giving them part of the oranges and citrons which the prince had presented her with, which very much surprised them, for they did not know her. While Cinderella was thus amusing her sisters, she heard the clock strike eleven and three-quarters, whereupon she immediately made a courtesy to the company and hurried away as fast as she could.*
>
> *Arriving home, she ran to seek out her godmother, and, after having thanked her, she said she could not but heartily wish she might go to the ball the next day as well, because the king's son had invited her.*

We also see in this the desire by many writers not only to sanitize and moralize but to make the heroes and heroines selfless and kind; though this process started much earlier with characters like Robin Hood transforming into a giver to the poor rather than a rebellious figure.

These attempts to sanitize and perhaps find a brighter past also inspired the Romantics to begin their quest for a peaceful past ruled by a mother. They were jumping off of the Enlightenment notion that there was a single evolutionary truth—a truth they believed humans, interestingly enough, started with—that prehistoric religion was the...

Embodiment of sublime truths, which had degenerated and been forgotten among most modern tribal peoples... The Germans (Romantics) assumed that one of these eternal truths consisted of monotheism, and usually linked it to an instinctual understanding of the process of nature and human life. (Hutton, 2001)

In line with their already discussed notion of feminism, this idea eventually gave rise to the idea of a monotheistic earth goddess. Thus, with a few strokes of their pens and, oddly enough, a lot of bias against hunter-gatherers and the complex religions of previous peoples, philosophers such as Gerhard would advance theories that all Greek deities, even if they were deities of the moon, water, or war, had once all been a single Earth Mother. At its core, this idea that there was once a single monotheistic religion is yet another fairly racist notion about the evolution of human thinking—one that states that the spirituality of the Celtic, African, Native American, and Asian cultures was a violent subversion rather than a complex adaptation.

This is not to say that goddesses weren't important, but in places where they were of the utmost importance, there never was a single goddess. Instead, there was a multitude of goddesses, such as the Greek nymphs who acted as the founders of cities and muses to people or the Japanese Kami of the sun, wisdom and war with many brothers and sisters. There are goddesses everywhere, but none of these existed alone. The notion that all these thousands of diverse beings and cultures sprang from a single monotheistic belief that once stretched over the whole of the world yet somehow never existed anywhere with records that anthropologists could study is a fascinating new myth, one that has the power to...

Set a feminist and ecological ethical agenda, and incredibly change lives... this is precisely what myths do and this narrative of matriarchal utopia and patriarchal takeover was surely a myth, at least in a scholarly sense: it was a tale told repeatedly and reverently, explaining things otherwise thought to be painfully inexplicable. (Eller, 2001)

Like Cynthia Eller, I'm fascinated by the development of this myth and by the earlier Romantac creations that adopted and transformed old ideas for the modern era. In many ways, these changes are no different from what happened previously, with fairy tales morphing to fit the needs of the time period. The difference with literature, however, is that very few people get to control the fairy tales. Additionally, the speed with which the world is changing has been increasing, thus increasing the speed with which the stories based on fairy tales are changing.

There is, however, one more difference between literary fairy tales and the fairies of folklore. Fairy tales represented a longing for fairies living near people and for mystical help they believed in. Fairy literature is a longing for something believed to be distant, something off in Neverland or Fern Gully.

Literature, on the other hand, is a longing for the countryside and for the wilderness that perhaps never truly existed in the way we imagine—for a past that was never the way we picture it. In this sense, the dreams of fairies have changed from a way to escape from poverty, illness, and starvation to an escape from reality. Some have bemoaned such changes, but I would argue that nothing could be truer to the tradition of these stories than adapting them, for they were always told to help and entertain society; society wasn't made for them.

158

References:

Abbott, G. F. (1976) *Macedonian Folklore*. Folcroft, PA: Folcroft Libr. Ed

Abercromby, John (1898) *Magic Songs of the West Finns*.

Achilli, A., Rengo, C., Battaglia, V., Pala, M., Olivieri, A., Fornarino, S., ... Torroni, A. (2005). Saami and Berbers—An Unexpected Mitochondrial DNA Link. American Journal of Human Genetics, 76(5), 883–886.

Aldhouse-Green, Miranda and Aldhouse-Green, Stephen (2005) *The Quest for the Shaman: Shape-Shifters, Sorcerers and Spirit Healers in Ancient Europe*. New York, Thames & Hudson.

Africa, Thomas W. (1970) The One-Eyed Man against Rome: An Exercise in Euhemerism. Issue 19 pp. 528-538, *Historia: Zeitschrift für Alte GeschichteBd.*

Andrews, Alfred C. (1949) The Bean and Indo-European Totemism. *American Anthropologist* New Series, Vol. 51, No. 2 (Apr. - Jun., 1949), pp. 274-292

Andrews, Elizabeth (2011) *Ulster Folklore*. Gutenberg.org: http://www.gutenberg.org/files/37187/37187-h/37187-h.htm#Fairies_and_their_Dwelling-places3

Anthony, David W. (2007) The Horse, the Wheel, and Language: How Bronze-Age Riders from the Eurasian. Princeton University Press

Asbjørnsen, Peter Christen, Jørgen Engebretsen Moe, and George Webbe Dasent. (1900) *Popular Tales from the Norse*. London: G. Routledge

Atkinson, J. C. (1891) *Forty Years in a Moreland Parish*. London: Macmillan and CO.

Bain, R. Nisbet (2009) *Cossack Fairy Tales and Folk Tales*. Gutenberg.org: http://www.gutenberg.org/files/29672/29672-h/29672-h.htm

Balfour, M. C. (1904) *Examples of Printed Folk-lore Concerning Northumberland*. London: David Nutt.

Balzer, Marjorie Mandelstam (2009) Flights of the Sacred Symbolism and Theory in Siberian Shamanism. *American Anthropologist*. Vol 98, Iss 2, p. 305-318

Bandellow, Joseph A. and Cohen, Doy Patterns of Individualism and Collectivism Across the United States, Journal of Personality and Social Psychology, 1999, Vol. 77, No. 2, 279-292

Barber, Richard (2004) *Myths and Legends of the British Isles by Richard Barber*. Rochester, NY: Boydell Press

Bartlett, Sarah (2009) The Mythology Bible: The Definitive Guide to Legendary Tales. Sterling

Baumeister, Roy F. and Bratslavsky, Ellen (2001) Bad Is Stronger Than Good. *Review of General Psychology,* 2001. Vol. 5. No. 4. 323-370

160

Behringer, Wolfgang (2000) Shaman of Oberstdorf: Chonrad Stoeckhlin and the Phantoms of the Night. University of Virginia Press

Berezkin, Yuri (2005) The Black Dog at the River of Tears': Some Amerindian Representations of the Passage to the Land of the Dead and their Eurasian Roots. *Anthropological Forum 2. St. Petersburg*: Peter the Great Museum of Anthropology and Etnography (Kunstkamera); European University at St. Petersburg, pp. 174-211.

Beza, Marcu (1928) Paganism In Roumanian Folklore. https://archive.org/details/paganisminrouman009481mbp

Biti, Vladimir & Katusic, Bernarda & Lang, Peter (2010) *Märchen in den südslawischen Literaturen*

Black, George Fraser (1903) *County Folklore Vol. III – Orkney & Shetland Islands*. London, UK: David Nutt.

Blackburn, Barry (1991) *Theios Anēr and the Markan Miracle Traditions*. Tübingen : J.C.B. Mohr

Bloomfield, Maurice (1905) Cerberus, The Dog of Hades. http://www.gutenberg.org/files/19119/19119-h/19119-h.htm

Blumenthals, Verra (1903) *Folk Tales From the Russia*. Rand, Mcnally & Company.

Bock, E Wilbur (1966) Symbols in Conflict: Official versus Folk Religion. *Journal for the Scientific Study of Religion* Vol. 5, No. 2 (Spring, 1966), pp. 204-212 Published by: Wiley

Bottigheimer, R. B. (1986) To Spin A Yarn: The Female Voice in Folklore and Fairy Tale. *In Fairy Tales and Society*. Philadelphia: Univ. of Pennsylvania Press, pp. 53–74.

Bottrell, William (1873) *Traditions and Hearthisde Stories of West Cornwall*.

Boyer, Pascal (2008) Bound To Believe. *Nature* Vol 455, 23 p. 138-1039

Breeze, Andrew (2007) Britannia, Volume 35, p 228-229.

Briggs, Katharine Mary (1967) *The Fairies in Tradition and Literature*. London, UK: Routledge

Briggs, Katharine (1968) *Folktales of England*. Chicago: University of Chicago Press

Briggs, Katharine Mary (1976) *An encyclopedia of fairies: hobgoblins, brownies, bogies, and other supernatural creatures*. New York, NY: Pantheon Books.

Briggs, Katharine Mary (1978) *The Vanishing People.: Fairy Lore and Legends*. New York, NY: Pantheon Books.

Brodman, James (2009) Charity and Religion in Medieval Europe. The Catholic University of America Press

161

Brown, M. S. (1966) Buried Horse-Skulls in a Welsh House. *Folklore* Vol. 77, No. 1 (Spring, 1966), pp. 65-66 Published by: Folklore Enterprises, Ltd.

Brown, Norman Oliver (1947) *Hermes the Thief; The Evolution of a Myth*. Madison, WI: University of Wisconson

Bruchanov (1991) *Грузинские народные сказки*. Ростовское книжное издательство: http://skazki.yaxy.ru/52.html

Bryant, Adam (2013) A Boss's Challenge: Have Everyone Join the 'In' Group. *The New York Times*: http://www.nytimes.com/2013/03/24/business/neuroleadership-institutes-chief-on-shared-goals.html?pagewanted=1&_r=0

Bulbulia, Joseph and Slingerland, Edward (2012) Numen, Vol 59, Iss 5-6, 564-613

Bunce, John Thackray (2005) Fairy tales their orgin and meaning. Gutenberg. Org: http://www.gutenberg.org/files/8226/8226-h/8226-h.htm

Campbell, John Gregorson (1900) *Superstitions of the Highlands and Islands of Scotland*. Glasgow, England: James MacLehose and Sons.

Carey, John (1983) Irish Parallels to the Myth of Odin's Eye. *Folklore*, Volume 94, Issue 2, 1983

Carmichael, Alexander (1928) *Carmina Gadelica Hymns and Incantations*. Edinburgh, UK: Oliver and Boyd

Ceng, Joey T., Tracy, Jessica L., & Anderson, Cameron (2014) *The Psychology of Social Status. Personality & Social Psychology*

Chaucer, Geoffrey (2011) *Caterbury Tales*. Amazon Digital Services, Inc.

Conrad, Joseph L. (2001) *Male Mythological Beings Among the South Slavs*. Folklorica

Craigie, William Alexander (1896) Scandinavian Folk-lore: Illustrations of the Traditional Beliefs of the Northern Peoples. Detroit, Singing Tree Press

Crawford, John Martin (1888) *The Kalevala.*

Croker, Thomas (1834) *Fairy Legends and Traditions of the South of Ireland*. LONDON: John Murray.

Crossing, William (1890) *Tales of the Dartmoor Pixies*. Amazon Digital Services, Inc.

Curry, Andrew (2013) Archaeology: The milk revolution When a single genetic mutation first let ancient Europeans drink milk, it set the stage for a continental upheaval. *Nature, 500*

Curtin, Jeemiah (1895) *Tales of the Fairies and of the Ghost World*. Boston: Little Brown & Company.

Czaplicka, Mari Antoinette (2004) *Shamanism in Siberia*. Kessinger Publishing.

Dando, William (2012) Food and Famine in the 21st Century.

Daniels, Cora L. M. & Stevens, C. M. (1903) *Encyclopaedia of Superstitions, Folklore, and the Occult Sciences of the World*. Chicago: J. H. Yewdale & sons Company

Dasent, George Webbe (1906) Popular Tales from the Norse and North German. London: Norrcena Society

Davidson, Hilda Roderick Ellis and Chaudhri, Anna (2006) A Companion to the Fairy Tale. BOYE6

Deguignet, Jean-Marie (2004) Memoirs of a Breton Peasant. Seven Stories Press

Denning, Kathryn (2009) Ten Thousand Revolutions: Conjectures About Civilization. *Acta Astronautica*, Volume 68, Issue 3, p. 381-388.

Dequiqnet, Jean-Mari (2011) *Memoirs of a Breton Peasant*. New York: Seven Stories Press

Deusen, Kira Van (2001) The Flying Tiger: Women Shamans and Storytellers of the Amur. Mcgill-Queen's Native and Northern Series

Dewing, H. B. (1914) Procopius. https://archive.org/details/procopiuswitheng01procuoft

Djordjevic, Tihomir R. (1903) *Die Zigeuner in Serbien: ethnologische Forschungen*.

Dorcey, Peter F. (1989) The Role of Women in the Cult of Silvanus. *Numen* Vol. 36, Fasc. 2 (Dec., 1989), pp. 143-155

Douglas, George (1901) *Scottish Fairy and Folk Tales*. New York: A. L. Burt Company, Publishers

Eirik the Red's Saga. https://archive.org/details/eiriktheredssaga17946gut

Eller, Cynthia (2001) The Myth of Matriarchal Prehistory: Why an Invented Past Won't Give Women a Future. Beacon Press

Elliot AJ, Pazda AD (2012) Dressed for Sex: Red as a Female Sexual Signal in Humans. PLoS ONE 7(4): e34607. doi:10.1371/journal.pone.0034607

Ellis Davidson, H. R. & Ellis Davidson, Hilda Roderick (1989) *Myths and Symbols in Pagan Europe: Early Scandinavian and Celtic Religion*. Syracuse, NY: Syracuse University Press

Emerson, P. H. (2003) *Welsh Fairy-tales and Other Stories*. Gutenberg.org: http://www.gutenberg.org/files/8675/8675-h/8675-h.htm

Fairbanks, Arthur (1900) The Chthonic Gods of Greek Religion.

Fansler, Dean S. (1921) Filipino Popular Tales. http://www.gutenberg.org/files/8299/8299-h/8299-h.htm

Fee, Christopher R., & Leeming, David A. (2004) *Gods, Heroes, & Kings : The Battle for Mythic Britain: The Battle for Mythic*. New York: Oxford University Press

Fillmore, Parker (2010) *Czechoslovak Fairy Tales*. Gutenberg.org: http://www.gutenberg.org/files/32217/32217-h/32217-h.htm

Frater, Jamie (2014) Listverse.com's Epic Book of Mind-Boggling Lists: Unbelievable Facts and Astounding Trivia on Movies, Music, Crime, Celebrities, History, and More, Ulysses Press

Frazer, James George (2003) *The Golden Bough : a study of magic and religion*. Gutenberg.org: http://www.gutenberg.org/dirs/etext03/bough11h.htm

Gar, Azar (2000) The Human Motivational Complex: Evolutionary Theory and the Causes of Hunter-Gatherer Fighting. Part I. Pri-mary Somatic and Reproductive Causes. *Anthropological Quarterly* Vol. 73, No. 1, pp. 20-34

Gat, Azar (2000) The Human Motivational Complex: Evolutionary Theory and the Causes of Hunter-Gatherer Fighting, Part II. Proximate, Subordinate, and Derivative Causes. *Anthropological Quarterly* Vol. 73, No. 2 (Apr., 2000), pp. 74-88

Gathorne-Hardy, Jonathan () The Rise and Fall fo the British Nanny.

Ghirotto S, Tassi F, Fumagalli E, Colonna V, Sandionigi A, et al. (2013) Origins and Evolution of the Etruscans' mtDNA. PLoS ONE 8(2): e55519. doi:10.1371/journal.pone.0055519

Gianakoulis, Theodore P. & Macpherson, Georgia H. (1930) *Fairy Tales of Modern Greece*. Boston, MA: E. P. Dutton & CO

Ginzburg, Carlo (1966) The Night Battles: Witchcraft and Agrarian Cults in the Sixteenth and Seventeenth Centuries. Routledge.

Gibbings, W. W. (1889) *Folk-Lore and Legends, Scotland*. Gutenberg.org: http://www.gutenberg.org/files/17071/17071-h/17071-h.htm

Gimbutas, Marija (1974) Lithuanian God Velnias. *Myth in Indo-European Antiquity*

Gjorgjevic, Tihomi R. (1903) Die Zigeuner in Serbien: ethnologische Forschungen. Budapest: Thalia

Goodman, Katherine (1992) In the Shadow of Olympus: German Women Writers Around 1800. State Univ of New York P

Gorman, Marianne (1993) Influences from the Huns on Scandinavian Sacrificial Customs during 300-500 AD. The Problem of Ritual. Vol 15

Grautoff, Otto (1916) *Die Baltischen Provinzen: Märchen und Sagen*. Felix Lehmann Verla.

Graves, Robert (1992) The Greek Myths. Penguin Books

Gray, L. H. (1918) *The Mythology of All Races Vol. III*. Marshall Jones Company

Green, Miranda (1996) The Celtic World. Routledge Worlds

Gregoricka LA, Betsinger TK, Scott AB, Polcyn M (2014) Apotropaic Practices and the Undead: A Biogeochemical Assessment of Deviant Burials in Post-Medieval Poland. PLoS ONE 9(11): e113564. doi:10.1371/journal.pone.0113564

Gregory, Lady (1920) *Visions and beliefs in the west of Ireland.* New York and London: G. P. Putnam's Sons.

Griffis, William Elliot (2005) *Welsh Fairy Tales.* Gutenberg.org: http://www.gutenberg.org/cache/epub/9368/pg9368.html

Grimberg, Carl (1924) *Svenska Folkets Underbara Berättelser.* Stockholm, Sweden: L. J. Hjerta.

Grimes, Heilan Yvette (2010) *The Norse Myths.* Boston, MA: Hollow Earth Publishing.

Grimm, Jacob (1882) *Teutonic Mythology.* Londan, UK: George Bell and Sons.

Grimm, Jacob and Grimm, Wilhelm (2008) Gutenberg.org: http://www.gutenberg.org/files/2591/2591-h/2591-h.htm

Griswold, De Witt (1991) The Religion of the Rigveda. Motilal Banarsidass Publishers Private Limited

Gross, JH (2012) Toward a Neurobiological Understanding of Religion: Examining Ritual and the Body.

Grossberg, Lawrence and Polloc, Della () Cultural Studies 11.3. Routledge

Grummond, Thomson de (2006) Etruscan Myth, Sacred History, and Legend.

Guerber, H. A. (1988) Myths and Legends of the Middle Ages. Crescent

Guidera, Anita (2012) http://www.independent.ie/irish-news/land-of-the-fairies-28815367.html.

Gyula Pap (1896) The Folk-Tales of the Magyars. Zeluna.net

Haas, Alfred (1903) Rügensche Sagen und Märchen: Gesammelt und Herausgegeben. J. Burmeister

Hart, Terese B. and Hart, John A. (1986) The Ecological Basis of Hunter-Gatherer Subsistence in African Rain Forests: The Mbuti of Eastern Zaire. *Human Ecology*, Vol 14, No 1

Hartnup, Karen (2004) *On the Beliefs of the Greeks: Leo Allatios and Popular Orthodoxy.* Leiden, The Netherlands: Brill Academic Pub

Hartland, Edwin Sidney (1890) *English Fairy and Other Folk Tales.* London: The Walter Scott Publishing Co.

Hartland, Edwin Sidney (1891) The science of fairy tales : an inquiry into fairy mythology. https://archive.org/details/scienceoffairyta00hartiala

Headland, Thomas N. and Reid, Lawrence A. (1989) Hunter Gatherers and Their Neighbors from Prehistory to the Present. *Current Anthropology*, Vol 30, 1

Headland, Thomas (1999) Could 'Pure' Hunter-Gatherers Live in a Rain Forest? http://www-01.sil.org/~headlandt/wildyam.htm

Hedeagera, Lotte (2007) Scandinavia and the Huns: An Interdisciplinary Approach to the Migration Era Scandinavia and the Huns: An Interdisciplinary Approach to the Migration Era. Norwegian Archaeological Review Volume 40, Issue 1, p 42-58

Heesterman, J. C., Van Den Hoek, Albert W., Kolff, Dirk H. A., and Oort, M. S. (1992) Ritual, State, and History in South Asia: Essays in Honour of J.C. Heesterman. Brill

Heikkila, Mikko (2013) From Surging Waves to the Spirit of Waves – On the Germanic and Sami Origin of the Proper Names Ahti and Vellamo in Finnic Mythology. *SKY Journal of Linguistics*, Vol 26, p 71-86

Hellman, Roxanne and Hall, Derek (2011) *Vampire Legends and Myths*. New York: Rosen Publishing Group

Henderson, Lizanne & Cowan, Edward J. (2001) *Scottish Fairy Belief*. Google eBook

Henderson, William (1879) *Notes on the Folk-Lore of the Northern Counties of England and the Borders*. London: W. Satchell, Peyton and CO.

Hofberg, Herman (1890) Swedish Fairy Tales

Homer (1999) *The Odyssey*. (Samuel Butler. Trans) Gutenberg.org: http://www.gutenberg.org/ebooks/1727

Hori, Ichiro (1994) Folk Religion in Japan: Continuity and Change (The Haskell Lectures on History of Religions.)

Horizon Research Foundation. http://www.horizonresearch.org/main_page.php?cat_id=275

Horsley, Richard A. (1979) Further Reflections on Witchcraft and European Folk Religion. History of Religions Vol. 19, No. 1 (Aug., 1979), pp. 71-95 Published by: The University of Chicago Press

Hunt, Robert (1908) *Popular Romances of the West of England; or, The Drolls, Traditions, and Superstitions of Old Cornwall*. London: Chatto & Windus.

Hutton, Ronald (2001) The Triumph of the Moon: A History of Modern Pagan Witchcraft Paperback. Oxford University Press

Hyde, Douglas (1890) *Beside the Fire : A Collection of Irish Gaelic Folk Stories*. London: David Nutt.

Ivanits, Linda J. (1992) *Russian Folk Belief*. Armonk, NY: M.E. Sharpe.

Jackson, Georgina Frederica (1883) Shropshire Folk-lore: A Sheaf of Gleanings, Part 1. Trübner & co.

Jacobs, Joseph (2004) *English Fairy Tales*. Gutenberg.org: http://www.gutenberg.org/files/14241/14241-h/14241-h.htm

Jacobs, Joseph (2011) *Folklore, Volume 13*. Ulan Press

Jana, Reena (2009) Innovation Trickles in a New Direction. http://www.bloomberg.com/bw/magazine/content/09_12/b4124038287365.htm

Jegerlehner, Johannes (1907) *Was die Sennen erzählen: märchen und sagen aus dem Wallis*. Budjdruckerel Buhler & Werder

Jettmar, K. (1986) *The Religions of the Hindukush 1: The Religion of the Kaffirs*. Aris & Phillips

Johns, Andreas (2004) Baba Yaga: The Ambiguous Mother and Witch of the Russian Folktale. International Folkloristics

Johnson, Walter (1912) Byways in British Archaeology. https://archive.org/details/bywaysinbritisha00johniala

Jolly, Karen Louise (1996) Popular Religion in Late Saxon England: Elf Charms in Context. The University of North Carolina Press

Kuhn, A. and Schwartz, W. (1846) Mahrt gefangen," Norddeutsche Sagen, Märchen und Gebräuche No. 16, p. 14-15

Kaplan, Robert (2006) The Neuropsychiatry of Shamanism. http://www.academia.edu/3549088/The_Neuropsychiatry_of_Shamanism

Keightley, Thomas (1892) *The Fairy Mythology*. London, UK: George Bell and Sons.

Kelly, Robert L. and Thomas, David Hurst (2012) *Archaeology*. Cengage Learning

Kelly, Walter Keating (1863) Curiosities of Indo-European Tradition and Folk-lore. Chapman & Hall

Kennedy, Patrick (1866) *Legendary Fictions of the Irish Celts by Patrick Kennedy*. London Macmillan and CO.

Keyser, Rudolph (1854) *The Religion of the Northman*. New York: Charles B. Norton.

Kieckhefer, Richard (1998) Forbidden Rites: A Necromancer's Manual of the Fifteenth Century.

Kirby, W. F. (1894) *The Hero of Esthonia*. London: John C. Nimmo

Kucharz, Christel (2009) *The Real Story Behind van Gogh's Severed Ear*. ABC News. http://abcnews.go.com/International/story?id=7506786&page=1

Kukharenko, Svitlana P. (2007) *Animal Magic: Contemporary Beliefs and Practices in Ukrainian Villages.* University of Alberta: https://journals.ku.edu/index.php/folklorica/article/viewFile/3784/3622

Lady Isabel and the Elf Knight: http://www.springthyme.co.uk/ballads/balladtexts/4_LadyIsabel.html

Laidoner, Triin. 2012. The Flying Noaidi of the North: Sámi Tradition Reflected in the Figure Loki Laufeyjarson in Old Norse Mythology. *Scripta Islandica* 63: 59–91.

Lang, Andrew (1897) *The Pink Fairy Book.* Gutenberg.org http://www.gutenberg.org/files/5615/5615-h/5615-h.htm

Larson, Jennifer (2001) *Greek Nymphs: Myth, Cult, Lore.* New York, NY: Oxford University Press

Lauder, Toofie (1881) *Legends and Tales of the Harz Mountains.* London: Hodder and Stoughton.

Lawson, John Cuthbert (1910) *Modern Greek folklore and ancient Greek religion: a study in survivals.* Cambridge University Press

Lecouteux, Claude (2003) *Lecouteux, Witches, Werewolves and Fairies: Shapeshifters and Astral Doubles in the Middle Ages.* Rochester, Vermont: Inner Traditions – Bear & Company

Lecouteux, Claude (2013) The Tradition of Household Spirits: Ancestral Lore and Practices.

Leland, Charles Godfrey (1892) *Etruscan Roman Remains in Popular Tradition.* New York, NY: Scribner's Sons.

Leung, Ak; Maddux, WW, Galinsky AD, and Chlu Cy (2008) Multicultural experience enhances creativity: the when and how. *NCBI*, Vol 63(3) p. 168-181

Lewis, Jerome (2002) http://discovery.ucl.ac.uk/18991/1/18991.pdf

Lincoln, Bruce (1976) The Indo-European Cattle-Raiding Myth. *History of Religions*, Vol. 16, No. 1 (Aug., 1976), pp. 42-65

Linden (2007) The accidental mind: how brain evolution has given us love, memory, dreams, and God. Cambridge, MA: Belknap Press

Linnell, J; Odden, John; Kaczensky, Petra & Swenson, Jon (2002) The fear of wolves: A review of wolf attacks on humans. *NINA NIKU Stiftelsen for naturforskning og kulturminneforskning*

Linton, E. Lynn (1861) *Witch Stories.* London: Chapman and Hall

Lonnrot, Elias (2010) *The Kalevala.* Gutenberg.org: http://www.gutenberg.org/cache/epub/5186/pg5186.html

Lorrits, Oskar (1998) The Stratification of Estonian Folk-Religion. *The Slavonic and East European Review*, Vol. 35, No. 85, p. 360-378

Macculloch, J. A. (1911) *The Religion of the Ancient Celts*. Edinburgh, UK: Morrison & Gibb.

Mackenzie, Donald (1912) Teutonic Myth and Legend
https://archive.org/details/teutonicmythandl027797mbp

Maenchen-Helfen, Otto J. (1973) The World of the Huns: Studies in Their History and Culture. University of California Press

Magliocco, Sabina (2009) Italian Cunning Craft: Some Preliminary Observations. *Journal for the Academic Study of Magic*. Vol 5

Mallarach, Josep-Maria; Papayannis, Thymio; and Vaisanen, Rauno (2010) The Diversity of Sacred Lands in Europe. Proceedings of the Third Workshop of the Delos Initiative. http://cmsdata.iucn.org/downloads/delos3_publication_the_diversity_of_sacred_lands _in_europe_9mb.pdf

Mallory, J. P. and Adams, Douglas Q. (1997) Encyclopedia of Indo-European Culture. Routledge

Maple, Eric ()Cunning Murrell. A Study of a Nineteenth Century Cunning Man in Hadleigh, Essex. *Folklore* Vol. 71, No. 1 (Mar., 1960), pp. 37-43

Masson, Elsie (1929) *Folk Tales of Brittany*. Philadlephia: Macrae, Smith, Company.

McCall, Andrew (1979) *The Medieval Underworld*. H. Hamilton

McRobbie, Linda Rodriguez (2013) The History and Psychology of Clowns Being Scary You aren't alone in your fear of makeup-clad entertainers; people have been frightened by clowns for centuries. : http://www.smithsonianmag.com/arts-culture/the-history-and-psychology-of-clowns-being-scary-20394516/#lxerAcab4j5rVJVB.99

Melton, J. Gordon (1998) *The Vampire Book: The encyclopedia of the Undead*. Canton, MI: Visible Ink Press.

Meyer, Kuno (1895) *The Voyage of Bran, Son of Febal*. London: David Nutt.

Mikhailovskii, V. M. and Wardrop, Oliver (1895) Shamanism in Siberia and European Russia, Being the Second Part of "Shamanstvo". *The Journal of the Anthropological Institute of Great Britain and Ireland* Vol. 24, (1895), pp. 62-10

Miller, David Harry (1993) The Case of Frankish Origins. *Journal of World History*, Vol. 4, No. 2, pp. 277-285

Monaghan, Patricia (2008) The Encyclopedia of Celtic Mythology and Folklore. Checkmark Books

Morrison, Sophia (1911)*Manx Fairy Tales*. London: David Nutt

Mortimer, Ian (2008) *The Time Traveler's Guide to Medieval England*. London: Touchstone

Müllenhoff , Karl (1845) Sagen, Märchen und Lieder der Herzogthümer Schleswig, Holstein und Lauenburg

Murphy, Caitriona (2011) http://www.independent.ie/business/farming/land-blessing-tradition-survives-as-farmers-seek-to-ward-off-piseogs-26729121.html

Narvaez, Peter (1997) *The Good People: New Fairylore Essays*. University Press of Kentucky

Näsman, Ulf (2008) Scandinavia and the huns : a source-critical approach to an old question. *Journal of Swedish Antiquarian Research*, Vol 103, p. 111-119

Nilsson, Martin P. and Nock, Arthur Darby (1972) Greek Folk Religion. University of Pennsylvania Press

Norenzayan, A., Atran, S., Faulkner, J., & Schaller, M. (2006). Memory and mystery: The cultural selection of minimally counterintuitive narratives. *Cognitive Science*, 30, 531-553.

Ó Giolláin, Diarmuid (1994) The Image of the Vikings in Irish Folk Legends. *Sounds from the Supernatural: Papers Presented at the Nordic-Celtic Legend Symposium*, pp. 163-170 Published The Folklore of Ireland Society

Olcott, Frances J. (1928) *Wonder Tales From Baltic Wizards*.

Oliver, Mary Beth and Sanders, Meghan (2004) The Horror Film "The Appeal of Horror and Suspense." Rutgers UP

Oppenheimer, Stephen (2007) Origins of the British: The New Prehistory of Britain. Robinson Publishing

Ostry, Elaine (2013) Social Dreaming: Dickens and the Fairy Tale. Routledge

Page, John Lloyd Warden (1892) An Exploration of Dartmoor and Its Antiquities: With Some Account of Its Borders. Seeley and Co.

Parnia, Sam; Spearpoint, Ken; de Vos, Gabriele; et al (2014) AWARE—AWAreness during REsuscitation—A prospective study. *Resuscitation*, http://www.resuscitationjournal.com/article/S0300-9572(14)00739-4/abstract

Patch, Haward Rollin (1918) Some Elements in Medieval Descriptions of the Otherworld. *Modern Language Association*, Vol. 33, No. 4 (1918), pp. 601-643

Palsson, Hermann (1999) Sami People in Old Norse Literature. Nordlit : Tidsskrift i litteratur og kultur

Paulson, Ivar (1965) Outline of Permian Folk Religion. *Journal of the Folklore Institute* Vol. 2, No. 2 (Jun., 1965), pp. 148-179

Petreska, Vesna (2008) *The Secret Knowledge of Folk Healers in Macedonian. Folklorica*: Vol 13

Petrovic, Sreten: *СРПСКА МИТОЛОГИЈА*
http://svevlad.org.rs/knjige_files/petrovic_mitologija.html#vampir

Petrov, Vlerv (1995) Vital Energy, Spirits, and Gods in Mari Folk Medicine. *Folk Belief Today*, Tartu

Philips, Sarah D. (2004) Waxing Like the Moon: Women Folk Healers in Rural Western Ukraine. *Folklorica, Journal of the Slavic and East European Folklore Association.*

Phelps, David (2013) Worcestershire Folk Tales

Polimen, Joseph (2003) Evolutionary Perspectives on Schizophrenia. *Can J Psychiatry* - Vol. 48 - Issue 1

Porter, C. C. and Marlowe, F. W. (2007) How marginal are forager habitats? *Journal of Archaeological Science.*

Purkiss, Diane (2007) *Fairies and Fairy Stories: A History.* Stroud, Gloucestershire: Tempus

Ralph P, Coop G (2013) The Geography of Recent Genetic Ancestry across Europe. PLoS Biol 11(5): e1001555. doi:10.1371/journal.pbio.1001555

Ralston, W. R. S. (2007) *Russian Fairy Tales.* Gutenberg.org
http://www.gutenberg.org/files/22373/22373-h/22373-h.htm

Rhys, John (1901) *Celtic Folklore: Welsh and Manx.* Oxford: Clarendon Press.

Richards, M. P. (2002) A brief review of the archaeological evidence for Palaeolithic and Neolithic. *European Journal of Clinical Nutrition*, Vol 56, N 12, p. 1270-1278

Richard, M. P.; Jacobi, R.; Cook, J.; Pettitt, P. B.; & Stringer, C. B. (2005) Isotope evidence for the intensive use of marine foods by Late Upper Palaeolithic humans. *Journal of Human Evolution* 49 p. 390-394

Richards, Michael P.; Pettitt, Paul B.; Stiner, Mary C.; & Trinkaus, Erik (2001) Stable isotope evidence for increasing dietary breadth in the European mid-Upper Paleolithic. *PNAS* vol. 98 no. 11

Riordan, James (1991) *The Sun Maiden and the Crescent Moon: Siberian Folk Tales.* Northampton, MA: Interlink Publishing Group

Rochholz, Ernst Ludwig (1856) Schweizersagen aus dem Aargau, vol. 1, no. 222, p. 312.

Rodgers, Charles (1884) *Social Life in Scotland, From Early to Recent Times.* Edinburgh, UK: William Patterson.

Sager, Sumatra Steven (2008) The Sky is our Roof, the Earth our Floor Orang Rimba Customs and Religion in the Bukit Duabelas region of Jambi. A thesis submitted for the degree of Doctor of Philosophy of The Australian National University

Savina, Magliocco (2009) *Italain Cunning Craft: Some Preliminary Observations.* Journal for the Academic Study of Magic.

Schaefer, Charles E. (2002) Play Therapy with Adults. Wiley

Schneller, Christian (1867) Das Rothhütchen," Märchen und Sagen aus Wälschtirol: Ein Beitrag zur deutschen Sagenkunde. *Innsbruck: Verlag der Wagner'schen Universitäts-Buchhandlung*, 1867), no. 6, pp. 9-10.

Sebeok, Thomas Albert (1956) *Studies in Cheremis: The Supernatural.* New York: Wenner-Gren Foundation for Anthropological Research

Seymour, John D. (2013) *Irish Witchcraft and Demonology.* Gutenberg.org: http://www.gutenberg.org/files/43651/43651-h/43651-h.htm

Sikes, Wirt (1880) *British Goblins Welsh Folk Lore, Fairy Mythology, Legends and Traditions.* London: Sampsons Low Marston, Searle, & Rivington.

Sky, Jeanette (2002) Myths of Innocence and Imagination: The Case of the Fairy Tale. *Literature and Theology*, Vol. 16, Iss 4. 363-376

Spence, Lewis (2010) *Legends & Romance of Brittany.* Gutenberg.org: http://www.gutenberg.org/files/30871/30871-h/30871-h.htm

Spence, Lewis (2005) *Hero Tales and Legends of the Rhine.* Guternberg.org: http://www.gutenberg.org/files/16539/16539-h/16539-h.htm

Speranza, Francesca (1887) Ancient Legends, Mystic Charms, and Superstitions of Ireland.

Spigel, Lynn (2001) Seducing the Innocent. Childhood and Television in Postwar America. Welcome to the Dreamhouse: Popular Media and Postwar Suburbs.

Stafford, Tom (2014) Why is all the News Bad. BBC http://www.bbc.com/future/story/20140728-why-is-all-the-news-bad

Stramberg, Susan (2007) The Color Red: A History in Textiles. http://www.npr.org/templates/story/story.php?storyId=7366503

Stroheker, Heinz, Karl & Walser, Gerold (1975) Historia: Zeitschrift für Alte Geschichte. Franz Steiner Varlog

Strong, W. D. (2009) North American Indian Traditions Suggesting a Knowledge of the Mammoth. *American Anthropologist*, Vol 36, Iss 1.

Stuart, John (1843) *Extracts from the Presbytery book of Strathbogie.* Aberdeen, Printed for the Spalding Club

Sugiyama, Michelle Scalise (2004) Predation, Narration, and Adaptation: "Little Red Riding Hood". Interdisciplinary Literary Studies Vol. 5, No. 2 (Spring 2004), pp. 110-129

Tacitus, Cornelisus (2012) *The Germania.* Gutenberg.org http://www.gutenberg.org/files/39573/39573-h/39573-h.html

172

Talhelm, T., Zhang, X., Oishi, S., Shimin, C., Duan, D., Lan, X., and Kitayama, S. (2014) Large-Scale Psychological Differences Within China Explained by Rice Versus Wheat Agriculture. *Science* 9 May 2014: vol. 344 no. 6184 pp. 603-608 DOI: 10.1126/science.1246850

Tarmo, Kulmar (2005) On Supreme Sky God from the Aspect of Religious History and in Prehistoric Estonian Material. *Folklore*

Tatar, Maria (1999) The Classic Fairy Tales. Norton Critical Editions

Taylor, Timothy (2007) The Real Vampire Slayers. *The Independent*. http://www.independent.co.uk/news/world/europe/the-real-vampire-slayers-397874.html

Tehrani JJ (2013) The Phylogeny of Little Red Riding Hood. PLoS ONE 8(11): e78871. doi:10.1371/journal.pone.0078871

Templin, Thor Heidrek The Specter of Wotan: Evolution of Proto-Indo-European God of Death. *Journal of Germanic Mythology and Folklore*, Issue 1

Thompsongaug, Derek (2012) The Case for Vacation: Why Science Says Breaks Are Good for Productivity. http://www.theatlantic.com/business/archive/2012/08/the-case-for-vacation-why-science-says-breaks-are-good-for-productivity/260747/

Thorms, William John (1865) Tree Notelets on Shakespeare

Tian-Shanskaia, O. S., & Ransel, D. L. (1993) *Village Life in Late Tsarist Russia*. Indiana University Press

Till, Rupert (2010) Pop Cult: Religion and Popular Music. Bloomsbury Academic

Tučkova, Natal'â Anatol'evna, Vladimir Vladimirovič Napol'skih, Anna-Leena Siikala, Mihály Hoppál, Sergěi Viktorovič. Gluškov, and Clive Tolley (2010) Selkup Mythology. Budapest: Akadémiai Kiadó

Tugend, Alina (2012) March 23rd, Praise Is Fleeting, but Brickbats We Recall. *The New York Times,* http://www.nytimes.com/2012/03/24/your-money/why-people-remember-negative-events-more-than-positive-ones.html?pagewanted=all&_r=1&

Turi, Johan (2011) An Account of the Sámi. Nordic Studies Press
Vadeysha, Masha (2005) The Russian Bathhouse: The Old Russian Pert' and the Christian Bania in Traditional Culture. *Folklorica, Journal of the Slavic and East European Folkore Association*

Uppsala University. (2009, September 25). Scandinavians Are Descended From Stone Age Immigrants, Ancient DNA Reveals. ScienceDaily. Retrieved February 17, 2015 from www.sciencedaily.com/releases/2009/09/090924141049.htm

Vajda, Edward J. (2011) Siberian Landscapes In Ket Traditional Culture. Landscape & Culture in Northern Eurasia, ed. Peter Jordan, Walnut Creek, CA: Left Coast Press, 2011. Pp. 297-314.

Vaz Da Silva, Francisco (2000) Complex Entities in the Universe of Fairy Tales. *Marvels and Tales*, Vol. 14 No. 2 p. 219-243

Vajda, Edward J. (2011) Siberian landscapes in Ket Traditional Culture. *Landscape and Culture in Northern Eurasia.*

Vandello, Joseph A. and Cohen, Dov (199) Patterns of individualism and collectivism across the United States. *Journal of Personality and Social Psychology*, Vol 77(2), Aug 1999, 279-292.

Västrik , Ergo-Hart (1999) The Waters and Water Spirits in Votian Folk Belief. *Folklore*, Vol 12 http://www.folklore.ee/folklore/vol12/spirits.htm

Veselica, Lajla (2006) *Croatian 'Dracula' Revived to Lure Tourists.* http://www.mg.co.za/article/2006-04-24-croatian-dracula-revived-to-lure-tourists

Vivian, Herbert (1908) The Perchten Dancers of Salzburg. *The Wide World Magazine: An Illustrated Monthly of True Narrative*, Volume 21

Waites, Margaret C. (1920) The Nature of the Lares and Their Representation in Roman Art. *American Journal of Archaeology*, Vol. 24, No. 3 (Jul. - Sep., 1920), pp. 241-261

Waller, Steven J. and Kolar, Miriam A. (2014) Shamans and Other "Magico-Religious" Healers: A Cross-Cultural Study of Their Origins, Nature, and Social Transformations. Acoust. Soc. Am. 136, 2270 (2014); http://dx.doi.org/10.1121/1.4900201

Wang, Hao-Chuan; Russell, Susan R. & Cosley, Dan (2011) From Diversity to Creativity: Stimulating Group Brainstorming with Cultural Differences and Conversationally-Retrieved Pictures. Department of Information Science, Cornell University.

Warner, Marina (1995) From the Beast to the Blonde: On Fairy Tales and Their Tellers. Farrar Straus & Girou

Watt, Diane (2001) Secretaries of God: Women Prophets in Late Medieval and Early Modern England. D.S.Brewer

Wigzell, Faith (2003) The Ethical Values of Narodnoe Pravoslavie: Traditional Near-Death Experiences and Fedotov. *Folklorica, Journal of the Slavic and East European Folkore Association.*

Wentz, W. Y. Evans (2011) *Fairy Faith in the Celtic Countries.* Gutenberg.org: http://www.gutenberg.org/files/34853/34853-h/34853-h.htm

Wibly, Emma (2006) *Cunning-Folk and Familiar Spirits: Shamanistic Visionary Traditions in Early Modern British Witchcraft and Magic.* Sussex, UK: Sussex Academic Press.

Wibly, Emma (2010) *The Visions of Isobel Gowdie: Magic, Witchcraft and Dark Shamanism in Seventeenth-Century Scotland.* Sussex, UK: Sussex Academic Press.

Wiessner, Olly (2014) Firelight talk of the Kalahari Bushmen: Did tales told over fires aid our social and cultural evolution? *PNAS*, September 2014 DOI: 10.1073/pnas.1404212111

Wigström, Eva (1881) *Folkdiktning : Visor, Folktro, Sägner, Och en Svartkonstbok.*

Wilde, Jane F. E. (1902) *Ancient Legends, Mystic Charms & Supersitions of Ireland.* London, UK: Chatto & Windus.

Winlow, Clara Vostrovsky (2014) Our Little Czecho-Slovak Cousin. http://www.gutenberg.org/files/45616/45616-h/45616-h.htm

Wlislocki, Heinrich von (1891) *Märchen und Sagen der Bukowinaer und Siebenbürger armenier.* Google eBook: http://google.com/books?id=dkoTAAAAYAAJ

Winkelman, Michael (2002) Shamanism as Neurotheology and Evolutionary Psychology. American Behavioral Scientist, Vol 45 No 12

Winkelman, Michael James (1990) Shamans and Other "Magico-Religious" Healers: A Cross-Cultural Study of Their Origins, Nature, and Social Transformations. Ethos Vol. 18, No. 3 (Sep., 1990), pp. 308-352 Published by: Wiley

Wood-Martin, W. G. (1902) Traces of the Elder Faiths of Ireland; a Folklore Sketch; a Handbook of Irish Pre-Christian Tradition. London: Longmans, Green, and CO.

Wratislaw, A. H. (1890) *Sixty Folk-Tales from Exclusively Slavonic Sources.* London Ellion Stock.

Young, Ella (1910) *Celtic Wonder Tales.* Maunsel & Company.

Yeats, W. B. (1888) *Fairy and Folk tales of the Irish Peasantry*

Zillmann, Dolf and Vordere, Peter (2000) Media Entertainment: The Psychology of Its Appeal. Routledge

Zipes, Jack (2013) The Irresistible Fairy Tale: The Cultural and Social History of a Genre. Princeton University Press

Made in the USA
Middletown, DE
27 March 2023

27710083R00104